PREFACE TO CRITICAL READING

THIRD EDITION

Richard D. Altick

Professor of English, The Ohio State University

HENRY HOLT AND COMPANY   New York

20357-0316
Printed in the United States of America

Preface to the Third Edition

In this freshly revised edition of *Preface to Critical Reading,* at least two-thirds of the illustrative and exercise material is new. The number of exercises has been increased, so that teachers may have a wider range of selection to suit the needs of the individual class and the amount of time that can be spent on the book.

Once again it is a pleasure to thank the companies which have generously consented to my quoting from their advertisements, as well as the owners of other copyright material, specific acknowledgment of which occurs at the appropriate places in the text. The sources of all quotations are listed, as before, in a Teacher's Guide which may be obtained from the publishers.

For valuable assistance I am indebted to Miss Wanda Petty, of the reference department of the Ohio State University Library. I am grateful also to the many teachers who have offered suggestions for the improvement of this book. As they look through the present edition, they will understand the extent of my obligation to them.

R. D. A.

Columbus, Ohio
October 15, 1955

Contents

Foreword

THIS BOOK is meant to help you learn to read.

To be sure, you already know how to read—in one sense. You read constantly—newspapers, novels, textbooks, *Life,* printed captions and slogans on television, advertising cards on buses. And in general you know what is being said. You can report to someone else the main gist of a passage of writing.

But reading is much more than this. Let's take two examples to show what we mean, and to provide a foretaste of the kind of thing we shall be doing throughout this book. First, here is a short speech. Read it once at your normal speed; then read it again, more slowly, pausing to decide just what each sentence says. What does the whole speech add up to? What are the speaker's ideas? What are his purposes in communicating them? How plainly and effectively does he present them? Before what sort of audience might the speech be delivered?

Mr. Chairman, Ladies and Gentlemen:

It is indeed a great and undeserved privilege to address such an audience as I see before me. At no previous time in the history of human civilization have greater problems confronted and challenged the ingenuity of man's intellect than now. Let us look around us. What do we see on the horizon? What forces are at work? Whither are we drifting? Under what mist of clouds does the future stand obscured?

My friends, casting aside the raiment of all human speech, the crucial test for the solution of all these intricate problems to which I have just alluded is the sheer and forceful application of those immutable laws which down the corridor of Time have always guided the hand of man, groping, as it were, for some faint beacon light for his hopes and aspirations. Without these great vital principles we are but puppets responding to whim and fancy, failing entirely to grasp the hidden meaning of it all. We must readdress ourselves to these questions which press for answer and solution. The issues cannot be avoided. There they stand. It is upon you, and you, and yet even upon me, that the yoke of responsibility falls.

What, then, is our duty? Shall we continue to drift? No! With all the emphasis of my being I hurl back the message *No!* Drifting must stop. We must press onward and upward toward the ultimate goal to which all must aspire.

But I cannot conclude my remarks, dear friends, without touching briefly upon a subject which I know is steeped in your very consciousness. I refer to that spirit which gleams from the eyes of a new-born babe, that animates the toiling masses, that sways all the hosts of humanity past and present. Without this energizing principle all commerce, trade and industry are hushed and will perish from this earth as surely as the crimson sunset follows the golden sunshine.

Mark you, I do not seek to unduly alarm or distress the mothers, fathers, sons and daughters gathered before me in this vast assemblage, but I would indeed be recreant to a high resolve which I made as a youth if I did not at this time and in this place, and with the full realizing sense of responsibility which I assume, publicly declare and affirm my dedication and my consecration to the eternal principles and receipts of simple, ordinary, commonplace *justice*.

If, after having carefully read and reread this speech, you haven't got much out of it, we don't blame you. It is a blast of hot air. The only positive point the speaker makes is that he is in favor of justice, which is not surprising, since practically everybody is in favor of justice, just as practically everybody is against sin.

But the speech as a whole isn't about justice. In fact, it isn't about anything. It opens (Paragraph 1, Sentence 2) with a platitude—a statement of the obvious couched in worn-out language. Then it asks a series of questions to which we might reasonably expect to get the answers before the speaker finishes. We never get them. Nor do we ever find out what is meant, in Paragraph 2, by "all these intricate problems," "those immutable laws," "these great vital principles," "these questions which press for answer and solution," "the issues." "We" (who?) are said to be "drifting," but we must keep working toward "the ultimate goal" (what?). A "spirit" is mentioned in Paragraph 4; it is also an "energizing principle." But again—to what does the speaker refer?

The most evident quality of the speech, looked at in this way, is that it is composed of five paragraphs of high-sounding but *empty* language. The unwary might jump to the conclusion that the speaker is a deep thinker, uttering immortal truths—but that is only because his words are chosen to give that impression. Actually, the speech is like a soap bubble that a child blows. It gives off pretty colors, for the moment; its words (for example, "mist of clouds," "faint beacon light," "that spirit which gleams from the eyes of a new-born babe," "the crimson sunset," "the golden sunshine") please us, just because we are accustomed to react in certain ways to such language. But when we prick the bubble with our critical intelligence, its substance proves so frail that it simply vanishes.

Look at the first sentence in Paragraph 2. Analyze it logically, word by word. If we take "casting aside the raiment of all human speech" at its face value, we have to assume that the speaker is no longer going to use "human speech." What, we may ask, does he plan to use instead? What is meant by "the crucial test for the solution of all these intricate problems" to which he says he has "just alluded" (but he hasn't)? What sort of picture is evoked by the hand of man groping for a beacon light?

We could say much more about this pompous speech. It is filled with trite phrases ("a great and undeserved privilege," "the corridor of Time," the yoke of responsibility," "onward and upward," "the toiling masses," "this vast assemblage"). It employs a variety of cheap oratorical tricks ("dear friends," "with all the emphasis of my being I hurl back the message *No!*"). It uses both short sentences (Paragraph 3) and a long one (Paragraph 5) to produce a desired effect upon the audience. But since these first pages are intended simply as a preview and we shall go into such matters more thoroughly in the chapters to follow, we shall not pause here for further analysis. We have not answered all the questions we raised before quoting the speech, but answering the remaining ones for yourself can give you a little preliminary practice in the techniques you will learn as you progress through this book.

The vital point of what we have done, however, is this: By keeping a few pertinent questions in mind as you read, you can strip away the pretensions of deliberately vague and "impressive" language and discover that, as in the case of this speech, what you are reading is as worthless as a three-dollar bill.

Having seen how critical reading can expose emptiness, if not actual fraud, let us now turn to the positive, constructive use of the same techniques. Here is part of a review of a movie. The reviewer has said that the film lasted 114 minutes. Then he goes on:

A hundred and fourteen minutes is damn near two hours. You can fly from here [New York] to Cleveland in a hundred and fourteen minutes. Roger Bannister can run twenty-eight miles in a hundred and fourteen minutes. In a hundred and fourteen minutes, you can get from here to Forest Hills on the Long Island Rail Road. But a hundred and fourteen minutes of "King Richard and the Crusaders" got me exactly nowhere.

What do these five short sentences, written by a talented journalist, accomplish? It takes close, thoughtful reading to get his full message and appreciate his true intention. He begins with the indisputable statement that 114 minutes is almost two hours. What can be done in 114 minutes? Well, you can fly from New York to Cleveland. That, too, is indisputable. So far, we are dealing with sober fact. Then our writer continues: Roger Bannister (the British athlete who was the first to run a mile in less than four minutes) can spend 114 minutes in running twenty-eight miles. At this point the alert reader does a double take: What was that last statement? A man who can run a mile in less than four minutes can run twenty-eight miles in 114 minutes. Theoretically, yes; actually, no. Bannister would have to be a superman indeed to keep up his record-breaking pace for almost two hours! The reviewer knew very well that his statement was absurd, but the absurdity, as we shall see, was part

of his plan. He has suddenly switched from the demonstrably
true to the obviously impossible—for a purpose. Next, he says,
you can ride from New York to the suburb of Forest Hills, a
distance of 8.7 miles, in 114 minutes. The full point of this
probably would be appreciated only by New Yorkers, for whom
the review was primarily intended. The Long Island Rail Road
for many years has been notorious for its slowness. Its timetable
says that the running time between New York's Penn Station
and Forest Hills is sixteen minutes, but the writer, now turning
cynical, implies that there is a pretty broad gap between the
railroad's promise and its actual performance. Furthermore, by
saying in effect that in 114 minutes a fast runner could go 19.3
miles farther than a passenger could go on the Long Island Rail
Road, the reviewer has capped his first absurdity (the assumption that a man can run twenty-eight miles in 114 minutes) with
a second (the assumption that he can outrace a train—even a
Long Island train).

Yes, but what has all this to do with the movie? The next
sentence makes it clear: "But a hundred and fourteen minutes
of 'King Richard and the Crusaders' got me exactly nowhere."
In other words, *even* the Long Island Rail Road, synonymous
with slowness, a road whose trains (it has been humorously implied) travel less than a third as fast as a human being on two
legs, moves faster than the picture does.

The reviewer could have said, in so many words, that the film
drags, and let it go at that. But then he would not have had his
fun, nor would his alert readers have had theirs. What he did
was begin with the idea of high speed (flying to Cleveland, running a four-minute mile) and then suddenly shift into the contrasting idea of slow motion (the weary railroad)—the two ideas
being ingeniously connected by the use of Roger Bannister.
The chain of reasoning from sentence to sentence is faulty, but
the fallacies were entirely intentional and the readers were
expected to recognize them as such. What our critic did, therefore, was to express his essentially serious comment on a movie
he didn't like in subtly humorous terms—to entertain his read-

ers with a bit of mental gymnastics which they could appreciate only if they read his review sentence by sentence, weighing the meaning and implication of each carefully wrought statement. At this point you are doubtless getting alarmed. "Do you mean to say that I'll have to read everything as closely—word by word, phrase by phrase, sentence by sentence—as we've read that little quotation from a movie review?" The answer is Yes—for the time being. Only by such close and admittedly time-consuming analysis can you hope to develop your critical faculty. It will do you little good to skim over the text of the exercises in this book, for the whole book is designed to show you the pitfalls that lie in such superficial reading. We do not mean that henceforth, to the end of your days, you must read everything so minutely; but you must get into the habit of watching for certain tricks of style and rhythm and logic, and the only way to develop that habit is to practice it intensively for a while. Obviously, you cannot spend as much time in your general reading as you are expected to do in working out the exercises in this book; but it is necessary to learn certain principles thoroughly, and the only way to do so is to observe their operation in detail. The exercises have the same basic importance for the novice critical reader that practicing scales has for the beginning musician. Once the habits that the book is planned to help you acquire are well established, you will find that you are able to read at your accustomed speed. But the time you spend in reading will be *better* spent, because you will be getting more out of the printed page. So don't give up before you begin. You have too much at stake.

Which brings us to a more direct statement of the whole purpose of this book. What is this "critical reading" spoken of in the title? What good is there in learning to read more analytically, more critically?

To begin with, critical reading involves digging beneath the surface, attempting to find out not only the whole truth about what is being said, but also (and this is, in the long run, more important) the hidden implications and motives of the writer

When a reader finds out not only *what* is being said, but also *why* it is said, he is on the way to being a critical reader as well as a comprehending one.

It is in these two respects, thorough comprehension and criticism, that the reading capacities of college students have been found seriously lacking. In recent years there has been much discussion about it, both in and out of academic circles, because it is recognized that slipshod, careless reading frustrates the whole aim of college education. Unless you can read accurately for meaning, and at the same time are able to discriminate between the genuine and the false, the important and the trivial, you will be wasting a great part of your time in college.

The practice and advice offered you in this book have a vital bearing upon all the work you are now doing, or plan to do, in college. Formal practice in reading is usually assigned to the course in freshman English, perhaps on the theory that any study of what is written belongs naturally and properly to the English Department. But actually, in how many college courses can you get along without reading? And in how many courses would your performance not be improved if you could do a better job in reading your textbooks and the collateral library assignments you receive from time to time? What this book teaches you can be applied to almost every subject you will ever take in college. It can reduce the number of occasions upon which you will have to tell your instructor that you have spent so many hours "reading" a certain assignment, but that you feel you have got nothing out of it.

Most college students have already had some practice in intensive reading, even though they may not have known it at the time. Mortimer Adler, in his book on *How to Read a Book*, says:

If we consider men and women generally, and apart from their professions or occupations, there is only one situation I can think of in which they almost pull themselves up by their bootstraps, making an effort to read better than they usually do. When they are in love and are reading a love letter, they read for all they are worth. They read every word three ways; they read between the lines and in the margins; they read the whole in terms of the parts, and each part in terms of the whole; they grow sensitive to context and ambiguity, to insinuation and implication; they perceive the color of words, the odor of phrases, and the weight of sentences. They may even take the punctuation into account. Then, if never before or after, they read.*

But the necessity for close reading is not confined by any means to affairs of the heart or the performance of college assignments. It is impossible to be a genuinely intelligent member of society without the ability to discriminate between the sincere and the fraudulent in all that is spoken or written concerning the affairs of society, and especially concerning politics. You have already become aware that there is such a thing as propaganda, which is an attempt by one group to persuade other people to think and act the way in which that group wants them to think and act. No doubt you feel confident of your ability to "see through" and resist unfair propaganda appeals. Perhaps so; perhaps you can at least detect and reject a particularly blatant example of unfair propaganda. But what of the more subtle kind, which is much more prevalent? Can you distinguish between the statement of an idealistic member of Congress, who is genuinely concerned with the larger issues, and that of a veteran congressman who is concerned only with the winning of the next election and thus says only what nobody could possibly take issue with? On the surface, the two statements may seem quite alike; it is only after some analysis that a reader begins to realize that one statement is sincere, meaty, informative, and that the other is composed of nothing but weasel words. Yet, since the second contains nothing to offend, it will often succeed in winning more votes than the first, which, because it speaks out, will necessarily make enemies.

And since our democratic system of government is based on representation, and effective representation in turn depends on communication between candidate and voter, it is clear that the success of our form of government hinges to a great extent upon

* Quoted by special permission of Simon and Schuster, publishers.

the use made of language. If voters are taken in by skillful politicians who know how to say what the public, in its uncritical way, wants to hear, they deserve the sort of representatives they often get. If, on the other hand, voters can tell when they are being imposed upon—when a candidate is saying one thing and meaning another—then they can exercise their right to reject him in favor of one who talks to them honestly.

At a time when the very destiny of civilization, indeed of the human race itself, depends upon the ability of the average citizen to understand the fateful issues which the free governments of the world—his elected representatives—must decide, the urgency of this problem of intelligent communication cannot possibly be exaggerated. Not only national but international affairs are at the mercy of language. The two greatest powers in the world today, the United States and Russia, both maintain that they are dedicated to the task of preserving and extending the blessings of *democracy*. Obviously the word means very different things to a sincere believer in American values and to an equally sincere believer in those of Communism. One can understand the confusion of the millions of men and women, the world over, who are besieged by the propaganda issued by both sides; both sides, however different their respective philosophies may be, seem to be advocating the same goal. Only when the meaning of *democracy* is made clear and concrete, in terms of actual values and ways of life, does the vast difference between the western world's definition of the term and that of Soviet Russia appear. Multiply such an instance by many hundreds every year—pronouncements by presidents, prime ministers, secretaries of state, chairmen of the Senate foreign affairs committee, and ordinary congressmen and members of Parliament—and you see why the state of the world demands more critical reading and listening habits on the part of the people who elect the governments. Because the use and misuse and abuse of words determine how people make up their minds, in a very real sense words are constantly shaping our destiny.

Or we can use another appeal—to your pocketbook. Indolent,

uncritical reading habits cost you money, and plenty of it. When you read an advertisement in a magazine or a newspaper, an attempt is being made to persuade you to buy something; and the chief means of persuasion are what advertising men call "eye-appeal" and "copy." With "eye-appeal"—illustrations, layout, and typography—we have nothing to do here; with "copy" we have much to do. The art of writing advertising copy is based upon the skillful, purposeful use of language: language that will subtly flatter you, whet your interest, entice you to buy. It is language specially chosen to do this job. You read, you believe, and you buy. But how many times are you being misled? How often do you buy a product, on the strength of the advertiser's sly persuasion, when you should have bought another brand, which is cheaper and better? We are prone too often to forget that the product which is most attractively and glibly advertised may well be inferior to other brands. If you question this, spend a half hour some time with the current report of one of the consumers' research organizations, which dispassionately rank various brands on the basis of laboratory tests.

The chief agencies of political and commercial persuasion, growing more powerful year by year, are the so-called "mass media," especially the big-circulation magazines and newspapers, and television. Thoughtful observers of modern society have become increasingly disturbed over the way in which these agencies (along with others, such as radio and the movies) tend to make people think or react alike, have the same tastes and biases—in a word, *conform*. The techniques used in the mass media are not 100 percent effective (sometimes they boomerang on the users); but they are certainly effective enough to worry all who believe that each individual should think for himself. The "big lie," ceaselessly drummed into a nation's consciousness until independent judgment is lulled to sleep and the lie becomes accepted as absolute truth, is a major weapon in the hands of dictators and demagogues. In totalitarian countries, the channels of communication are controlled by the government; hence they are all a gigantic mouthpiece for one set of ideas. In free nations, they are not as a rule government-controlled, but in America especially, the concentration of mass media in the hands of relatively few owners has sharply reduced the variety of viewpoints that can find widespread expression. For example, fifty years ago every large American city had a number of newspapers, independently owned, briskly competing, and uttering diverse opinions. Today there are few cities in which such healthy competition exists.

Like every modern American, therefore, you are in growing danger of having your opinions ready-made for you. You need at all costs to preserve and cultivate your capacity for seeing all sides of an issue and making up your own mind after careful weighing of the pros and cons. You need to develop an I'm-from-Missouri attitude toward the political and commercial messages that bombard you from every direction. This book will help you do so.

It has still another purpose: to increase your enjoyment and understanding of general reading. In these pages you will find suggestions that will enable you to derive more profit from all the reading you do, whether it be a story in the *Saturday Evening Post,* a factual article in *Holiday,* a best-selling novel, or a commentary on the present stage of the world crisis. This is not a book specifically on imaginative literature; we shall make no attempt to show you the structure of a novel or a play or a poem, or to discuss the many problems confronting writers in these forms. Nor shall we attempt to develop "literary taste"— that is something which takes years of extensive and thoughtful reading. But we can point out some of the elements that distinguish good writing from bad: elements of style, of organization, of logic. When you reach the end of this book you should be more impatient of shoddy, "hack" writing, of stuff that obviously is written for a market of undiscriminating people who read with their mental eyes shut; and on the other hand you should have a more acute sense of what is genuinely good writing.

At the present stage of your life, the great bulk of the reading you do is confined to material written especially for you. Newspaper reporters, magazine writers, the authors of "popular" novels and nonfiction works, all assume (necessarily) that the great reading public is made up of people who want to be amused or instructed without pain, cost or obligation. They want what they read to be custom-made for them. It must contain few words they do not understand, few allusions to anything they have not learned in high school, few ideas that force them to do some serious thinking. The "average" reader, including the college freshman, who is an "average" young American, is assumed to be quite indolent in his reading habits. If he cannot have his reading spoon-fed, he wants none of it.

You can go through life quite easily without reading anything beyond this wide but still limited area of material specially designed for the "average" reader. But how much you will be missing! The fact is that most of the great writers of the past—the men and women who said things that are still vitally meaningful to us today—have written for an audience of men and women of superior education and of cultivated reading habits. Seldom have they "written down"; they have written for their intellectual equals. This is true also of the contemporary writers whose work is most worth reading. They refuse to make concessions to the unambitious reader. And yet what these people say can make a tremendous difference in your life—if only you will read them.

The only solution is for you to equip yourself to become a member of the superior audience to which the superior writers address themselves. You do not have to renounce your taste for popular magazine articles or Book-of-the-Month Club fiction; and there are plenty of highly intelligent and cultivated people who love detective stories, just as the late Justice Holmes is said to have been fond of a good earthy burlesque show. But you should also be *able* to read material that is several notches higher, both in content and in style. Although we cannot show you in detail how you can train yourself to do so, we can give you some useful hints.

There is a simple way by which you can measure your progress. About halfway through the book, if you have done the exercises carefully and profited by class discussions, you should be worried because you no longer believe anything you read. Wherever you turn, you should be seeing clichés, "glittering generalities," fallacious reasoning, cunning manipulation of sentence rhythms; and you should be bothered. This is the healthiest possible sign, because it means that you have lost your faith in many false gods; you are wiser, even if, for the time being, you are sadder. You have been divested of lifelong prejudices, biases, and reliance on what has proved to be fraudulent.

Don't worry. This is only half the process of becoming an intelligent reader. The other half, the constructive half, requires the establishment of positive critical standards by which you may detect what is good and credible and sincere in what men write. The establishment of this wiser faith is a slower process, but it will come if you allow it to do so. No one need be, or indeed should be, a mere scoffer, a cynic who maintains that nothing is written but to deceive. But in order to recognize the true you must first be prepared to recognize the false. That is the first, and major, job confronting you. And if you somehow regret the loss of those old prejudices which you so carefully cherished, remember the slogan of that cigarette ad compaign a few years ago: "It's fun to be fooled, but it's more fun to know." With that one advertising sentiment, at least, we can be in complete agreement.

To the conscientious student we can guarantee a reward, one which is inevitably the result of close analysis of the ways of language and of thought. You will emerge from this work a more matured person. You will have had a glimpse into the way your mind operates, and you will have had some exercise in making it operate more efficiently and more acutely. You will have made a start toward separating the vain illusions of this world from the substantial realities. You will have dis-

covered the satisfaction of being able to expose the emptiness
of much that is written for your personal consumption and at
the same time to profit by what intelligent and honest men and
women have written for other intelligent and honest men and
women to read. In a word, these pages are designed to show you
the direction in which intellectual maturity lies.

CHAPTER ONE

Denotation
and Connotation

NCIDENTS like this are happening every day. A teacher in a
college English course has returned a student's theme on the
subject of a poem (a stanza of which is printed on page 13 of
this book). One sentence in the theme reads, "Like all of Keats's
best work, the 'Ode to Autumn' has a remarkably sensual quality that makes it especially appealing to me." The instructor's
red pencil has underscored the word *sensual,* and in the margin
he has written "Accurate?" or whatever his customary comment
is in such cases. The student has gone home, checked the dictionary, and come back puzzled. "I don't see what you mean,"
he says. "The dictionary says *sensual* means 'of or pertaining to
the senses or physical sensation.' And that's what I wanted to
say. Keats's poem is filled with words and images that suggest
physical sensation."

"Yes," replies the instructor, "that's what the word *means*—
according to the dictionary." And then he takes his copy of the
American College Dictionary, which contains the definition the
student quoted, and turns to the word *sensual.* "Look here," he
says, pointing to a passage in small type just after the various
definitions of the word:

SENSUAL, SENSUOUS, VOLUPTUOUS refer to experience through the
senses. SENSUAL refers, usually unfavorably, to the enjoyments de-

1

rived from the senses, generally implying grossness or lewdness: *a sensual delight in eating, sensual excesses.* SENSUOUS refers, favorably or literally, to what is experienced through the senses: *sensuous impressions, sensuous poetry.* VOLUPTUOUS implies the luxurious gratification of sensuous or sensual desires: *voluptuous joys, voluptuous beauty.**

The student reads the passage carefully and begins to see light. The word *sensual* carries with it a shade of meaning, an unfavorable implication, which he did not intend; the word he wanted was *sensuous.* He has had a useful lesson in the dangers of taking dictionary definitions uncritically, as well as in the vital difference between denotation and connotation.

The difference between the two is succinctly phrased in another of those small-type paragraphs of explanation, taken this time from *Webster's New Collegiate Dictionary:* "Denote implies all that strictly belongs to the definition of the word, *connote* all of the ideas that are suggested by the term; thus, 'home' *denotes* the place where one lives with one's family, but it usually *connotes* comfort, intimacy, and privacy. The same implications distinguish *denotation* and *connotation.*"† The denotation of a word is its dictionary definition, which is what the word "stands for." According to the dictionary, *sensuous* and *sensual* have the same general connotation: they agree in meaning "experience through the senses." Yet they *suggest* different things. And that difference in suggestiveness constitutes a difference in connotation.

Nothing is more essential to intelligent, profitable reading than sensitivity to connotation. Only when we possess such sensitivity can we understand both what the author *means,* which may be pretty plain, and what he wants to *suggest,* which may actually be far more important than the superficial meaning. The difference between reading a book or story or essay or

* Reprinted by courtesy of the publishers from *The American College Dictionary.* Copyright 1947 by Random House, Inc. (textbook edition by Harper & Brothers).

† By permission. From *Webster's New Collegiate Dictionary,* copyright, 1949, 1951, 1953, by G. & C. Merriam Co.

poem for surface meaning and reading it for implication is the difference between listening to the New York Philharmonic-Symphony Orchestra on a battered old radio and listening to it on a high-fidelity record player. Only the latter brings out the nuances that are often more significant than the obvious, and therefore easily comprehended, meaning.

An unfailing awareness of the connotative power of words is just as vital, of course, to the writer. His eternal task is to select the word which will convey, not approximately but exactly, what he wants to say. He must remember that two words may be "synonymous" in respect to denotation; that is, they *mean* the same thing. But to the practiced writer, as to the practiced reader, few if any words are exactly synonymous in connotation; in a given context one particular word will convey the precise implication the writer desires to communicate to his reader. The inexperienced writer, forgetting this, often has recourse to Roget's *Thesaurus,* where he finds, conveniently marshaled, whole regiments of synonyms; not knowing which to choose, he either closes his eyes and picks a word at random or else chooses the one that "sounds" best. In either case he is neglecting the delicate shadings of implication which differentiate each word in a category from its neighbors. To be certain that the word he has selected conveys exactly the sense he has in mind, he should check it in those invaluable little paragraphs in the dictionary.* For further help, he can look up the fuller discussions in *Webster's Dictionary of Synonyms.*

EXERCISE 1

Explain why the italicized words in the following sentences reflect the writer's insensitivity to connotation, and in each case supply a more accurate word.

1. Although she was really twenty-one, there was a certain *childish-*

* If the definition of the word in question is not followed by a paragraph discriminating between its "synonyms," there is a cross-reference to the place where this paragraph occurs.

ness in her voice and manner which set her apart from the other girls and delighted everyone who met her.

2. Some of the members of the party were not at all interested in modern art; however, they *gaped* politely at the various exhibits as they plodded along after the guide.

3. What especially interests newcomers is the absolute *smoothness* of the countryside.

4. When she got out of the hospital she was pretty *lean*, but a good wholesome diet of home cooking soon remedied that.

5. Attractive though it was in terms of pay and prospects for advancement, Clem decided finally to *spurn* the offer and look for some other job.

6. I've been taking aspirins by the carload, but they haven't *healed* my headache.

7. I knew she had studied the lesson thoroughly, so after asking my question I waited a little. Finally the *retort* came, in her usual quiet, almost hesitant manner.

8. One of the best things the Scouts and Hi-Y did for him was to develop genuinely *mannish* qualities. He's a fine, upstanding youth.

EXERCISE 2

Explain the differences in connotation among the members of each of the following groups of words:

1. dash, hurry, race, gallop, speed, hurtle, run
2. corpulent, plump, obese, heavy-set, fleshy, fat, paunchy, burly, overweight, rolypoly, bulky
3. mansion, dwelling, domicile, residence, house, home
4. racket, uproar, hubbub, clatter, noise, commotion
5. titter, giggle, chuckle, guffaw, laugh, roar
6. dress, frock, costume, outfit, gown, ensemble, get-up, apparel
7. dilapidated, ramshackle, ruined, neglected, deteriorated, tumbledown
8. shrewd, cunning, calculating, sly, adroit, knowing, clever, astute
9. cheat, phony, quack, crook, impostor, charlatan
10. admire, love, relish, like, approve, idolize, respect, revere, esteem

11. snooty, arrogant, conceited, cocky, egotistical, proud, high-and-mighty, overbearing, high-hat
12. colleague, ally, associate, sidekick, partner, mate, confederate, comrade, buddy, accomplice

———

Not all words possess connotative powers. Articles, conjunctions, prepositions, many common adverbs (*well, badly, thoroughly*, etc.) lack connotative qualities because they are words used to connect ideas and to show relationships between them, or to modify their meaning; these parts of speech do not themselves stand for ideas. But most words which stand for ideas have connotations, even though they are often scarcely perceptible. That is because ideas themselves have connotations: they produce some sort of intellectual or emotional reaction inside us.

Connotations: Personal and General

There are two types of connotation: personal and general. Personal connotations are the result of the experience of the individual man or woman. The way we react to ideas and objects, and thus to the words that stand for those "referents," is determined by the precise nature of our earlier experience with the referents. Taken all together, the connotations that surround most of the words in our vocabulary are a complex and intimate record of our life to date. Our present reaction to a word may be the cumulative result of all our experiences with the word and its referent. In the case of other words, our reaction may have been determined once and for all by an early or a particularly memorable experience with them. A student's reaction to the word *teacher*, for instance, may be determined by all his experience with teachers, which has been subtly synthesized, in the course of time, into a single image or emotional response. In it are mingled memories of Miss Smith, the first-grade teacher who dried his tears when he lost a fight in the schoolyard at recess; of Miss Jones, the sixth-grade teacher who bored her pupils with thrice-told tales of her trip to Mexico ten years earlier; of Mr. Johnson, the high school gym teacher who merely laughed when he saw the brush burns a boy sustained when he inexpertly slid down a rope; of Mr. Miller, the college professor who somehow packed a tremendous amount of information into lectures that seemed too entertaining to be instructive. Or, on the other hand, when the student thinks of *teacher* he may think of a particular teacher who for one reason or another has made an especially deep impression upon him— the chemistry teacher in high school, for instance, who encouraged him, by example and advice, to make chemistry his life work.

A moment's thought will show the relationship between personal and general connotations as well as the fact that there is no line of demarcation between the two types. Since "the mass mind" is the sum total of the individual minds that comprise it, general connotations result when the reaction of the majority of people to a specific word is substantially the same. The reasons why one word should possess a certain connotation, while another word has a quite different connotation, are complex. We shall spend a little time on the subject later. Here it need only be said that differences in general connotation derive from at least two major sources. For one thing, the exact shade of meaning a word possesses in our language is often due to the use to which it was put by a writer who had especially great influence over the language because he was, and is, so widely read. The King James version of the Bible, for instance, is responsible for the crystallizing of many connotations. People came to know a given word from its occurrence in certain passages in the Bible, and thus the word came to connote to them on *all* occasions what it connoted in those familiar passages; it was permanently colored by particular associations. Such words include *trespass, money-changers, manger, Samaritan* (originally the name of a person living in a certain region of Asia Minor), *salvation, vanity, righteous, anoint,* and *charity.* The same is true of many words used in other books which, being widely read and studied, influenced the vocabularies of following generations—

Malory's *Morte d'Arthur,* for example, or Shakespeare's plays, or the essays of Addison and Steele.

But general connotation is not always a matter of literary development. It can result also from the experience that men as a social group have had with the ideas which words represent. Before 1938, the word *appease* had an inoffensive connotation. In the edition of *Webster's Collegiate Dictionary* current in that year it was defined simply as "to pacify, often by satisfying; quiet; calm; soothe; allay." But then the word became associated with the ill-fated attempts of Neville Chamberlain to stave off war with Hitler by giving in to his demands, and that association has now strongly colored its meaning. The latest edition of the same dictionary adds to the meaning quoted above this newer one: "to conciliate by political, economic, or other considerations;—now usually signifying a sacrifice of moral principle in order to avert aggression." Laden as the word is with its suggestions of the disaster of Munich, no British or American official ever uses it in referring to an aspect of foreign policy for which he wants to win public acceptance. On the other hand, opponents of that policy use the word freely to arouse sentiment against it, even though the situation in question may have little or no resemblance to that of Munich. In other words, events have conditioned us to react in a particular way to the verb *appease* and the noun *appeasement.* If our support is desired for a policy of *give-and-take,* or *live-and-let-live,* in international relations, its advocates will use the terms just italicized, as well as *negotiation* and *compromise,* which convey the idea of mutual concessions without sacrifice of principle; or *horse-trading,* which has a homely American flavor, suggesting shrewd bargaining with the additional implication that a good profit can be made on the deal.

All general connotations thus have their origin in private connotations—in personal, individual, but generally shared reactions to words and the ideas for which they stand. But later, after general connotations have been established, the process works the other way: the individual, who may have had no personal experience with the idea represented by a given word, may acquire a personal attitude toward it by observing how society in general reacts to the word. In the future, men and women who were babes in arms when Klaus Fuchs and other men stole American and British atomic secrets and relayed them to Russia may react negatively to mention of such names. If they do, it will be because they have acquired the feelings of revulsion that people associate with the names of traitors—just as Americans almost two centuries later still react to the mention of Benedict Arnold.

Every writer is obliged to differentiate between general connotations and personal ones, and to rely only upon the former. He can transmit his full message to the reader only when the reader finds in his words the same shade of meaning the author intended, and that is possible only when the commonly established distinctions among words are fully recognized. A writer who uses words which have special connotations for himself alone is writing in a private shorthand to which only he holds the key.

The Uses of Connotations

What forms do our reactions to words take? By no means all words evoke any distinguishable emotional response; *delusion* and *illusion,* for instance, probably do not do so for most people. Here the response is largely an intellectual one, a recognition that the two words are customarily used in different contexts, that they "imply" slightly different things.

But for our purposes the most important categories of words are the ones which touch the emotions of those who hear or see them. They are words that arouse people to a pleasant or unpleasant judgment—words that often stir them to decision. *Atheist* arouses deep-seated prejudices for or against the ideas that the word is said to represent, for or against people who are said to be atheists. *Streamlined* connotes modern design, clean lines, efficiency, and thus has a generally pleasant suggestion. (On the other hand, like many words that become too fashionable and thus are overused and even abused, *streamlined* has come to have a negative connotation to many fastidious readers. Too often it has been loosely used as a means of glossing over, skimping and corner-cutting—as in *streamlined* education.) *Gardenia* may suggest to some a corsage sent to a girl before a high school prom—and to others a principal ingredient* in a funeral spray. Mention of *F.D.R.* evokes fervent sentiments, of very diverse quality, from both those who voted for him and those who did not. *Sub-deb* eases the selling of clothing to adolescent girls, of whom not one in a hundred thousand will ever have a debut. *Nigger* connotes very different things to a champion of white supremacy in Mississippi, a member of the National Association for the Advancement of Colored People, and a Londoner whose only experience of Negroes has been in connection with jazz bands. *Draft* and *selective service* mean the same thing, but one term has a more unpleasant connotation than the other. And so on, *ad infinitum*.

EXERCISE 3

In Bliss Perry's *A Study of Poetry* (p. 140) is printed the following list of words which are part of the basic vocabulary of poetry because they possess particularly strong emotional appeal. Why are they so filled with suggestion? How many are part of the basic vocabulary of today's popular songs?

age, ambition, beauty, bloom, country, courage, dawn, day, death, despair, destiny, devotion, dirge, disaster, divine, dream, earth, enchantment, eternity, fair, faith, fantasy, flower, fortune, freedom, friendship, glory, glow, god, grief, happiness, harmony, hate, heart, heaven, honor, hope, immortality, joy, justice, knell, life, longing, love, man, melancholy, melody, mercy, moon, mortal, nature, noble, night, paradise, parting, peace, pleasure, pride, regret, sea, sigh, sleep, solitude, song, sorrow, soul, spirit, spring, star, suffer, tears, tender, time, virtue, weep, whisper, wind, youth†

* Does the use of *ingredient* here seem inappropriate? Why?
† By permission of Houghton Mifflin Co., publishers.

EXERCISE 4

What are the present connotations of the following words? To what extent do your answers agree with those of others in the class?

Winston Churchill, egghead, Pentagon, censorship, security, United Nations, socialized medicine, minority group, Hitler, concentration camp, thermonuclear warfare, imperialism, witch hunt, welfare state

EXERCISE 5

1. What reaction, if any, do you have when you hear the name "Gwendolyn"? Do you see any specific picture in your mind? How can you account for it? Try the same experiment with "Elmer."
2. What personal connotations does each of the following names have to you? Do your reactions match those of others in the class? Explain why they do—or don't.

    Bill, Will, Willy, William, Billy
    Meg, Margie, Margaret, Peg, Peggy, Marge

EXERCISE 6

What do the following words connote to you personally?

serenade, Texas, examination, sandpaper, romantic, wryly, skunk, Inquisition, mangled, primitive, prudish, kiss, trample, messily, slither, mother, doleful, crackle, ostentatiously, sunrise, cooperate, refresh, bleak, celestial, chocolate, orchid, gurgle, midnight oil, Hawaii, crimson, soggy

EXERCISE 7

What do the following words connote to you?

soubrette, ogle, sycophant, quaternary, torsibility, Rhadames, exacerbate, congeries, barratry

EXERCISE 8

Which of these two lists contains the greater number of terms having connotative value? Why?

1. salt, nightingale, violet, werewolf, grizzly bear, brain fever, nylon, opium, sugar, turkey vulture
2. sodium chloride, Luscinia megarhyncha, Viola cucullata, lycanthrope, Ursus horribilis, encephalomyelitis, product of the interaction of a dicarboxylic acid with a diamine, inspissated juice of Papaver somniferum, $C_{12}H_{22}O_{11}$, Cathartes aura

---

Intimately associated with emotional response, and often directly responsible for it, are the images that many words inspire in our minds. The commonest type of image is the visual: that is, a given word habitually calls forth a certain picture on the screen of our inner consciousness. Mention of places we have seen and people we have known produces a visual recollection of them. Of course the precise content of these pictures is determined by the sort of experience one has had with their originals. *Mary* may not recall the picture of one's childhood sweetheart, but it may evoke instead a picture of a pink hair-ribbon which Mary must once have worn. *Boston* may recall only the picture of a street accident, which was the most vivid memory one carried away from that city. And so on! It is a fascinating game to examine in this fashion the mental images thus spontaneously conjured up by words; equally rewarding is the effort to explain why many words evoke images which on first thought seem so completely irrelevant to their denotations.

It is not only words referring to concrete objects which have this power of evoking a visual response in the imagination. Our picture-making faculty also enables us to visualize abstractions in concrete terms—and, as we shall see, it gets us into a great deal of trouble on that account. *Capitalist* is an abstract noun; it denotes a person who has a certain function in a certain kind of economic system. But to many people it connotes a definite picture, obviously derived from the cartoonist's stock figure, of a bloated banker in striped pants, cutaway coat, top hat, and spats; he is smoking a Corona-Corona cigar, on his fingers are rings with huge stones, and across his middle reposes a gold watch chain with links as thick as frankfurters. To many, in a similar way, the noun *liberal* conjures up a picture of an intellectual-looking man with thick glasses, bushy hair, wrinkled clothes, and a wild expression on his face. Thus abstractions are made concrete, and our reactions to the words that represent those abstractions are patterned in terms of that visual image. What visual images do the words *statesman* and *politician* suggest to you?

In addition to visual responses in the imagination, words evoke responses associated with the other senses. Many words have connotations that appeal to our inward ear: *tick-tock, harmony, squeak, trumpet, dirge, static, thunder, croon, lisp*. Others appeal to our sense of touch—*gritty, needle, ice-cold, lather, soft, kiss, baby's cheek, woolen underwear*. Another class invites palatal responses—*buttermilk, spicy, mellow, roast beef, castor oil, menthol, mild*. And a final group invites olfactory responses—*burning dump, incense, new-mown hay, sweaty, coffee roaster, fragrance, diesel fumes*. Many words, like some already mentioned, appeal to two or more senses at once: for instance, *dry, bubbly, satin, wine, wrinkle, mossy, sea breeze, snowy, cigarette, sugar*.

Since our sensory experience may be either pleasant or unpleasant, the words that evoke their imaginative equivalents have the power to sway us to accept or reject an idea. "So soft, yet manageable . . . so sweetly clean! Come-hither loveliness— that's what your hair has after a luxurious Prell shampoo! It's caressably soft, yet so *obedient*! Yes, angel-soft, smooth as satin, glowing with that 'Radiantly Alive' look *he'll* love!" Thus exclaims the advertising man who wants millions of women to buy a certain solution for washing their hair. Or: "It's a foul, evil-smelling mess!" Thus speaks a minority-party congressman who is dissatisfied with something the administration has done.

But sometimes men employ words lovingly, unschemingly, wishing only to enchant:

> Season of mists and mellow fruitfulness,
>   Close bosom-friend of the maturing sun;
> Conspiring with him how to load and bless
>   With fruit the vines that round the thatch-eaves run;
> To bend with apples the mossed cottage-trees,
>   And fill all fruit with ripeness to the core;
>   To swell the gourd, and plump the hazel shells
>   With a sweet kernel; to set budding more,
> And still more, later flowers for the bees,
> Until they think warm days will never cease,
>   For Summer has o'er-brimmed their clammy cells.

Or:

> It is a beauteous evening, calm and free,
> The holy time is quiet as a Nun
> Breathless with adoration; the broad sun
> Is sinking down in its tranquillity;
> The gentleness of heaven broods o'er the Sea:
> Listen! the mighty Being is awake,
> And doth with his eternal motion make
> A sound like thunder—everlastingly.

And then we have literature.

Now we need to look a little more closely at these three main uses of connotation.

Connotations in Advertising

If advertising copywriters were less skillful masters of word connotations, we should spend far less money than we do. They know how to cultivate our responses, always evoking pleasant pictures, making us yearn for what we lack—and all without our being aware of it. On the other hand they have a formidable list of taboos—words which must never be mentioned because they have negative connotations of one sort or another. In advocating the purchase of a product because (they say) it doesn't cost very much, they never use the word *cheap: cheap* connotes shoddiness, as well as pennypinching. And so they appeal to our sense of *thrift,* which is more fashionable perhaps because it has the approval of Ben Franklin, an American folk-hero. In promoting a large-size package of their product, they call it the *economy size*—"You save when you buy it!" *Fat* is never used except in the reducing-course ads; you can never induce a woman to buy a dress or a corset by calling her fat. Instead there are dresses for *the larger figure.* And when it is a matter of selling pipe tobacco, perfume, coffee, or even Air-Wicks, *smell* is absolutely interdicted.

It is not hard to find out for oneself exactly how advertising men work: a half-hour with one or two current magazines, keeping in mind the evocative powers of connotation, will supply abundant examples of the way in which a product is always presented in the most enticing light. Here are a few instances culled at random. In brackets are inserted alternative words which the writer of the advertisement may have considered and then rejected. Can you account for each rejection—or do you think some of the rejected words might have been more effective?

1. Superb craftsmanship [talent, know-how, proficiency]—achieved by no other potters [pottery company, china makers, pottery manufacturers]—fuses Franciscan's strong [tough, durable, breakage-resistant], pearl-toned [pearly, pearl-colored], china-body with china of subtle [delicate, faint, hardly perceptible] nature colors, then encircles them with gleaming [shining, bright, flashing] platinum. Encanto is a luxury to own—economy [cheap, thrifty, inexpensive] to buy.

2. For more years than you can probably remember, women have been using crisp [brittle, fragile], perky [jaunty, sharp] Heinz Pickles to tempt lagging appetites [to get their families to eat more, to stimulate hunger] . . . and spark [spice up, give zest to] plain economy dishes [ordinary food, routine meals] with a cool, green touch of spring! We've been making [putting up, bottling, processing] pickles the same careful [precise, meticulous, loving] way for over 80 years—using treasured [precious, valuable] home recipes, pedigreed [specially developed, cultivated] cucumbers, our own fine Heinz Vinegar and rare [out-of-the-way, exotic,

unusual], fragrant spices—and, naturally, most people like Heinz
Pickles best!*

3. New styling [design, shape] plus dramatic advancements [new
features, novelties, innovations] in exclusive [our very own,
unique, patented] "Unimatic Construction"! Gives you smooth-
top comfort [is comfortable, feels good, has no humps] and
healthfully-correct support [firmness, solidity, suspension]! Here
is sleep at its most refreshing best [finest, soundest, most delect-
able] . . . freed at last from the uncomfortable tenseness and ir-
ritations caused by old-fashioned buttons and bumps. The reasons for this are as sound as the sleep you enjoy. For the daring
[audacity, ingenuity, bright ideas] of Serta's engineers [makers,
draftsmen], coupled with scientific medical research [fresh medical data, knowledge of sleeping habits], has created [made, inspired, suggested] this ultra-modern [new, up-to-date, futuristic]
mattress that is so much better for you in three vital [important,
noteworthy, remarkable] ways.

4. It's like starting life all over again, with a brand new complexion
[facial hue, coloration]! Just smooth on [apply, rub in] a few
drops with your fingertips [fingers, by hand]. Pat on [follow up
with, add] powder. You'll be astounded [startled, surprised,
thunder-struck] at the change! Your skin has new color, a finer
[better, improved, closer-grained] texture [surface, feel], a glowing [shining, bright, smoldering] look you thought you'd lost
forever [you'd never get back, you were too old to regain]!†.

Obviously the precise choice of words a writer makes depends
to a great extent upon the audience to which he is addressing
his message. Confronted by four possible alternatives, all of
which are pleasing, he selects the one which in his practiced
estimation will be most effective with the people he has in
mind. Thus if he is writing an ad intended for the widely diversified readers of *Time,* he chooses words whose connotations
would most affect them; but if he is writing an ad for *Harper's
Bazaar,* let us say, or *The New Yorker,* his audience, having
special tastes, will be moved by a completely different set of

---

* Courtesy of H. J. Heinz Company.
† Courtesy of Revlon Products.

words. We shall have more to say later of this matter of writing for a specific audience.

All this is very interesting; but is it important? The answer is a decided "Yes." Assuming, as we no doubt have a right to do, that your money is not unlimited and that you like to get as much as possible for it when you spend it: how many times in the course of a year do you buy something on the strength of the words some advertising agency magician has spoken to you, rather than on the actual merits of the product? Perhaps you really do not need it, but the words of the advertiser (*luxurious . . . smart . . . efficient . . . delicious . . . figure-flattering*) have made you want it so badly that you buy it. Or perhaps you do need it; but why buy Brand A instead of Brand B, which is indisputably better? Brand A's advertising writer did a better job with words (*independent laboratory tests have proved . . . up-to-the-minute smartness . . . matchless flavor . . . super- swift . . . a little higher in price, but what a world of difference in wearability . . . the best-groomed men everywhere . . .*). But how much that is really worth knowing have you learned from Brand A's advertisements? Or has the writer been craftily playing upon your weak spots—your vanity, your envy of some- one else, your fear of not being in step with the latest fashions, your desire for greater personal beauty or more leisure or more friends? You can find out, very easily, if you analyze his words for their connotative overtones. It is a salutary exercise to ex- amine the advertisements in a single issue of a widely circulated magazine to find out how many real *facts* they contain; you will learn that for every nugget of information you find, you must burrow your way through mountains of fine-sounding words. In the end you must decide whether it is sensible to let your emo- tions rule your pocketbook.

EXERCISE 9

The following advertisement appeared in *The New Yorker*— a magazine read by people in the "higher income brackets."

From each group of alternatives, select the word you think the copywriter chose:

A [mixture, hodgepodge, concoction, blending] of subtle French [skill, genius, artistry, craftsmanship] with the [intrepid, audacious, courageous, bold], [sprightly, vivacious, animated, peppy] American touch—this accounts for its very [peculiar, distinctive, special, unmistakable] [style, character, nature, makeup]. [Bouncy, Lively, Buoyant, Volatile], dry yet [intoxicating, dizzying, heady, stimulating], [indescribable, defying classification, too wonderful for words, unutterable], Escapade is—above all—Adventure in [Odor, Fragrance, Perfume, Aroma]. Eleven Escapades [intended, contrived, designed, manufactured] to [solve the gift problem for, satisfy, gratify, please] all who give, [enchant, stun, hypnotize, fascinate] all who receive.

EXERCISE 10

How informative is the use of language in this advertisement?

Our Famous Hard Water Soap is carefully compounded to the original formula brought from France more than fifty years ago by John Wanamaker. It combines premium fats and cocoanut oil with nourishing buttermilk, and is pure enough for a baby's tender skin. It is economical because it is hardmilled, and usable right down to the last sliver. It gives a rich, creamy lather in either hard or soft water.

EXERCISE 11

Analyze a group of current advertisements in one field—for example, cigarettes, television sets, automobiles, men's or women's clothing, or liquor—to find the chief selling points which the copywriter wishes to impress upon his readers, and to see how he uses language to make them wish to buy his product. What are the words now most fashionable among the writers of advertisements for a certain class of products? How much testable *information* can you find in each advertisement?

EXERCISE 12

Compare these two advertisements for (a) connotative value,

(b) the amount of solid information conveyed, and (c) their probable effectiveness with the audience for which each seems to have been written:

1. As surely as sunshine follows rain, romance follows the girl whose hair is bright to see, soft to touch, fresh as a spring breeze —the kind of hair you always have when you use New White Rain. This fabulous shampoo sprinkles your hair with sunlight. And with sunshine all around you, love and laughter follow after. Love and laughter . . . the essence of romance. Ask for White Rain . . . the lotion shampoo that gives you results like softest rain water.

2. Specifically designed to inactivate calcium and magnesium plus all traces of iron. In alkaline processing liquors, calcium and iron sequestering is accomplished simultaneously. Cheelox B-14 is the new, all-purpose chelating agent which is soluble and stable at all temperatures in neutral, acid and alkaline solutions. For economical control of metal ions, regardless of the problem, Cheelox B-14 is the product to use. To determine the effectiveness and economy of Cheelox B-14, we suggest you compare this new sequestering agent with the product you are now using.

EXERCISE 13

At the time this edition of *Preface to Critical Reading* was being prepared, these were some of the coined terms, many of them trademarks, used in advertising campaigns. How much connotative value has each?

Cushionaire (tires)
Grip-Seal construction (tires)
Magic Margin (device on typewriters)
Glide-Ride suspension (automobile springs)
Luxury Lounge interiors (automobiles)
Gardol ("decay-fighter" ingredient in toothpaste)
Halo Light (television)
Power-Mesh (suggests an automobile transmission, but actually refers to a fabric used for girdles)
Wrinkl-Shed (cotton fabrics)
Supersorb (terry cloth)

Chromspun (fiber for swimming suits and other garments)
Foam-Ease (mattresses)
Spiffy-Glo (paints)
Foodarama (electric refrigerators)
Nylovent (women's gloves)

EXERCISE 14

1. A newspaper advertisement announces a "MONSTROUS THREE-DAY FOURTH OF JULY CELEBRATION," including auto and horse races, boxing matches, band concerts, and fireworks. From the way the ad is worded, would you be justified in expecting something out of the ordinary?
2. A highway sign tells you that you are nearing a roadside restaurant called "THE CHAT AND CHEW." Are you inclined to stop there for dinner?
3. A sign in a department store window during the Christmas season proclaims "SUGGESTIVE TOYS." Why do so many people stop for a closer look? How should the sign have been worded so as to convey what the management really meant?

Connotations in Political Persuasion

Now let us consider the reader not as a consumer, a buyer of things so temptingly advertised in the magazines and on television, but as a citizen of a free society, whose personal opinions, when joined with those of millions of other citizens, constitute public opinion. Every day representative men and women of America are being interviewed for the public opinion polls. They are being asked what they think on this or that current issue, and most of them turn out to have some sort of view. Where and how do they get their opinions?

Public opinion is being formed wherever and whenever one person expresses his opinion on a topic to someone else. Unless the hearer or reader has already made up his mind and refuses to change it (in which case his own opinion, whether in agreement or opposition, will be confirmed simply by hearing the arguments restated), he will be influenced by what he is told—and thus where before there was only one man who believed such and such, now there are two. And just as is the case with commercial advertising, in persuasion designed to make someone think thus-and-so about a public issue, the emotion-producing powers of words are a vast force for good or evil.* Used in one way, they are a means of spreading and intensifying the basest sort of prejudice and bigotry; used in another, they are a means of stirring the human spirit to heights of nobility and courage.

We wish at all costs to avoid the suggestion that words, used for the purposes of persuasion, are always either evil or empty. Mankind would never have risen from barbarism had there not constantly been men—poets, orators, preachers—to stir it to action. If you condemn all persuasive language as being sinister in motive, designed to make men respond to empty symbols rather than to reality, you condemn a great body of our finest literature, from the Old Testament prophets with their sulphurous denunciations of a godless people to Winston Churchill's speech which rallied the British people to a defense of their island even after the catastrophe of Dunkirk. The Welsh hymn "Men of Harlech," Wordsworth's sonnet "Milton! thou shouldst be living at this hour," Milton's *Areopagitica,* Pericles' funeral oration, MacLeish's "Lines for an Interment," Hood's "The Song of the Shirt," John of Gaunt's "This England" speech in Shakespeare's *Richard II*—all are, in one way or another, pieces of persuasion. But they are all on a high plane; they are designed to stir men to positive, constructive action by appealing to their loftiest emotions, emotions of pride and honor and courage and pity. They inspire.

But much, indeed most, persuasion does no such thing. It operates on a much lower plane, reaching into those regions of men's spirits which harbor their intolerance, their vanity, their hankering for superiority, their suspicion of the new or different, their jealousy, their fear. All of us are prejudiced; we dis-

* Nowadays, to be sure, photography also has a great part in forming and spreading public opinion—as cartoons have had for almost a century and a half.

like certain people, certain activities, certain ideas—in many cases, not because we have reasoned things out and found a logical basis for our dislike, but rather because those people or activities or ideas affect our less noble instincts. Of course there are also positive prejudices, by which we approve of people or things—perhaps because they please our lower emotions (vanity, sense of superiority, etc.) or perhaps because we have always been taught that they were "good" and never stopped to reason why. In either case, it is these prejudices and biases, irrational and unfair though they are, which words can and do arouse. Two principal means by which this is accomplished are name-calling and the use of the glittering generality. They are alike in that they depend upon the process of association, by which one idea (the specific person, group, proposal, or situation being discussed) receives emotional coloration from another idea placed close by.

Name-calling is the device of arousing an unfavorable response by such an association. There is a whole treasury of words which connote things unpleasant to most Americans: *un-American, alien, Communist, Fascist, bureaucratic, dictator, subversive, rabble rouser, totalitarianism, free spending, agitator, reactionary, radical* are a few of them. If, then, a speaker or writer wishes to sway his audience against a person or party or principle, he will often use such terms in his persuasion. "The bill now before Congress is un-American and will take us another long step on the road toward totalitarianism." "The Republican party is made up largely of smug, die-hard reactionaries." "The Democratic party is riddled with second-generation New Dealers and radicals." Name-calling is not confined to political discussion. It is found in every argument, on whatever topic, in which more heat than light is generated. "The preachers who want to padlock the movies on Sundays are strait-laced, bluenosed hypocrites who want nothing more than to spoil the poor man's only day of recreation." "The liquor dealers' association that is agitating for the emasculation of the state law is composed of racketeering saloon keepers and greedy proprietors of dives where every sort of sin and debauchery rages unchecked; every one of them is an agent of Satan." Every sentence we have quoted contains words loaded with unpleasant emotional suggestion. And inevitably their evil connotations spill over into the ideas with which they are associated and hide the real point at issue.

The glittering generality, on the other hand, involves the use of agreeable connotations. Most people automatically react favorably to such words and phrases as *American, freedom, democracy, national honor, patriotism, Constitution, statesman, human rights, peace, liberty, economy, equality of opportunity, prosperity,* and *higher standard of living.* Words like these therefore shed a pleasant glow upon the ideas with which they are associated. "The bill now before Congress is based on true principles of American democracy and will provide us with a strong bulwark against alien ways of life." "The Republican party is the party of men and women united for the preservation of private enterprise and the right to earn an honest living." "The Democratic party is composed of practical idealists who are working for a better America—a land of peace, prosperity, and security." Nor is the glittering generality confined to political discussion. "The ministers who are urging Sunday closing are honest, unselfish servants of God and man, who have at heart the best interests of the community." "The liquor dealers' association that is recommending the liberalization of the state law is composed of substantial tax-paying citizens who are well aware that their success depends upon the maintenance of order and decency in their establishments." In every sentence occur words designed to soothe the reader, make him feel good—and incline him to accept the idea which the words so agreeably clothe.

These two categories in no way exhaust the methods by which words can be used to condemn or approve without reference to evidence or logic; you will be able to find many pieces of persuasion in which there is not a single example of name-calling or a glittering generality. These devices have been sin-

gled out for notice because they are very common and because
their unfairness is so easily seen. (Several more devices will be
discussed and illustrated in Chapter Three.)

The irrationality of the use of such words and the injustices—
indeed, the grave harm—that result from it can be illustrated by
a brief analysis of the actual process.

The speaker: "Mr. X (a government official, a writer, a college professor, an artist, a scientist, a television performer) is a
Communist sympathizer!"

The evidence: None. As a matter of fact, Mr. X, while a man
of relatively liberal leanings in politics, believes firmly in the
soundness of the capitalistic system, disagrees with those who
think Russia's economic and political system is better, and is an
indisputably loyal American.

The man in the crowd: "I don't like Communists. You say
this man is a Communist? All right, throw him out of his job,
put him in jail, send him back to Russia where he belongs—
anyway, do something about him!"

What are the principal errors here? One is that the speaker
calls Mr. X a Communist sympathizer without producing any
evidence to support his accusation; a second is that the listener
translates "Communist sympathizer" into the more blunt
"Communist"—a very common habit, because the human mind
loves to simplify, distort, and exaggerate; a third is that the
listener reacts promptly and violently to a word, without stop-
ping to ask by what right the speaker uses it. What does *Communist* mean to the listener? Plainly it has some strong and
unpleasant connotation. But if he were asked to explain *why*
the word touches off so disagreeable a reaction, he might turn
out to have only the vaguest idea of what *Communist* stands for.
Several years ago, reporters from the *Capital Times,* a newspaper in Madison, Wisconsin, asked 197 people chosen at random, "What is a Communist?" Of these 197 people, 123 admitted that they didn't know. Presumably typical of the latter
were a farmer who said, "They are no good to my notion. I can't
figure out what they are," and a housewife who said, "I really

don't know what a Communist is. I think they should throw
them out of the White House." (In other words, I don't know
what Communists are, but whatever they are, I'm against them.)
Of those who attempted a definition, a stenographer said, "If a
person didn't have a religion I would be tempted to believe he
was a Communist"; a high-school student said, "A Communist
is a person who wants war"; an office worker said that a Communist is "anyone that stands for things that democracy does
not." (By this last bit of "reasoning," a Communist could be
identical with a Fascist.)

To every thoughtful person, it is horrifying that so many
people are ready, even eager, to condemn an individual or party
or philosophy on the strength of a word alone, without knowing
what it means, or with only the haziest idea of its meaning, or
with a positively wrong idea of its meaning. And just as dangerous to the successful operation of a democracy is the willingness
to accept an *unsupported* accusation. The listener quoted above
may have substantial reasons for hating Communists; he may
be able to list, on request, a large number of perfectly sound
arguments against Communism. Yet if he censures a man on
someone's mere say-so, he is as unthinking and unjust as the
people in Madison who admitted they didn't know what a
Communist was but still had an opinion to offer.

The above example has been chosen merely because in the
middle of the twentieth century the Communist issue has
haunted America. It is not only in politics, however, but in
every sphere of life—on campus, in factory, office, home—that
we run across such groundless denunciations and irrational
responses. To paste a ready-made label on a bottle is far easier
than going to the trouble of analyzing its contents.

Try the same procedure with the second device, the glittering
generality.

The candidate: "We must protect our sacred heritage, the
American way of life!"

First listener (a mechanic): "Good stuff! American way of life
—high wages, profits of big business limited by taxation, monop-

olies forbidden, labor unions protected by law, equal opportunity for all, nobody too rich, nobody too poor . . . I'll vote for him!"

Second listener (owner of a small factory): "My sentiments exactly! American way of life—government keeps its hands off business, no excess profits tax, labor unions kept in hand by restrictive laws. If a man has the brains and the aggressiveness he can make a million dollars and it'll be his own . . . I'll vote for him."

Who is going to be disappointed after the candidate takes office and begins making decisions on specific issues? He cannot serve two masters; yet both voted for him because he favored what they favored—a vague phrase which was bound to please them, *so long as it remained undefined.* The simple, devastating test to apply to every such word or phrase, so agreeable, so unexceptionably fine, is this: What *in particular* does it mean to the person who utters it? Is it as beautiful in practice as it looks on paper? Would you agree with the sentiment if you knew the specific things the man proposes to do?

The peril in all such easygoing use of language is a lack of definition, which allows the emotions and prejudices free play. Wrenched loose from what it "stands for"—its strict dictionary definition—or from specific applications, a word can be used indiscriminately. *The New Yorker* once printed a shrewd comment on the way in which the word *Fascist* can serve anyone who wants to attack anyone else:

. . . It is getting so a Fascist is a man who votes the other way. Persons who vote *your* way, of course, continue to be "right-minded people."

We are sorry to see this misuse of the word "Fascist." If we recall matters, a Fascist is a member of the Fascist party or a believer in Fascist ideals. These are: a nation founded on blood lines, political expansion by surprise and war, murder or detention of unbelievers, transcendence of state over individual, obedience to one leader, contempt for parliamentary forms, plus some miscellaneous gymnastics for the young and a general feeling of elation. It seems to us that there are many New Deal Democrats who do not subscribe to such a program, also many aspiring Republicans. Other millions of Americans are nonsubscribers. It's too bad to emasculate the word "Fascist" by using it on persons whose only offense is that they vote the wrong ticket. The word should be saved for cases where it applies, as it does to members of our Ku Klux Klan, for instance, whose beliefs and practices are identical with Fascism.*

When, as is often the case with terms used in name-calling and the glittering generality, a word refers to a large and variegated group of people, it can be used with equal effectiveness to condemn *or* to praise, depending on the writer's motive. *Management* is a typical dual-purpose word. Someone writing from the viewpoint of militant labor might use it in the expectation of arousing a negative reaction, stemming from its suggestion of the predatory, public-be-damned "robber baron" capitalism of the nineteenth century; another writer, however, might adopt it to evoke the favorable connotations associated with the modern enlightened businessman who has a highly developed sense of responsibility toward employees and public alike. Again, what is *labor*? A clique of racketeering union bosses, with criminal convictions in their past and no doubt in their future, or sober, impeccably honest and intelligent leaders who are devoted to the welfare of the rank and file? Everything hinges on who uses the term, and why he does so.

This is not to say that so-called "omnibus" words are useless. On the contrary, they are indispensable, because otherwise we could not talk about large entities such as parties, religions, institutions, philosophies. But the obligation of the intelligent man and woman is plain and urgent. Everyone must get into the habit of responding not to the prejudices a word evokes but to the specific ideas behind it. If he takes the trouble to inquire what those ideas really are, he may well respond in a manner quite different from the one that his first impulse seemed to demand.

* Permission of *The New Yorker*. Copyright 1943 by the F.-R. Publishing Corporation.

EXERCISE 15

Analyze the following passage for appeals to prejudice rather than to reason, and explain in detail why an intelligent reader or listener would refuse to be swayed by such methods of persuasion:

My fellow citizens, strange as the words may sound coming from one who has no greater pride than that which springs from his life-long devotion to the ideals of the Democratic party, in a way it has been a blessing in disguise for us to be out of office. Now the country has had a bitter but eye-opening taste of what Republican rule means. The events of the past few years have exposed with the piti-less spotlight of truth the emptiness and hypocrisy of the promises foisted on the people by the New York advertising men who have been the G.O.P.'s propaganda hirelings.

Instead of the forward-looking, dynamic action—end quote—that the slick-penned sloganeers promised during the last campaign, we have witnessed reaction—reaction that has saddled us with the kind of government we once thought had ended forever in the Coolidge-Hoover era—government by and for the privileged few. The G.O.P. still lives in the horse-and-buggy days, even though it rides around in Cadillacs. We must never forget that no sooner had the Grand *Old* Party taken office than one of its top cabinet members let the cat out of the bag when he publicly announced that "What is good for General Motors is good for the country!"

The babble, bungle, and muddle in Washington is incredible. Faithful public servants, career people who had long experience in administering government affairs efficiently and economically, with favoritism toward none, have been shoved out to make room for high-paid executives from our giant corporations. As you and I know full well, you can't run a government the same way you run a big business. It takes special talents of the sort that thousands of loyal Democrats possess. But those talents aren't being used. No wonder we have government by confusion.

You are hard-working laboring people, the backbone and sinews of the nation. What have the Republicans done for the common man? Have they ever welcomed union leaders into their councils? Have they repealed the Taft-Hartley slave labor law? Have they cut your taxes, while they slashed the tax rates for those who live in the lap of luxury from dividends, dividends made possible by the sweat of your brow?

You are the people who have come from the melting pot that has made America the greatest nation on earth. Our names may be Italian or Polish or Greek or Czech, but above all, you and I, every one of us gathered here tonight, are Americans. We share a precious common heritage of the country's natural resources—the vast and magnificent forests, the rushing streams, the awe-inspiring national parks. They are the God-given possession of the people. But the Republicans, the party of Teapot Dome, have done their best to aid and abet one of the most shameless grabs in American history. They have given away these priceless assets for the exploitation of the predatory lumber and power interests, whose greed for huge profits at public expense grew all the keener through the years when they were kept at bay by the enlightened power and conservation policies of our great leaders, Franklin D. Roosevelt and Harry S. Truman.

Now is the time to redeem America from the money-changers. We must replace the men who swing the golf clubs with men who are ready and able to wield new brooms—brooms that will clean out the mess in Washington. This is our shining moment of opportunity. Only under a Democratic administration can our beloved country move onward to a brighter future of peace and plenty.

EXERCISE 16

In the above discussion, the comparatively neutral word *persuasion* was used instead of *propaganda,* a "loaded" word that probably would have aroused prejudices in your mind and thus would have unfairly affected your response to what was being said. But it is necessary always to remember that, as a book on *How to Understand Propaganda* says, "Propaganda is not all lies. It can be the simple truth. It can be safe or dangerous. By all odds, the things that should concern the consumer is the way he permits himself to react to propaganda."

1. Exactly what connotations does *propaganda* have to you? Looking back on your experience with the word and what it

represents, how can you account for your present attitude? What is the word's denotation?

2. Collect some current examples of "good" and "bad" propaganda. (Don't forget that propaganda is in no way confined to political persuasion. It may be used in behalf of, or against, any cause— from world calendar reform to temperance.) What standards do you use in classifying each example as "good" or "bad": your personal attitude toward the subject discussed, your estimate of the fairness or unfairness of the methods the propagandist uses, or both?

3. This book is itself a piece of propaganda. In what sense? Is it "good" or "bad"?

EXERCISE 17

Make a list of the catch-words and -phrases most in favor with propagandists at the moment. If a political campaign is going on, what are the terms most used to praise or condemn a candidate or party?

Connotations in Literature

When we turn from these aspects of practical persuasion to imaginative writing—poetry, drama, fiction, and the rest—our duty as intelligent readers is quite different. Here the writer usually has no ax to grind, no product to sell, no vote to win, no policy to put over. His intention is not to deceive; on the contrary, it is to offer his readers a vivid experience, the essence of which is the transmutation of life, of actuality, into an imaginative adventure. He may wish to present before our inward eye a person or a scene that he himself has either actually witnessed or imagined, and to present it with as much color and credibility and meaningfulness as he can; or he may wish to play upon our emotions, so as to make us feel as he has felt concerning love or death or courage or religious devotion; or he may wish to communicate an intellectual idea to us in such terms that we cannot help apprehending its force and truth. Whatever the writer's precise intention as an observer and

interpreter of life, one of the major means by which he makes
us see and hear and think and feel with him is the skillful use
of word-connotations. And now, instead of being on guard
against deception, we must become completely receptive to the
subtleties of language, allowing them to sway us as the author
desires.

A great part of the pleasure of reading poetry is due to the
manner in which the poet is able to crowd the reader's mind
with a rapid pageant of impressions, which the poet may select
and control in order to produce a single powerful effect. In the
"Calais Beach" sonnet quoted on page 13, Wordsworth seeks
to produce the single impression of quietness and serenity, and
he does so by the conscious selection of words which connote
those qualities. Sometimes, too, the poet relies upon the con-
notativeness of words to transport his reader from the world of
actuality into a realm of the pure imagination, a never-never
land of magical fascination created solely by language:

> In Xanadu did Kubla Khan
> A stately pleasure-dome decree:
> Where Alph, the sacred river, ran
> Through caverns measureless to man
>   Down to a sunless sea.
> So twice five miles of fertile ground
> With walls and towers were girdled round:
> And there were gardens bright with sinuous rills,
> Where blossomed many an incense-bearing tree;
> And here were forests ancient as the hills,
> Enfolding sunny spots of greenery.
>
> But oh! that deep romantic chasm which slanted
> Down the green hill athwart a cedarn cover!
> A savage place! as holy and enchanted
> As e'er beneath a waning moon was haunted
> By woman wailing for her demon-lover!

Often a single line or two may contain a wealth of suggestiveness. To one who knows the story of the fall of Troy, Marlowe's
lines

> Was this the face that launched a thousand ships,
> And burnt the topless towers of Ilium?

contain all the emotional values implicit in the story of a
beautiful woman for whose love a civilization was almost destroyed. Or take a minute to examine the manner in which the
connotations of the separate words in such a passage as this
merge to produce a simple but powerful emotional effect:

> Your low voice tells how bells of singing gold
> Would sound through twilight over silent water.

Of course it is not only the poet who makes constant use of
word-connotations. The writer of imaginative prose uses them
just as often, and for the same reasons. Here is a brief excerpt
from Van Wyck Brooks's *The Flowering of New England,* in
which the writer, by presenting a succession of connotative
images, evokes the flavor of a particular time and place in
history:

> The Cambridge flowers had a moral meaning, as good New Eng-
> land flowers ought to have; but they had a poetical meaning that
> was even more apparent. So did the sounds one heard on summer
> evenings, the bells of the cows ambling home at twilight, the lullaby
> of the crickets in early autumn, the hymns of the frogs, in spring, in
> some neighbouring swamp, not to speak of the creaking of the winter
> wood-sleds, dragging their loads of walnut over the complaining
> snow. Every sound and odour had its value. One heard the carpenter
> smoothing his knotty boards, and the whips of the four-horse coaches
> rattling by; one heard the ticks in the joints of the old bedsteads;
> one smelt the salt of the sea in the summer breeze. What a store of
> allusions and similes, drawn from the homely facts of his daily
> living, a Cambridge boy might pack into his poems!*

The importance of connotation in creative literature is illustrated by a paraphrase of a familiar lyric by Shelley. Note that
the paraphrase closely reproduces the denotations contained in
the original—it "means" the same. But the emotional qualities,
supplied by words of rich and colorful suggestiveness, have

---

* Quoted by permission of E. P. Dutton & Co., Inc., publishers.

completely evaporated. What is left is a dull, drab string of words.

(a)	(b)
My soul is an enchanted Boat,	My inner self resembles a marine craft under a spell,
Which, like a sleeping swan, doth float	Which, like a dormant member of the subfamily *Cygninae* of ducks, is suspended
Upon the silver waves of thy sweet singing;	On the light-reflecting grayish undulations of your agreeable vocalism;
And thine doth like an Angel sit	And yours is seated like a supernatural being
Beside the helm conducting it,	Next to the steering apparatus guiding it,
Whilst all the winds with melody are ringing.	While all the air currents reverberate with a pleasant succession of sounds.
It seems to float ever, for ever,	It appears to remain permanently, yes permanently, on the surface
Upon that many-winding river,	Of that circuitous water-filled channel,
Between mountains, woods, abysses,	Between rocky elevations, dense arboreal growths, precipitous gaps,
A Paradise of wildernesses!	A euphoria-producing but imaginary area comprising uncultivated tracts!
Till, like one in slumber bound,	Until, like a hypnotized individual,
Borne to the ocean, I float, down, around,	Transported to a large body of saline H_2O, I proceed, simultaneously dropping and spinning,
Into a sea profound, of ever-spreading sound.	Into (metaphorically speaking) an aqueous region of considerable depth, made up of interminably diffusing auditory sensations.

What we are doing here is simply restating, from a new point of view, what is stressed over and over again in every course in English composition: avoid general, abstract words in your writing; wherever possible, select words which are concrete and particular, which evoke vivid responses in your readers' consciousness. Only when you do this are you able to draw upon the rich storehouse of word-connotations. When you neglect this advice, your writing inevitably is pale and dull; it fails to stir the reader. When you follow this advice, your writing can be so persuasive that the reader cannot help heeding what you have to say.

EXERCISE 18

Comment on the connotative power of the following passages:

1.
    Dark house, by which once more I stand
      Here in the long unlovely street,
      Doors, where my heart was used to beat
    So quickly, waiting for a hand,

    A hand that can be clasp'd no more—
      Behold me, for I cannot sleep,
      And like a guilty thing I creep
    At earliest morning to the door.

    He is not here; but far away
      The noise of life begins again,
      And ghastly thro' the drizzling rain
    On the bald street breaks the blank day.

2.
When icicles hang by the wall,
    And Dick the shepherd blows his nail,
And Tom bears logs into the hall,
    And milk comes frozen home in pail,
When blood is nipped, and ways be foul,
Then nightly sings the staring owl:
"Tu-whit, tu-who!" a merry note,
While greasy Joan doth keel the pot.   [*keel:* cool, skim]

When all aloud the wind doth blow,
   And coughing drowns the parson's saw,   [*saw:* preaching]
And birds sit brooding in the snow,
   And Marian's nose looks red and raw,
When roasted crabs hiss in the bowl,   [*crabs:* crabapples]
Then nightly sings the staring owl:
"Tu-whit, tu-who!" a merry note,
While greasy Joan doth keel the pot.

3. It is common knowledge that water may exist in three very different physical states, namely, gaseous, liquid, and solid. Existence in all these three states is not peculiar to water but is the common behavior of the great majority of substances. Experiment has shown that every substance, whether element or compound, tends to pass into the gaseous state if its temperature is raised sufficiently, although it is not always possible actually to bring about such a change. In some cases the temperature required is so high that it cannot be obtained by laboratory methods; in others, the substance decomposes before the required temperature is reached.*

4. But Herr Hitler is not thinking only of stealing other people's territories or flinging gobbets of them to his little confederate. I tell you truly what you must believe when I say this evil man, this monstrous abortion of hatred and deceit, is resolved on nothing less than the complete wiping out of the French nation and the disintegration of its whole life and future.

    By all kinds of sly and savage means he is plotting and working to quench forever the fountain of characteristic French culture and French inspiration to the world. All Europe, if he has his way, will be reduced to one uniform Bocheland, to be exploited, pillaged and bullied by his Nazi gangsters.†

5. At length she came home one night after one of these saunterings and mounted to her bedroom. She took off her laced coat and stood there in shirt and breeches looking out of the win-

---

* From McPherson, Henderson, Mack, and Fernelius, *Chemistry: A Textbook for Colleges,* by special permission of Ginn & Co., publishers.

† From *Blood, Sweat, and Tears,* copyright 1941 by Winston S. Churchill. Courtesy of G. P. Putnam's Sons.

dow. There was something stirring in the air which forbade her to go to bed. A white haze lay over the town, for it was a frosty night in midwinter and a magnificent vista lay all round her. She could see St. Paul's, the Tower, Westminster Abbey, with all the spires and domes of the city churches, the smooth bulk of its banks, the opulent and ample curves of its halls and meeting-places. On the north rose the smooth, shorn heights of Hampstead, and in the west the streets and squares of Mayfair shone out in one clear radiance. Upon this serene and orderly prospect the stars looked down, glittering, positive, hard, from a cloudless sky. In the extreme clearness of the atmosphere the line of every roof, the cowl of every chimney was perceptible. Even the cobbles in the streets showed distinct one from another.*

EXERCISE 19

1. The power of connotation is further illustrated in the selection of titles for books. What connotative value have the following titles?

> *All the King's Men.—Winterset.—The Newcomes.—This Side of Paradise.—North of Boston.—Brave New World.—The Grapes of Wrath.—Gone with the Wind.—The Heart is a Lonely Hunter.—A Stillness at Appomattox.—The Plough and the Stars.—The Remembrance of Things Past.—The Death of a Salesman.—The Autocrat of the Breakfast Table. —Death Be Not Proud.—Passions Spin the Plot.*

(Often, as is true of more than half a dozen examples in the above list, book titles are quotations from earlier literature, perhaps a phrase from a poem. The meaning of the whole book becomes clearer to us if we recognize the context from which the title comes. For instance, the title of Thackeray's *Vanity Fair* is relatively meaningless unless we grasp the connotations the phrase acquired in Bunyan's *Pilgrim's Progress*.)

2. Certain novelists and playwrights have had the habit of

* From *Orlando,* copyright, 1928, by Virginia Woolf. By special permission of Harcourt, Brace & Co., Inc.

giving their characters names that help the reader decide
what sort of people they are. What descriptive value do these
names have?

> Mrs. Slipslop.—Lydia Languish.—Molly Brazen.—Sir Epicure
> Mammon.—Mr. Feathernest.—Sir Toby Belch.—Rawdon
> Crawley.—Lord Frederick Verisopht.—Amelia Roper.—
> Count Smorltork.

EXERCISE 20

1. Examine a recent issue of *Time* to discover how the writers'
   choice of connotative adjectives and verbs affects your attitude towards the subjects discussed. Pay particular attention
   to the magazine's practice of describing a man or woman by
   two or three colorful adjectives. Does the use of these epithets help the reader to form a just opinion of the person,
   or does it unfairly affect one's attitude toward him?
2. Try rewriting a *Time* article, using only words of minimum
   connotative value. Which version—yours or the original—
   would give the reader a more objective view of the topic?
3. Read Geoffrey T. Hellman's scalpel-sharp dissection of
   Time-style, " 'Time' Lumbers On," in *The New Yorker*
   for April 16, 1955.

———

How Connotation Changes

One of the chief difficulties students have in reading literature
written a hundred or more years ago is that they encounter
words which do not seem to make sense in the way they are
used, even though they are words which are in daily use today.
For example, the diarist Samuel Pepys, writing in 1660, described the execution of a leader of the Puritan rebellion of
1649. "I went out to Charing Cross," Pepys writes, "to see
Major-general Harrison hanged, drawn, and quartered; which
was done there, he looking as cheerful as any man could do in
that condition." Immediately one stops short at that word
cheerful: is it very probable that a man who was in the process

of being hanged, drawn, and quartered maintained what we could call a "cheerful" countenance? Obviously Pepys meant nothing of the sort; *cheerful* in his day connoted something unlike what it connotes today. To him it suggested "tranquil," "calm," "resigned," not "full of good spirits," "buoyant," "optimistic." Such instances can be multiplied without end. We encounter them on every page of Shakespeare, Milton, Pope, Johnson, Wordsworth. What can we make of the lines in which Wordsworth is praising his wife for her manifold virtues—

> A Creature not too bright or good
> For human nature's daily food;
> For transient sorrows, simple wiles,
> Praise, blame, love, kisses, tears, and smiles.

> *And now I see with eye serene*
> *The very pulse of the machine.*

The word *machine* jolts nearly every reader who comes to it; what business has such a word, with its connotations of steel and gears and motors, in such a poem? What has machinery to do with Mary Wordsworth? The answer is that to Wordsworth and his contemporaries *machine* had a much more general connotation; the line might be paraphrased, "The very pulse [or heart] of her being." The word *engine,* incidentally, causes similar trouble to modern readers who run across it in older literature. What does "two-handed engine" mean in Milton's "Lycidas" (line 130) or "the fatal engine" in Pope's *The Rape of the Lock* (canto III, line 149)?

Connotations are in a constant state of flux; the writings of our own contemporaries will be as troublesome to readers a century or two hence as the English classics sometimes are to us. We have already seen the reasons why words acquire certain connotations which are agreed upon by all literate readers and writers: the practice of the most influential writers, and the attitude of society toward the ideas which certain words have come to represent. But these general connotations are by no means permanently established, because few writers remain influential indefinitely and no social attitude fails to undergo some modification. Although the usage of Addison and Steele "set" many connotations in their own day, the time came when other writers had more influence, and thus, gradually and almost imperceptibly, Addison and Steele began to seem old-fashioned in their use of words. The influence of social attitudes upon connotations is well illustrated by the history of *Roman Catholic,* which was brought into use when the older words used to designate a member of that faith, *Romanist, Roman,* and *Papist,* had acquired so heavy a stigma that a substitute was necessary—one which lacked the bad connotations that the other words possessed in Protestant England. The subsequent history of *Roman Catholic* is in effect a history of shifting winds of feeling. In England it gradually lost the stigma it had inevitably acquired, in time, as a substitute for *Papist;* but wherever there is anti-Catholic feeling today, it retains its negative connotations. The histories of such words as *Methodist* and *Quaker* offer similar illustrations of the evolution of social feeling.

Suppose that a word with an established denotation acquires a new connotation which in time becomes as firmly established as the denotation itself. If it becomes customary to use the word only in the sense implied by this new connotation, the original denotation is forgotten, and the dominant connotation becomes the new denotation. In brief, change in connotation, if carried far enough, becomes change in actual meaning. Since there is no sharp dividing line between denotation and connotation, it is impossible to say just when change of connotation results in change of meaning. But it has happened in the case of thousands upon thousands of words, whose meanings have been completely transformed by a series of shifts in connotation. These changed meanings of course introduce further difficulties in the reading of older literature. Take as an example of both types of change the opening sentences of Bacon's essay "Of Studies":

Studies serve for delight, for ornament, and for ability. Their chief use for delight is in privateness and retiring; for ornament, is in discourse; and for ability, is in the judgment and disposition of business. For expert men can execute, and perhaps judge of particulars, one by one; but the general counsels, and the plots and marshalling of affairs come best from those that are learned. To spend too much time in studies is sloth; to use them too much for ornament is affectation; to make judgment wholly by their rules is the humour of a scholar.

One can grasp the general sense at a first reading; but that is because enough of the words Bacon uses retain the denotations they possessed in his day to give us clues. Yet no one will say that this is modern English, or even close to it. What if we are asked to rewrite the passage so that every trace of its late sixteenth-century origin is removed? *Delight* is too strong a word for this context; we should use *pleasure* instead. *Ornament* is no longer used in Bacon's sense of "social advantage"; *ability* stands for our modern "practical profit" or "usefulness." *Privateness* has gone almost completely out of use; taken together with *retiring* (people of Bacon's day loved to couple two virtually synonymous words) it means "our personal, or home, life." *Discourse* now means "talk by one person"; to Bacon it meant what we now call *conversation*. *Judgment and disposition* can be modernized as *conduct*. *Expert* to Bacon suggests "accomplished, competent" in general; in our time its use is restricted to suggest skill in certain techniques. And so on. Scarcely a noun of Bacon's could be retained if the passage were to be made intelligible to, let us say, a prospective student in a correspondence course.

It takes constant vigilance to allow for these changed connotations and meanings as we read, but the result is worth the effort, because when we read some piece of old writing with full understanding we have succeeded in cheating Time himself; we have received the message that the author, long since dead, intended for us. And that can often be a considerable satisfaction.

There is no royal road to such comprehension. The simplest

way to improve one's ability to read material written in previous centuries is to read more of it. If a child has much contact with a very old great-grandparent, who uses English words in ways that were proper two or three generations ago, the child will gradually acquire a "feeling" for such usages, and they will seem entirely natural to him. Likewise if an adult reads more widely in older literature than is customary nowadays, he will find himself gradually acquiring a similar feeling. His vocabulary habits will come closer to those of Malory or Shakespeare or Milton; such frequently used words as *humor* will no longer perplex him by the oddness of their use. He will automatically think in the language of his author.

Shakespeare, because he made such audaciously individual use of the English language, is somewhat harder to read than his contemporaries, and is nearly always read in annotated editions, with the uncommon words explained in footnotes. But most of the other great authors of the past must be read without such easily available help. For the really inquisitive reader there exists the *Oxford English Dictionary*, which is an encyclopedia of the history of English words. In the *OED* (or *NED*), as it is usually called, one can check up on all the shades of meaning which a word had at any given time in its history. One's education is not complete until he has had the experience of tracing the history of a few selected words in the pages of the *OED*.

EXERCISE 21

In the following quotations, the meaning of the italicized words differs from the meaning (or the connotation) they have in today's common usage. Try to determine the meaning of each word by fitting it into the general sense of the sentence, and then check your answers by reference to the *Oxford English Dictionary*.

1. [As] for the lawyer, . . . as our wickedness maketh him necessary, and necessity maketh him *honorable,* so is he not in the deepest truth to stand in rank with these, who all endeavor to take

naughtiness away and plant goodness even in the secretest *cabinet* of our souls. (Sidney, ca.1585)

2. An ant is a wise creature for itself, but it is a *shrewd* thing in an orchard or garden; and certainly men that are great lovers of themselves *waste* the public. [In this sentence, *shrewd* is a pun. What makes it so?] (Bacon, 1612)

3. "I fear," replied Neander, "that in obeying your commands I shall draw some *envy* on myself." (Dryden, 1668)

4. Most of the quarrels I have ever known have proceeded from some valiant coxcomb's persisting in the wrong, to defend some prevailing folly, and preserve himself from the *ingenuity* of *owning* a mistake. (Steele, 1709)

5. But most by *numbers* judge a poet's song,
And smooth or rough with them is right or wrong. (Pope, 1711)

6. In the *nice* bee what sense, so subtly true,
From pois'nous herbs extracts the healing dew? (Pope, 1732)

7. With sweet May dews my wings were wet,
And Phoebus fir'd my vocal *rage*. (Blake, 1783)

8. A good that seems at an immeasurable distance, and that we cannot hope to reach, has therefore the less influence on our *affections*. (Cowper, 1786)

9. Nor will it seem to thee, O Friend! so prompt
In sympathy, that I have lengthened out
With *fond* and feeble tongue a tedious tale. (Wordsworth, 1805)

10. The language was not only *peculiar* and strong, but at times knotty and contorted, as by its own impatient strength.
(Coleridge, 1817)

EXERCISE 22

1. First, write down the usual meaning(s) each of the following words has today: *head, extravagant, probation, cousin, admiration, doubt* (verb), *shrewdly, eager, fee, toys* (noun), *lets.* Then, using a well-annotated edition of *Hamlet,* find out what each word meant in Shakespeare's time, in the particular passages noted. All are in Act One.

Scene One: line 106 (*head*), 154 (*extravagant*), 156 (*probation*).

Scene Two: line 64 (*cousin*), 192 (*admiration*), 256 (*doubt*).

Scene Four: line 1 (*shrewdly*), 2 (*eager*), 65 (*fee*), 75 (*toys*), 85 (*lets*).

2. If a modern architect's plan for a large building were described as "artificial" and "awful," would the words indicate praise or condemnation? The same adjectives were used in high praise of Sir Christopher Wren's design for St. Paul's Cathedral in the latter part of the seventeenth century. What did they mean then?

EXERCISE 23

As we saw in Exercise 8 (pages 10-11), many words, especially in the scientific vocabulary, have little or no connotative quality; they are as devoid of emotional suggestion as an algebraic formula. Sometimes, however, a turn of events suddenly gives them connotative power. Before 1945, *radioactivity* and *nuclear fission* were almost wholly denotative. Then what happened to them? Can you think of any other words that have gone through the same process recently?

The Importance of Context

We were able to understand the general sense of the passage quoted from Bacon because some of the words it contained had not shifted so radically in meaning as to conceal Bacon's thought, and they threw light on the words whose meaning had changed more completely. Thus we had a brief glimpse of the meaning and usefulness of context, which is the reciprocal relationship between a given word and the words which surround it in any passage. Think of a sentence as a row of highly polished vases (the important words—nouns, verbs, and modifiers). What we see when we look at each of those vases includes not only the form of the vase itself but also reflections of the adjacent vases. Those reflections are what we mean by context. Each word has a meaning in and of itself, but as we read along, we find that that meaning is affected by the meanings of the words which precede and follow.

The use of context to clarify individual words and phrases can, when the process is understood, be a most entertaining and instructive mental exercise. The reader should try to solve as many as possible of the riddles confronting him without recourse to a dictionary. In many cases the meaning of a certain word is hinted at by the words that surround it. The momentum of the preceding thought may carry us right to the explanation we require. Or if we are still puzzled, it often pays to go past the word in question to see what follows; perhaps the sentences immediately following it will throw light on its meaning.

Determining what a word means in a given context is made much easier by some knowledge of foreign languages, especially Greek, Latin, and French, from which many thousands of our English words are derived. A student who has had as little as a year or two of these languages in high school or college has a tremendous advantage over those who have not. His native ingenuity is strengthened by a knowledge of word roots which can help him over innumerable obstacles in his everyday reading.

Of course the method of trying to guess the meanings of words is by no means foolproof; mere ingenuity can lead one far astray, inviting him to interpret passages in a way the author never intended. Therefore the dictionary should always be kept close at hand for the resolution of difficulties. Under the word in question, the dictionary lists a number of definitions. The trick then is to select from the list the meaning which best fits the context. Often it may be a difficult matter to decide which of two or three meanings, each of them apparently fitting the context, the author intended. Then the reader should return to the context, rereading the whole passage more carefully, until he is able to reject certain definitions as not being *precisely* what the author meant and to emerge with the one meaning which, he feels, adequately conveys the author's intention.

Here is part of the conclusion of Henry James's essay on Emerson, which took the form of a review of Cabot's biography of the essayist:

It has not, however, been the ambition of these remarks to account for everything, and I have arrived at the end without even pointing to the grounds on which Emerson justifies the honors of

biography, discussion, and illustration. I have assumed his importance and continuance, and shall probably not be gainsaid by those
who read him. Those who do not will hardly rub him out. Such a
book as Mr. Cabot's subjects a reputation to a test—leads people to
look it over and hold it up to the light, to see whether it is worth
keeping in use or even putting away in a cabinet. Such a revision
of Emerson has no relegating consequences. The result of it is once
more the impression that he serves and will not wear out and that
indeed we cannot afford to drop him. His instrument makes him
precious. He did something better than anyone else; he had a particular faculty, which has not been surpassed, for speaking to the
soul in a voice of direction and authority.*

As was the case with the selection from Bacon printed above,
we are probably able to understand the general sense on first
reading. James is saying in effect that the test of a great man's
permanent worth is whether his fame can survive a biography
like Cabot's, and that Emerson triumphantly passes the test.
(The fourth and fifth sentences say as much.) But a careful
reader will wish to know more. Since James presumably wrote
each sentence for a particular purpose—to advance and add to
his earlier argument, to clinch a point, to prepare for a new
idea—each sentence should be considered and understood. And
upon closer examination we find a number of words and locutions which need explanation:

Ambition. "Remarks" are not usually thought of as having
ambition; normally we think only of people as having it. But
the meaning is clear from context: "design," "purpose," "intention."

Illustration. Since James has already used the word in the
same sense earlier in the essay, the careful reader will already
have discovered its meaning: "quotation," "the selection of examples to clarify certain aspects of the subject."

Continuance. By "importance and continuance" James
means "his present and future importance," or, as we should
say, more simply, "his continuing importance."

* From Henry James's *Partial Portraits.* By permission of The Macmillan Company, publishers.

Gainsaid. The context suggests the idea of opposition. The conjunction *and* implies agreement or similarity between the two parts of the sentence; therefore the second part should be in essential harmony with the first. "I have thought so-and-so," says James, *"and* others will probably agree with me." *Gainsaid* is more commonly used to mean "denied" ("The assertion will not be gainsaid") but its meaning here ("I shall probably not be opposed") is plainly similar.

Revision. This can be attacked in two ways. Obviously the word does not mean "change [of opinion]" or "new edition." The reader with a smattering of Latin will recognize the prefix *re* (again) and the root *vis* (seeing, looking—as in *vision, visual, visionary*). He then realizes that James is using the word in its original, literal sense of "looking over again." And if he reviews the context, he will find that the preceding sentence had already explained the word to him!

Relegating. Latin is of some help here, but again the context is sufficient; "putting away" in the preceding sentence is the literal meaning of *relegating.* In other words, in the preceding sentence James has said in Anglo-Saxon-derived words what he now says in Latinized diction.

Serves. Definition 6 under *serve* (verb, intransitive) in *Webster's Collegiate Dictionary:* "to answer a purpose." But the meaning can be inferred from the following, "and will not wear out."

Instrument. This is explained by what follows. "Not *what* he said so much as *how* he said it."

Direction. Definition 2 in the *Collegiate:* "That which is imposed by directing; command; also, authoritative instruction." Definition 4: "The line or course upon which anything is moving or aimed to move, or to which anything is pointing." The latter meaning is more familiar to us; but the context, especially the proximity of "authority," shows plainly that the former meaning is intended.

It is by such a combination of methods as this that the full purport of a passage can be arrived at. Analyzing a few paragraphs, word by word, for complete, rather than superficial, meaning will impress you with the importance of each individual word in context. In the best writing there are no superfluous words or sentences; each small brick in the structure has its own particular function and cannot be removed without loss.

EXERCISE 24

Here is a good opportunity to measure how much you have learned in this chapter. The following quotation is from a work written almost two hundred years ago; but the ideas it contains are essentially the same as those we have set forth in this chapter. With this hint, read carefully through the selection, sentence by sentence, relating each idea which the author discusses to points already covered in this book. Some of the words (e.g., *passions, eloquence*) have changed connotations; substitute for them the equivalent modern words used in the preceding discussion. You will thus be testing two things: (1) your comprehension of the subject-matter of pages 8-36 (the fundamental importance of word-connotations) and (2) your ability to read noncontemporary writing.

How Words Affect the Passions. Now as words affect, not by any original power, but by representation, it might be supposed that their influence over the passions should be but light; yet it is quite otherwise; for we find by experience that eloquence and poetry are as capable, nay indeed much more capable, of making deep and lively impressions than any other arts, and even than nature itself in very many cases. And this arises chiefly from these three causes.

First, that we take an extraordinary part in the passions of others, and that we are easily affected and brought into sympathy by any tokens which are shown of them, and there are no tokens which can express all the circumstances of most passion so fully as words; so that if a person speaks upon any subject, he can not only convey the subject to you, but likewise the manner in which he is himself affected by it. Certain it is, that the influence of most things on our passions is not so much from the things themselves, as from our opinions concerning them; an these again depend very much on the opinions of other men, conveyable for the most part by words only.

Secondly, there are many things of a very affecting nature, which can seldom occur in the reality, but the words that represent them often do; and thus they have an opportunity of making a deep impression and taking root in the mind, whilst the idea of the reality was transient, and to some perhaps never really occurred in any shape, to whom it is notwithstanding very affecting—as war, death, famine, etc. Besides, many ideas have never been at all presented to the senses of any men but by words, as God, angels, devils, heaven and hell, all of which have however a great influence over the passions.

Thirdly, by words we have it in our power to make such *combinations* as we cannot possibly do otherwise. By this power of combining, we are able, by the addition of well chosen circumstances, to give a new life and force to the simple object. In painting we may represent any fine figure we please, but we never can give it those enlivening touches which it may receive from words. To represent an angel in a picture, you can only draw a beautiful young man winged; but what painting can furnish out anything so grand as the addition of one word, "the angel of the *Lord*"? It is true, I have here no clear idea; but these words affect the mind more than the sensible image did; which is all I contend for. . . .

Now as there is a moving tone of voice, an impassioned countenance, an agitated gesture, which affect independently of the things about which they are exerted, so there are words, and certain dispositions of words, which, being peculiarly devoted to passionate subjects, and always used by those who are under the influence of any passion, touch and move us more than those which far more clearly and distinctly express the subject-matter. We yield to sympathy what we refuse to description. The truth is, all verbal description, merely as naked description, though never so exact, conveys so poor and insufficient an idea of the thing described, that it could scarcely have the smallest effect, if the speaker did not call in to his aid those modes of speech that mark a strong and lively feeling in himself. Then, by the contagion of our passions, we catch a fire already kindled in another, which probably might never have been struck out by the object described. Words, by strongly conveying the passions, by those means which we have already mentioned, fully compensate for their weakness in other respects.

CHAPTER TWO

Diction

L ET US NOW do a little detective work.

1. "When I told Dad how I'd goofed that exam, he literally blew his top." *Who is writing (or speaking)? In England or America? At the present time, or at some time in the past? How sure a sense of words has he (or she)?*

2. "There was a constable on point duty just where we stopped, and he came over and lifted the bonnet and made ineffectual motions with a spanner. And then—what do you think?—we found we were out of petrol!" *What is the nationality of the speaker?*

3. "We don't keep nothing like that here, but maybe we could order it for you special. Not in a hurry for it, was you?" *How well educated is the speaker?*

4. "I had him on the ropes in the fourth, and if one of those short rights of mine had connected, he'd have gone down for the count. I was aiming for his glass chin, but I couldn't seem to reach it." *What activity has the speaker been engaged in?*

5. "A close examination and correlation of the most reliable current economic indexes justifies the conclusion that the next year will witness a continuation of the present upward market trend, though this may be accompanied by seasonal fluctuations in respect to certain areas of the economy." *How much of a gift for clear, concise expression has this writer?*

6. "We were loading hay in the west forty when we saw the twister in the distance." *From what section of the United States does the speaker come?*

7. "Both the Oriental romance and the picaresque narrative

48

have been favorite vehicles for the satirist, the romance because it permits a handy and vivid way of contrasting western manners with those of a very different culture, the picaresque tale because the hero's adventuresome career, spiced as it is with all sorts of roguery, gives an excellent excuse for pungent comment on the errant ways of mankind." *What can you infer about the education, professional interests, and writing skill of the author?*

8. "The female operatives in this mill seemed well content with their lot, laughing and singing as they emerged at the end of the day." *When was this sentence written?*

9. "Have you noticed how perfectly lovely the sunset is?" *What is the sex of the speaker?*

10. "The ominous final movement begins with a toccata in the horns, punctuated by glissando effects in the tympani, and then develops, in the middle section, into a lyric coda." *How much does the writer know about music?*

If we have a moderately dependable sense of language, we should have no trouble answering these questions somewhat as follows:

1. That this sentence probably was spoken, not written, is suggested by the presence of a contraction *(I'd)* and of slang *(goofed, blew his top).* Contractions and colloquial or slang expressions are used more often in informal speech than in writing. Still, it is perfectly conceivable that the sentence occurred in a letter. That the speaker (or writer) is young is revealed not only by the reference to an exam but by the use of current slang; older people normally do not pick up and use contemporary slang, but rather retain the slang that was in fashion when they were younger and their language habits more flexible. There is no sure evidence whether the speaker is a young man or a girl. He (or she) is American and speaking at the present time. Finally, the use of *literally* indicates a certain carelessness in language, though it is an error common to many presumably well-educated people, including professional writers. If Dad *"literally* blew his top," he was lucky to escape with his life. *Literally* never belongs with an expression intended merely as a figure of speech; the correct adverb, if any is needed, would be *figuratively.* Keep this in mind whenever you read, and you will soon amass an entertaining collection of howlers. ("The audience literally sat on

its hands through the whole show." "The tennis champion literally blasted his opponent out of the court." "It's literally true to say that 'our language is a cemetery of dead metaphors.' ")

2. The speaker is British. A *constable on point duty* is an English traffic cop; *bonnet, spanner,* and *petrol* are, respectively, the English equivalents of the American *hood* (of a car), *wrench,* and *gasoline.*

3. The speaker is very poorly educated: note the ungrammatical double negative *(we don't keep nothing);* the use of an adjective *(special)* where an adverb would be correct (or, better yet, the speaker should say, "We could get it for you on special order") ; and the mismatching of verb and subject *(was you).*

4. The speaker is, or has been, a boxer. He uses five terms associated with prize fighting.

5. This writer has no gift at all for plain communication. What he says in forty-five words could be said, far more clearly and economically, in seventeen: "The present signs are that stock prices will continue to rise, though certain stocks may temporarily decline." The original sentence is an example of what we call inflated writing.

6. The speaker—or writer—is from the middle west. *Forty* designates a forty-acre tract, a customary division of land in that region, and *twisters* (tornadoes) are most common in the middle west.

7. The writer is well educated, has a greater-than-ordinary interest in various types of literature (the Oriental romance, the picaresque narrative), and writes clearly. He may be a professional critic or literary historian. The sentence, though fairly long, is maturely constructed; observe how the opening clause (down to *satirist*) is developed by what follows—two parallel elements, the first expanding on the idea of the Oriental romance, the second on the idea of the picaresque tale. The words chosen are familiar to any reasonably intelligent reader, and convey accurately the point the writer wishes to make.

8. This sentence was written perhaps a hundred years ago; certainly not in recent times. *Female operatives* is an old-fashioned way of referring to "girls and women that tend the machines."

9. The speaker is a woman. *Perfectly lovely* is a characteristically feminine expression. Can you imagine a man using it—even in speaking of a girl he admires?

10. The writer is either simply deceiving himself or else deceiving himself that he is deceiving others; in either case, the sentence is nonsense. A *toccata* is a "touch-piece" designed to exhibit the dexterity of an organist or a pianist, not of a horn player; nor is it likely to appear in an "ominous" musical passage. Tympani cannot produce *glissando* effects (see your dictionary). A *coda,* being the concluding portion of a composition, would not occur in the middle section.

From these examples we can draw one extremely important conclusion: that words not only connote shades of meaning, but also contain valuable clues to the background, the personality, and often the attitude and the intention of the writer or the speaker. Thus it is possible to supplement what we are told outright with data shrewdly inferred from the *manner* in which the information is given.

Some of the following material is found in college textbooks of composition under the heading of "Diction." There it is intended primarily to help you achieve a good writing style by the selection of words and idioms appropriate to such writing; here it is intended primarily to show the technique by which we can extract more information from what we read. Of course the two purposes are closely associated. Just as the chapter on denotation and connotation has made you more aware of the necessity for accuracy in the selection of words when you are doing your own writing, so the present chapter should enable you to avoid some of the other common pitfalls in writing.

Elementary Clues of Diction

1. *Geographical clues.* Though both are called "English," there is a great difference between the British and American vocabularies. No constant reader of British essays or fiction can long remain unaware that our *electric cord* is the Englishman's *flex,* our *wheat* is his *corn,* and, in turn, his word for what we call *corn* is *maize.* In Britain, a *biscuit* is our *cracker* (but one of the largest American producers of crackers is the National *Biscuit* Company!); at the same time, the British *cracker* refers to one

of those party favors that give a loud pop when pulled apart. An American *furniture van* is known in England as a *pantechnicon,* and on the British Railways a *luggage van* is what we call a *baggage car.* American and British idioms differ also: an American is said to be *in the hospital,* but in British usage the *the* is dropped. Americans *take* (subscribe to) newspapers; the British *take* them *in.* *

Similarly there are vocabulary differences between the various sections of the United States. In the Boston area, a soda fountain is a *spa;* in certain parts of the midwest a chocolate sundae is a *dope,* but in the South, a *dope* is a Coca-Cola. A New England *stone wall* is a *stone row* in northern New Jersey, a *stone fence* in Pennsylvania, and a *rock fence* from West Virginia southward. What is known in general American usage as a *baby carriage* is called by other names in certain localities— *baby coach, baby buggy, baby cab.* North of the Mason-Dixon line one *wheels* the baby; south of the line, one *rolls* or *rides* him.

2. *Occupational clues.* Every profession and occupation has its own slang as well as its own technical vocabulary. If a woman speaks of being on *O.B.* duty she is probably a nurse in the obstetrical section of a hospital. (However, someone else using the same abbreviation may turn out to be a school psychologist— *O.B.* is also a polite abbreviation for "orthogenic-backward"— i.e., "problem"—children.) If a doctor speaks of a colleague as "a good G.I. man" he does not mean the latter is a soldier; *G.I.* is medical shorthand for *gastrointestinal.* Mention of a *widow* or a *river* identifies the printer; *fluff* or *snow* the television repairman; *feather-bedding* or *highballing* the railroad man; *tailgating,* the truck-driver.

Often, however, what began as a term peculiar to one occupation or another ends as a member in good standing in the general vocabulary. *On the nose,* which in the sense of *on time*

* Long and interesting lists illustrating this difference are printed in H. L. Mencken's *The American Language,* 4th edition, pp. 233-237, and *Supplement One* thereto, pp. 457-487.

originated in the broadcasting studio, now is common slang; *top brass,* originally an Army term, is widely used for bosses, executives; the noun *complex,* recently the possession of the psychologists, has been taken over and manhandled by the general public. Sometimes, therefore, what seems at first glance to be a clue to a man's occupation actually has no value as such.

3. *Educational clues.* Bad grammar, such as the use of the double negative, the placing of the object of a verb in the nominative case, and the mismatching of verb and subject ("she don't"), marks the man or woman who either has never had an opportunity for education or has failed to profit by his advantages. It would not do, of course, to go farther and say that a person using such poor grammar is obviously a member of the lower classes. In practice, however, this is often true, if only because there is a certain amount of pressure higher up in society which requires people to speak correctly.

It must be remembered that modern standards allow the genuinely literate person quite generous leeway in English usage. Only those who have been reared in outmoded, unnaturally rigid traditions of language censure the splitter of infinitives or the supposed ignoramus who ends a sentence with a preposition. Probably no reputable modern grammarian will deny that "It is me" is perfectly good colloquial English or that there are many situations in which it is conspicuously awkward *not* to split an infinitive. Only when a writer or speaker indulges in errors which are not condoned, even by the most liberal arbiters, are we justified in calling him uneducated. In the case of the person in Example 3, page 48, we are amply justified.

Grammar is the most obvious clue to a person's educational background. Another, equally important, clue is vocabulary. The writer or speaker who uses words accurately and appropriately, as does the writer of Example 7, is well educated beyond question—whether formally, in college or university, or informally, by wide and thoughtful reading, is immaterial. On the other hand, the person who strays beyond the confines of his established vocabulary and misuses words, either by mistaking their meaning or by insensitivity to connotation, is not soundly educated, because one of the first purposes of education is to teach a man to use his native language with *accuracy*. Again, the verbose market prophet in Example 5, although he uses words correctly, is just as ignorant as the man who uses words of whose meaning or connotation he is not sure, for he fails to understand that stilted language is entirely out of place in a simple statement. The only way we can be fair judges of another person's use of language is to be accurate users of it ourselves. Only when we are ourselves certain of the meaning and connotation of a word can we justly call someone else to account for his clumsiness in expression.

4. *Time clues.* We have already seen, in Chapter One, how words shift in meaning through the years. Many other words, once in common use, have disappeared except in historical references, either because the object they designated has itself vanished or become simply a museum piece *(Dundreary whiskers, sponging house, carpet bag, gig)*, or because other words took their place *(rubberneck wagon, watering place, dead beat, pantaloons, counting house)*. The occurrence of a word whose meaning has changed, or of a word that is obsolete, is a clue to the date of the passage in question. If we know approximately when the word was current, we have an approximate dating for the passage. The *Oxford English Dictionary* and its American counterpart, the *Dictionary of American English*, are the standard sources of information on this subject.

The occurrence of slang or colloquialisms is a particularly important clue to the time background of a passage. A letter in which a young man speaks of a fraternity stag party or a musical comedy as having been "bully" can be dated with fair accuracy about fifty years ago; Theodore Roosevelt, one recalls, was particularly addicted to the use of the word as a general mark of enthusiastic approval. A young lady's characterization of a picnic supper as "elegant" would probably belong to the nineteenth century—or to one who dates from that period; *elegant* once served all the purposes which *swell* or *super* served more recently. *Hooch, lounge lizard, tin lizzie, make whoopee, sheik, the cat's pajamas, banana oil, baloney* suggest that a certain piece of writing dates from the 1920's, although if they occur in dialogue they may simply show that a more recent author wants to represent the flavor of talk in that era. *Boondoggle, corny, ruptured duck,* and *zoot suit* are slang of a more recent vintage. It would be interesting to gather a list of all the words that have been used, at one time or another, to designate the activity once known as *sparking* or *spooning,* later as *pitching woo,* and still later as *smootching.* What are the current slang terms? And while you are at it, what are the terms now popular among high-school and college students to express strong approval or disapproval of a member of the opposite sex? (In the 1920's, for example, it was high praise to say of a *flapper* that she had plenty of *"it." "It"* later became the somewhat more specific *sex appeal.* Twenty years later, the girl would speak of the *dreamboat* she was dating, or of the *drip* she wouldn't think of dating.)

Clues to Personality and Intention

The preceding types of clue are all fairly simple. Used cautiously, and with the realization that they are nothing more than indications, they often throw valuable light upon the social, occupational, and educational background of the writer or speaker. But language also contains subtle clues to the writer's character, personality, and intentions. "Style is the man," once remarked a famous critic; and it is true that a person's habitual manner of speaking or writing, or the manner he assumes for a particular occasion, reflects more of him than he is aware.

For example, compare two ways in which a man might express his desire to borrow five dollars: (1) "Listen, slip me a fin, will you? I'm in a jam. I'll pay you back Saturday." (2) "I'm awfully sorry to bother you, old man, but I wonder if you could possibly lend me five dollars. I'm in a sort of predicament. I will repay you on Saturday." The language in which the first appeal is couched suggests that the speaker is the kind of person to whom slang is the normal mode of expression. (With that clue, you can fill in the details of the portrait for yourself.) The meaning of the second appeal is identical, and the general approach is the same: "chummy" might be the word for it. But whereas the first speaker is unabashed and forthright, the other is diffident and, in the slang sense of the word, "smooth." The personalities of the two men, one is tempted to say, are as different as the connotations of *jam* and *predicament*. Would it be safe to say that the first man is used to borrowing from his friends, while the second is embarrassed to do so? Or is the seeming hesitancy of the latter just an affectation?

Again, take these two versions of another idea: (1) "She don't think much of him, but believe me, if I ever got my hooks into him, nobody else wouldn't ever have a chance at him." (2) "Poor Elsie treats him rather frivolously, I'm afraid. I confess I have a different feeling about men like him. I find them quite fascinating." What a difference between the two women, at least on the surface! The first, whatever the shortcomings of her grammar, is blunt, outspoken: let her once get that man into her clutches . . . The second girl, however, tries to disguise her eagerness for the man by a studiedly light, off-hand manner of speaking. She does not even come right out and say she wants *that* man—she merely is fascinated by his type! One could conclude, then, that she places more store upon outward appearance; she does not want to admit her feelings as candidly as does the plain-speaking girl. The *rather* and the *quite,* for their part, suggest that she is of a different social class from the other girl; they are mannerisms characteristic of a certain upper stratum of society, or of what would like to think of itself as being an upper stratum.

In Chapter One we saw how connotations are used to influence others to pass judgment upon a given idea or person. Connotations also reveal the writer's or speaker's own judgment, often without his knowledge or desire. This is one of the most valuable phases of intelligent reading—the analysis of a person's language to discover his true feelings about a matter. We often find that even though a man asserts he has no prejudice in a certain matter, his choice of words betrays his bias; or we may find that his true feelings on a question, as reflected by his diction, are the direct opposite of his alleged feelings. Examination of diction, therefore, helps us see the truth despite a writer's attempt to conceal it.

Suppose the second woman quoted above—the one who had designs on the man Elsie didn't appreciate—remarked, in another connection, that she came from a family of "simple, good-hearted mountain people." Quite plainly she would have been patronizing them—acknowledging their humble goodness while implying (by what she leaves unsaid) that they were, after all, a pretty uncultivated lot, whatever their rough native virtues. In other words, by casting emphasis upon the traits of simplicity and good-heartedness she avoided expressing a judgment, which might have been by no means flattering, upon their intelligence, social charm, cleanliness, and other characteristics. From her choice of words, therefore, we can infer something of her own personality: she has a definite sense of personal superiority but at the same time she wants to *appear* tolerant. But what if, on the other hand, those same "simple, good-hearted mountain people" had been described as being "one generation removed from the baboons, and they still feel uncomfortable when they sit in a chair"? Here the writer makes no effort to disguise the revulsion which these people breed in him; he even magnifies it by humorous exaggeration. He also is prejudiced, but at least he does not conceal his bias. He is an honest, if intolerant, man.

It is impossible to lay down any rules for this sort of character-reading through diction. It requires, far more than rules, two gifts: a sense of the implications of words—in what situation they would most likely be used, and by just what sort of person, and for what purpose—and, equally important, a shrewd sense of human nature. And it is always a dangerous game to play; there is always the possibility of serious error. We are dealing here with probabilities, never with certainties. But the attempt to read deeper into a passage of writing—to discover, by a careful consideration of the way in which the writer expresses himself, more than he chooses to tell you—often pays rich dividends.

EXERCISE 1

Use clues of diction to infer as much as you can about the person who wrote (or spoke) each of the following statements:

1. (a) He has no spunk.
   (b) He has no guts.
   (c) He has no intestinal fortitude.
   (d) He is regrettably lacking in determination.
   (e) The trouble with him, he's invertebrate.
   (f) I could make a better backbone out of a banana.

2. Just our luck. Don dug the obit out of the morgue a week ago and we had it in type, all ready for the word from Mac, who was standing the death watch at the hospital. So what happens? He calls ten minutes after the last edition has gone to bed.

3. I rang through to the theatre, but they couldn't give me anything but two seats in the stalls a fortnight from Boxing Day.

4. Oh, *Doris!* What a *delightful* surprise! I hadn't known you were coming to the reunion. My dear, why haven't I heard from you? It's been years and years!

5. I sure was aggravated when I heard he hadn't turned in that theme for me. When I saw him last night, he inferred that he had.

6. Despite the dark and ominous clouds that seem to hover everywhere we look, we can forge ahead to ever greater achievements if we but retain our faith in the eternal verities to which our grandparents clung and refuse to be daunted by the prophets of gloom and doom.

7. You take a very handsome guy, or a guy that thinks he's a real hot-shot, and they're always asking you to do them a big favor. Just because *they're* crazy about themself, they think *you're* crazy about them, too, and that you're just dying to do them a favor. It's sort of funny, in a way.

8. Look you, forsooth, I am, as it were, bound for the land of

matrimony; 'tis a voyage, d'ye see, that was none of my seeking, I was commanded by father, and if you like of it mayhap I may steer into your harbour. How say you, mistress? The short of the thing is, that if you like me, and I like you, we may chance to swing in a hammock together.

9. My friends, Peace be on this house! On the master thereof, on the mistress thereof, on the young maidens, and on the young men! My friends, why do I wish for peace? What is peace? Is it war? No. Is it strife? No. Is it lovely, and gentle, and beautiful, and pleasant, and serene, and joyful? O yes! Therefore, my friends, I wish for peace, upon you and yours.

10. When I struck the town I see there warn't nobody out in the storm, so I never hunted for no back streets but humped it straight through the main one, and when I begun to get towards our house I aimed my eye and set it. No light there; the house all dark—which made me feel sorry and disappointed, I didn't know why.

EXERCISE 2

The following letter was written by a prisoner in a state penitentiary to the police officer who had been largely responsible for his receiving a long-term sentence for robbery. How much can you infer about the prisoner's degree of education, his personality, and his outlook?

My dear Mr. Kauffman:

Another Christmas is about here and I am still in the process of social rehabilitation. Honestly John, do you think that I am so harden against the susceptibilities of reformation that all of these years are necessary for society to realize her objective? Sometimes while in one of those characteristic moods of retrospection I think of the true prophesy I made in regards to my present plight. Doubtless, you may also be able to recall the pronastication I made in regards to that magazine article, "Life begins at sixty-five." It is unnecessary for me to say I was not at all serious but somehow I have conceived the idea that his honor was. What do you think?

Well, John, as in Dante's "Inferno," I am at present enjoying that state of re-segration. Upon the termination of my quarantine period in May, I asked permission to go to school, which was granted. I was making good progress in my clerical work until I aspired to the more academic subject of geology. Naturally, I wished a little practical experience; therefore I made a couple of explorations into the more subterraneous cavaties of the institution for that purpose, and can you imagine my consternation upon being apprehended and having a misinterpretation taken of my geological propensities. During the earlier part of my incarceration I found a profound necessity for the sake of mental stability to accept some medium of philosophy which would make a partial alleviation of such a invariable routine of monotony. What would be more appropriate than for me to become a student of the old stoic Socrates? In accepting such a medium of philosophy I took their misconception with placid resignation, as I realize that they do not understand such an aspiration.

John, I wish to apologize to you for my conduct in court. Possibly I am presuming too much in thinking that my actions in any way affected you, but I remember the conversation we had on the road from Philadelphia to Lancaster and the magnanimous treatment I received while under your care; therefore I have no reason to doubt your integrity. Because of my negligence in writing as I promised is not that I in any way hold you responsible for such a sentence or any one, as I realize that I am the victim of my own avarice and jackass philosophy. I do not wish a misinterpretation taken of this letter. I wish only to express my appreciation for what you would have done and my admiration for you as a man.

Before ending this idiotic epistle, as I see paper is getting short, I wish to take this opportunity of wishing you a Merry X-Mas. So until next Christmas, good luck and health.

Gratefully yours,

———— ————

EXERCISE 3

In 1913, a young English poet announced his intention of traveling in America. He received the following reactions from various people. What does each comment reveal about the personality and attitude of the speaker? (Needless to say, some of these attitudes are no longer current.)

1. A philosopher: "A country without conversation."
2. A scholar: "The big land has a big heart."

3. A critic: "That land of crushing hospitality!"
4. An artist: "It's hell, but it's fine."
5. An Oxford man: "El Cuspidorado."
6. "One wiser than all the rest": "Think gently of the Americans. They are so very young; and so very anxious to appear grown-up; and so very lovable."
7. Nineteen different Americans: "Wal! it's a great country!"
8. "Ordinary English friends": "My God!"

EXERCISE 4

Each of the following groups is composed of words and phrases which, while having the same general denotation, vary in connotation. Examine each member of the group for clues to the kind of person who would use such a term (sex, occupation, age, nationality, etc.), his attitude toward whatever the word refers to, and his probable reason for selecting that particular term rather than another. Some words, of course, are richer in clues than others.

1. The War Between the States, The War to Free the Slaves, The War for Southern Independence, The War of the Rebellion, The Civil War
2. inventory adjustment, recession, decline, depression, slump, dip, leveling off
3. belly, stomach, abdomen, nether regions, gut, breadbasket, midriff, tummy, midsection
4. cinema, flickers, movies, show, motion pictures, picture show, film
5. whopper, fib, lie, story, prevarication, misrepresentation
6. senior citizen, codger, old gentleman, old man, elderly man, geezer, oldster
7. kid, boy, lad, urchin, brat, young person, tyke, member of the rising generation, future citizen, juvenile
8. village, community, crossroads, whistle-stop, jerkwater town, Podunk, rural settlement, hick town
9. nonintellectual type, dope, plodder, backward student, dull pupil, knucklehead, member of a slow group
10. undergarments, lingerie, unmentionables, underwear, underthings, intimate apparel

11. derelict, bum, gentleman of the road, hobo, person with no fixed abode, tramp, vagrant, drifter
12. traveling salesman, commercial traveler, drummer, pavement pounder

---

Talking the Language of the Audience

In Chapter One we pointed out that every writer who wishes to be understood must take care to select words that connote the same thing to his audience generally that they do to him personally; otherwise his message will not be received as he sent it. Not only must words be used whose connotations can be depended upon to convey shades of meaning from writer to reader; in addition, the writer's vocabulary must be that of his audience, and the way he says things—his use or avoidance of slang, for example—must accommodate the habits of his audience. Only then can he be certain that he is establishing successful rapport with those whom he wishes to inform or persuade.

The way in which diction is modified to suit the experience and limitations of the audience can be illustrated by the obvious differences between history books written for fourth graders, for high school students, for college students, and for historians. In these four examples we note a sharply ascending scale of complexity, from the very simple diction required to communicate ideas to a ten-year-old, through the somewhat more difficult diction (necessary to convey more complex ideas) of the books addressed to adolescents, to the diction of highly educated specialists. Each book is written for one particular audience, and no other audience could be expected to profit very much from reading it.

To appeal to the audience for which it is designed, every magazine must be carefully edited so that its language is the one with which its readers are most at home. *Boys' Life*, the Boy Scout magazine, must avoid the use of difficult, unusual words because its audience is composed largely of teen-aged boys. *Vogue* may allow itself more freedom in this respect, but on the other hand it must be careful always to use the diction most natural to women—such things, for instance, as the adjectives that appeal most strongly to feminine tastes, *pert, charming, sophisticated, youthful, alluring,* and so on. (One can imagine the results were the *Vogue* style to be transferred to *Boys' Life*—or *Esquire.*) The diction of a writer for *Good Housekeeping* must differ from that of a writer for *The American Scholar.* An article written to the specifications of *Fortune* would be out of place in the pages of *True Detective.*

This constant requirement, that the writer adapt his style to the tastes and habits of his audience, is most important when he is attempting to move them to a course of thought or action. Now he not only has to tell them something by way of information: he has to make them think and act in the way he desires. And there is no more effective device for doing so than speaking to them in their own language. "He speaks my language" is no empty compliment; it means that one likes a certain person because his manner of expression identifies him with one's own group. Suppose a professor of economics addresses a meeting of a steelworkers' union. If he speaks to them in the language in which he is accustomed to speak to his classes or to his colleagues, his chances of success with the steelworkers are slim. If, however, he has the knack of talking their own language— without their ever feeling that he is deliberately "talking down" to them—he can be a great success. As they leave the hall, they will be saying that he is a swell guy, even if he is a college prof— he didn't put on the dog but talked to them straight from the shoulder. And (and this is the important thing) they will be inclined to react favorably not only to his manner but to what he was saying to them. He may have been all wrong; the union perhaps would seriously jeopardize its strength if it were to act on his suggestions. But the members are in danger of being converted by his use of language alone.

Thus the use of appropriate diction to establish rapport between the writer or speaker and his audience can often become abuse of the worst kind. Just as is the case with words of highly emotional connotation, the employment of words and idioms designed to promote a fellow-feeling between the two parties can divert attention from the reasonableness of any argument. "We're pals, we see eye-to-eye, and of course you'll believe what I'm telling you."

BULL SESSION

. . . Sometimes it doesn't take much to get a guy wondering.

You probably never heard of me. I'm just a plain guy. Name of Joe Smith. But in a way I'm a pretty important fella. At least that's the way Doc Hibbard put it.

Guess I must have been really spouting off. But Doc just looked at me with those twinkling eyes of his. "Business profits too big?" he said, with a chuckle. "Why, son, they're as American as apple pie."

He pointed to little Tim Taylor—he's Ed Taylor's boy—selling newspapers on the corner.

"Tim there, for instance. When you talk about monopolies and more taxes on big business, that's the fellow you're attacking. 'Cause if you wrap up every big question about our free-enterprise economy, what he does answers it.

"Tim knows what the American Way is, all right. Lots of folks seem to think you can get something for nothing. Not Tim. No siree, you don't catch him running to the government for handouts. Don't hear him hollerin' about security, either."

Doc tapped his pipe and went on. "There was a fellow once put it pretty well—'Let not him who is houseless pull down the house of another.'"

Doc paused a moment and then, very softly, continued, "The codger who said that, son, was a fellow called Abe Lincoln."

I guess that's when I began to see things differently. And brother, take it from me, maybe it's time all of us did.

Maybe it's time we stopped biting the hand that feeds us. Maybe it's time we got behind the Tim Taylors.

Let's let the snake-oil peddlers yell all they want about their ism and their "security." Me . . . I'll take vanilla.

Yessiree, it doesn't take much to get a guy to wondering these days.

Everything is everybody's job*

The man responsible for this ad, a sophisticated writer, has a message to deliver—something about the superiority of "our free-enterprise economy," "the American way," over the "isms" vended by the "snake-oil peddlers." His intended audience is composed of "plain guys." And so he writes in the way he thinks plain guys talk. Count the number of times he uses words designed to make the reader identify himself with the supposed speaker: *guy, plain guy, fella, folks, brother.* . . . Note the free use of colloquialisms and slang, beginning with the title of the piece and including *spouting off, no siree, take it from me, I'll take vanilla.* . . . Sometimes the speaker omits the subject of his sentence, as is often done in informal talk: "Guess I must have been really spouting off," "Don't hear him hollerin' about security, either." Note, too, the short sentences and the frequent contractions *(doesn't, I'm, they're).*

The "logic" behind this cracker-barrel discourse is: (1) I talk like you. (2) Therefore (!) I'm really like you; we're buddies. (3) If we're buddies, neither of us is a high-dome intellect. We're just ordinary fellows, with plenty of horse sense. Like you, I wouldn't deceive anybody. And, since you have plenty of horse sense, I can depend on you to realize the truth of my argument. (4) So listen to what I tell you—man to man!

The reasoning is weak in every link. Swindlers have an art of talking like their prospective victims, too, but they can scarcely be trusted. The advertiser's manner—his diligent attempt to say his say in just the language that will make you feel most at home with him—has nothing at all to do with the soundness of his ideas. Maybe he is 100 per cent right; but has he *proved* to you that he is—or, indeed, given you any solid reason

* Quoted by permission of the author from William H. Whyte, Jr., *Is Anybody Listening?* (Simon & Schuster, 1952).

for *believing* that he is? Homely, familiar talk can often be a device for evading or concealing the real issue, for inducing the reader to relax his vigilance and take ideas on faith alone. The reader is in danger of buying a worthless package simply because it is attractively wrapped.

The same device is dear to all politicians, and for exactly the same reason. No candidate who cherishes votes can afford to allow himself to be thought of as several notches loftier than the common run of men. He therefore takes pains to convince his prospective electors that he is wood from the same fine block from which they themselves were carved. The baby-kissing expeditions, the "front porch" campaigns, the clam bakes, the publicity given to the simple, affectionate, moral domestic life of the candidate—all are designed to encourage the people's conviction that he is one of them, has the same tastes and hobbies—and therefore (that long-suffering word!) must be wise and honest, too. His language is designed to serve the same end, especially when he is meeting the electorate face to face. Public education has progressed to the extent that every politician above the rank of ward-heeler is expected to be reasonably grammatical in his public utterances; but his choice of words must convince the audience that this man talks their language (and thinks their thoughts).

The most famous example in recent history of the careful cultivation of rapport between speaker and audience was President Franklin D. Roosevelt's fireside chats. The magic of those radio talks lay not merely in the inspired name that was given to them (analyze the connotations of *fireside* and *chat*); it lay in the way in which Mr. Roosevelt's whole manner—his invariable use of simple words, his homely illustrations and analogies, his frequent use of the pronouns "you" and "I" instead of the impersonal diction of the statesman—fulfilled the promise of the name. Time after time he won public support for his side of a controversy by talking "with" the people, in their own language.

EXERCISE 5

What requirements of diction should be observed in writing the following items?

1. A direct-mail advertisement of this book, addressed to teachers who might be persuaded to adopt it in their classes.
2. An advertisement of a new antibiotic, to be published in the *Journal of the American Medical Association.*
3. Directions for assembling a model airplane bought through an ad in a teen-age boys' magazine.
4. Directions for assembling a high-fidelity record player.
5. A booklet, entitled "So You're Going to Have an Operation!", given to patients admitted to the surgical section of a hospital.
6. A story in a magazine intended for kindergarten-age children.
7. A talk to be delivered to the Kiwanis Club.
8. A talk to be given at a sorority meeting.
9. A letter to the dean, asking him to waive a certain requirement on the grounds that if it isn't waived, you can't accept a bid from the fraternity or sorority you want to join.
10. A bread-and-butter letter to your hostess after a recent weekend.
11. A letter to your congressman, protesting his announced stand on a certain issue.
12. An article on new trends in home decoration, to be published in one of the magazines especially intended for distribution through supermarkets.

EXERCISE 6

Comment on the following versions of a famous American speech. For what audience and what sort of medium (oral delivery, magazine article, business memo, etc.) might each have been designed? How does each version compare in effectiveness with the original?

1. Friends, it is now eighty-seven years since our beloved nation saw the light of day. Behind it was a new idea, the idea that one man is as good as another and every man deserves the blessings of liberty.

   We are met here today while the war clouds hang heavy over

us. Our brothers, husbands, and sons are giving their all to defend the sacred principles upon which our country was founded.
On this solemn occasion it is our purpose to do homage to them
by setting aside a portion of the rolling countryside about us,
in which they were recently locked in mortal combat, as a last
resting place for the departed heroes.

When we give way to reflection, however, it becomes plain that
we, who have not fought and bled here, are not the ones to "dedi-
cate" this cemetery. It has already been dedicated by the valorous
warriors who clashed in fierce struggle here last July. Our program today will not go down in the annals of time. That honor
is reserved, and justly so, for the magnificent deeds of those soldiers. Let us turn our thoughts instead to the unfinished business
remaining before us. We must carry on, with every ounce of
determination at our command, so that the great ideals that
our fallen brethren cherished in their stout hearts shall be fulfilled. Let us therefore partake of fresh inspiration from the
sacrifices they have made. Let us make a solemn vow that their
deaths were not in vain. The finest monument we can erect to
them will be the triumph of the high cause for which they laid
down their lives—the cause of democratic government. Then we
can rest assured that they are gone but not forgotten.

2. The present occasion of commemoration and dedication is an
appropriate moment at which to offer several observations.
These are as follows: (1) The current state of belligerency between two sections of the nation is traceable to a regrettable
divergence of opinion as to whether the aforesaid nation has an
indefinite life expectancy, predicated as it is upon certain novel
principles laid down 8.7 decades ago, viz.: that all members of
the commonwealth are (a) equal in status and (b) entitled to
freedom of intellect, expression, and action. (2) The ceremonies
attendant on the allocation, in perpetuity, of the acreage en-
vironing us as a memorial to the casualties of the late battle,
while they are indisputably honorable in intent, nevertheless
must not detract attention from the fact that the memorializing
has already been implemented by the sanguinary activities which
occurred here last July. (3) In view of this circumstance, it is
highly desirable that our motivations be directed instead toward

the finalization of the procedure which is already under way. (4) Such finalization should consist of an intensified application to the program for insuring the future stability of the nation, namely, for guaranteeing that the principles of liberty shall be resuscitated and that the concept of government, deriving its authority from, and operating through, the agency and in behalf of the best interests of the constituents shall be indefinitely preserved.

3.   IN MEMORIAM

Today, in the typically American countryside south of Gettysburg, Pa., a soldiers' cemetery is being dedicated.

Think what that means. Only a few months ago, a great battle was fought there. A battle that probably marked the fateful turning-point of the war—a war fought to preserve a free America—an America that owes its very being to the sacrifices of our grandfathers who believed, as we do, that all men are brothers.

The ceremonies at Gettysburg are a fitting gesture, but still only a gesture. We mustn't flatter ourselves that they are history-making. History has already been made there, and we can't possibly match that.

The *real* dedication must take place within ourselves.

The soldiers of the Union Army have done a wonderful job. But they can't do it all. We, who survive, must become, in a sense, their comrades-in-arms.

Every patriotic American must take a greater part in the affairs that concern us all. Every public-spirited citizen must contribute, in the way he is best fitted, to furthering the cause of freedom and democracy.

Join the great crusade—*today*!

EXERCISE 7

From one of the volumes of *The Public Papers and Addresses of Franklin D. Roosevelt,* select one of the fireside chats (or several of Mr. Roosevelt's informal speeches to people along the route of his train tours) and analyze the means by which he kept "the common touch."

EXERCISE 8

Each of the following advertisements is designed to appeal to a certain well-defined audience. How successfully does the writer "talk the language" of his intended readers?

1. Through all the higher phases of business and finance and industry, Cadillac is the overwhelming favorite.

   It is not at all unusual, in fact, for a fine American corporation to have its entire board membership represented on the Cadillac owner list.

   Needless to say, a motor car must offer many exceptional qualities in order to win the favor of so distinguished a group of motorists.

   And never have these been more clearly evident than they are today.

   There is Cadillac's inspiring new beauty, for instance . . . its great distinction . . . its magnificent performance . . . and its brilliant luxury.

   Of course, you don't have to be a member of a Board of Directors in order to enjoy a new Cadillac car.

   In fact, a Cadillac is one of motordom's greatest values—the ideal car, economically, for a very wide group of American motorists.

2. Are you the type that likes to breeze along the open road on a bright summer day with nothing above between you and the blue? Do you like the sound of rain against a snug fabric top? If so, the Chevrolet Convertible is for you! No question about it. For here's a car that's as young in spirit as you are—and looks it! Even the smart all-vinyl interior is made to live outdoors.

   But maybe you like a car that can carry anything from small fry to outboard motors with equal ease. That would be the "Two-Ten" Handyman Station Wagon (one of five Chevrolet wagons). Here's one car that's so versatile it practically makes you a two-car family all by itself. So low it sets a new height of fashion for station wagons! Practical? If the kids track sand inside, you can wash it out in a jiffy.

   On the other hand, if you go for hardtops—and like 'em long.

low and dashing—the Bel Air Sport Coupe is just your dish. It's a "show car" from the word go!

Whichever Chevrolet you choose, you're bound to have the driving time of your life!

3. Once there was a woman and that's how clothes began. As time went on, she needed more and more clothes in order to be well dressed. And that's really where all the trouble started. Because more and more clothes meant more and more and *more* money.

So she sat herself down to think. And she knitted one and she purled two—and she rocked and she thought and she rocked. And there was the answer as plain as day. It was simply perfect— and perfectly simple. And the word rang a bell in her head. "The *soul* of Simplicity," she'd heard someone say. And that's just precisely what Simplicity Printed Patterns *were*. Because being printed meant they were easier to follow than any pattern before or since.

So she made one dress and then another. And everyone said: "How grand, how clever, how smart!" And after that she made a discovery.

Everyone knows a girl never *really* has enough clothes—but she *was* better dressed, she *had* saved money, and something even more important had happened. She was proud of what she was doing—and her family was proud of her, too! And it was just because . . . she did it all by herself, with the help of Simplicity Printed Patterns.

4. What with the ballyhoo about ball-point pens, super-snorkle jobs, and such—you wouldn't think anyone would ever use a quill pen these days. Well, you'd be quite wrong.

There's a man in New Haven, Conn., Lewis Glaser is his name, and his full-time business is manufacturing quill pens. He cuts and mails 75,000 a year—all in a single, little room. His production equipment is a 49-cent penknife.

We know all about Pen-maker Glaser because we wrote a little story about him in January Nation's Business. He told us he got lots of nice mail from it, including a fine, fat order from a large insurance company—with an even larger one on the way.

Well, why not? He had a distinguished customer list. Not long ago, for example, he sold 1,800 quill pens to the United States

Supreme Court. These were made from the feathers of pure bred white Embden geese. The court paid him 15 cents each, after he trimmed them to the ten-inch size first specified by John Marshall, the court's fourth Chief Justice.

Who knows what other customers Nation's Business might dig up for him? After all, three-quarter-million men in every conceivable kind of business read this magazine every month . . . Nation's Business, *a magazine for businessmen.*

EXERCISE 9

This is a campaign biography of a candidate for mayor of a large American city. What considerations seem to have governed the writer's choice of words? How do the facts recited bear on the candidate's qualifications for this office? Do you think this is an effective piece of persuasion?

THE RIGHT MAN FOR A BIG JOB

The next chief executive of our great city, Walter ————, has in his veins an auspicious mixture of Scotch-Irish and German blood, an ideal combination for a public servant, mingling as it does the religious devoutness and regard for strict economy that are typical of the Scotch-Irish with the unquenchable zest for hard work and quiet living that is typically German. Though not born in a log cabin, his birthplace was modest enough—a clapboard home at Dublin Crossing, in the southern part of the state. His father was the owner of the village's general store and for many years was also the local justice of the peace, known far and wide for the fairness with which he dispensed justice. His mother, a gentle, self-sacrificing lady, contributed profoundly to the molding of Walter's sterling character. "All that I am, or ever hope to be, I owe to her," he says in a moving voice. Still alert though frail in body at eighty-two years of age, she has been spared by a kindly Providence to witness the full measure of her son's achievement.

Young Walt early knew the meaning of economy and diligence. As one of seven brothers and sisters, he had to hew his own path toward the fulfilment of his ambitions. When school was out for the day, and on Saturdays and in the summers, he clerked long hours in his father's store. Inspired with a thirst for learning, upon the com

pletion of his signally successful high school career he entered
————— College, where again he welcomed the opportunity to
forge ahead on his own. He eked out a frugal living by waiting on
tables and applying his talents for salesmanship in the college book
store. Although he modestly admits to having burned the midnight
oil on many occasions, he was no mere bookworm, for he found time
to become a track star and to participate in other college activities,
such as the glee club to which he added his fine baritone voice. No
one was surprised when he took his sheepskin with high honors.

Walt had early fixed his sights on a high professional goal, the
practice of law. After two years of selling insurance, an interim in
his career necessitated by the depression, he resumed his studies at
the University of ————— Law School, from which he emerged
with his accustomed academic accolades. Subsequently he hung out
his shingle in partnership with his old college chum, Paul —————,
and soon reached a position of enviable eminence in the local bar.

At this point in his career he married Miss Dorothy Jane —————,
his high school sweetheart. A winsome, efficient helpmeet, she has
contributed in no small measure to his success. Active in the P.T.A.,
Red Cross, Cancer Society, and other civic groups, she has still man-
aged to be an affectionate mother to the three children with whom
their union has been blessed. Walt, Jr., 20, is now following his
father's footsteps in college; blonde Beverly, 17, is a popular leader
in her class at Sherman High School; and the "baby" of the family,
"Bonnie Prince Charlie," as he is fondly called, is in grade school.

With the coming of Pearl Harbor, Walt ————— volunteered
immediately to serve the nation in its hour of peril. Although he
was offered a commission, his firm democratic convictions impelled
him to enlist as a private. He saw action in several theaters of war,
received three medals for distinguished service, rose to the rank of
captain, and in 1945 joined the staff of Gen. Patton, whom he accompanied in the last dramatic months of Victory in Europe.

With the country once again at peace, Walt doffed the khaki and
took up the threads of his interrupted civilian career. Although
often urged from many quarters to enter the political arena as
candidate for state assemblyman, district attorney, and common
pleas judge, he steadfastly declined to run for office until this past
year, when, as he says, "the call of duty became too clear and in-
sistent for me to turn a deaf ear to it." Having incurred no political

obligations in the past, he is completely unbossed. As mayor, he will have no debts to pay off to any pressure group or political faction, but instead will devote himself to the service of all the people.

An active member of many church, fraternal, and civic organizations, Walt's particular interest is in youth-group activities, since he recognizes the ever-mounting problem of juvenile delinquency and is determined to combat it with every resource at his command. Despite the manifold nature of his affiliations, he takes time off whenever possible "to go fishing with the kids," to quote his own phrase. At forty-nine, he is in the prime of life. Hiking and "puttering around in the garden" keep him in fit physical condition.

As befits the man, his philosophy of government is exquisitely simple and homespun, no doubt deriving in its essentials from the opinions he absorbed as a youth from the neighbors who congregated, after their day's work was done, on the straight-backed chairs on the porch of his father's store. "I am a middle-of-the-roader," he says with his characteristic directness. "I believe in dynamic conservatism in the handling of the city's affairs. The first duty of a mayor is to make sure that the people get one hundred cents' worth of municipal services for every tax dollar."

Here, then, is a man whom our city will be fortunate indeed to have at its helm for the next two years; a man of varied experience and unsullied integrity; a man sure of his own powers and yet humble before God. Privileged are we that next month we will have the opportunity to vote into office this distinguished citizen—Walt ————, the right man for a big job.

The Clues of Unnecessarily Difficult Language

We have remarked that every author, if he is to succeed in communicating his ideas, must address himself to his chosen audience in its own language. This fact may suggest to you that the obligation is all on the writer's side; that all you have to do is allow him to impart his information and his arguments to you, in your own terms. This is not true. You must go halfway to meet your author, whoever he is; as should be abundantly clear by now, intelligent reading is in no sense a process of passive absorption. Every reader, however, may expect a writer to express himself as clearly and directly as he can. Whenever he encounters language which seems unnecessarily difficult, he should follow this procedure:

1. Find out what is said—by use of context, dictionary, and brains.

2. Try to restate the meaning in simpler language, without using much more space—using less, if possible—and without changing or sacrificing any essential idea. If this experiment is successful, two preliminary conclusions may be made: (a) The difficult language is not justified because it saves space. Sometimes oversized words are chosen because the ideas they embody otherwise can be expressed only by awkward, space- and time-consuming clauses or sentences. Rightly used, this is a perfectly legitimate sort of shorthand. But if the big words can be replaced by short synonyms, obviously no space has been saved. Furthermore, if some words or phrases can be omitted without loss, space is being wasted. (b) The difficult language is not called for by the complexity of the idea. In a culture like ours there are many ideas which cannot possibly be expressed by the familiar, short words of our everyday vocabulary; they require the use of longer words, many of which were created expressly to stand for such ideas. If, however, you can be sure that your paraphrase in simpler language does preserve the sense of the passage, you have demonstrated that the language is unjustifiably complicated.

If, on the other hand, after conscientious effort you have failed to simplify the language of the passage, you probably have proved that the difficult language which the author used was necessary—and you have no choice but to dig in and try to understand him by learning his terminology. He cannot come any farther to meet you, so you must work toward rapport with him by equipping yourself with his vocabulary.

But if your experiment has proved that the author's use of difficult language was not justified—what then? Several possible inferences may follow:

1. The writer's mind does not function clearly and precisely,

and this lack of clarity and precision is reflected in his attempts at communication. If a man's thinking is muddled, his writing is likely to be muddled, too.

2. The writer may be a fairly incisive thinker, but he honestly assumes that he can convey his ideas only by the use of outsized words and roundabout expressions. He should be listened to with respect, because his ideas may be valuable; but he should be pitied for his ignorance of the art of communication.

3. The writer knows better than to clothe his ideas in language that is too big for them, but he goes ahead and does it anyway because he thinks he will impress his audience. He may be right. The uncritical reader will think, "Gosh, what complicated language; he must be a brilliant man to be able to write like that." But the critical reader will be impatient and suspicious: "Who do you think you are? I can write like that too, but I have more sense."

4. The writer is deliberately using such language, not to display his own talents (which may be pretty dubious anyway) but to hide something—perhaps his own ignorance, perhaps an idea of which his audience would not approve were he to express it so that they would immediately recognize it.

There is also a fifth inference, which may well accompany any of the preceding four. That is, the writer who uses an unnecessarily wordy or obscure style may have little sensitivity to the beauties of language. Writing that is full of polysyllabic words and hard knots and clusters of phrases is likely to offend not only the intellect but also the ear. We shall say more about the rhythm of language below, and again in Chapter Four. But as you read the examples of bad writing in this chapter, notice how jagged, heavy, cacophonous, the sentences often are, and try to discover the cause of this unpleasantness.

This brings us to the important topic of jargon, which is defined by a noted English critic of language as "talk that is considered both ugly-sounding and hard to understand; applied especially to the sectional vocabulary of a science, art, class, sect, trade, or profession, full of technical terms . . . and the use of long words, circumlocution, and other clumsiness." Or, to put it in terms familiar to you from your handbook of composition, jargon is that kind of bad writing which prefers the roundabout expression to the direct one, the long word to the short, the high-sounding word to the plain one, the abstract term to the concrete, the noun to the verb, and the "weak" passive to the "strong" active voice.

Jargon: (1) Dead Wood

In every handbook of composition at least one section is devoted to directions for expunging so-called "dead wood" from one's writing. Dead wood—words and phrases that add nothing to the meaning of a sentence or that could be drastically simplified—is the most obvious form of jargon. Strewn carelessly across the straight highway of thought, it forces constant and perfectly unnecessary detours. "The condition of redundancy that exists in such a great number of themes produced by college undergraduates should be eliminated by every means that lies at the disposal of the person who teaches them."—There is a sentence full of dead wood. Such phrases as *the condition of, the quality of, the state of, the nature of,* can nearly always be omitted without loss. *That exists* and many similar locutions are nearly always redundant. *Such a great number of* is a roundabout way of saying *so many. Produced by* is unnecessary, and *that lies at the disposal of,* like the concluding clause, can be greatly condensed. Thus the sentence could be revised to read, "The redundancy found in so many college students' themes should be eliminated by every means known to the teacher." This sentence, though much improved, is still not perfect; we shall return to it before long for further simplification.

It is a profitable exercise to make a list of the most frequent stereotyped phrases that clutter up our government documents, our newspaper articles, our business letters, our student themes. Among the most common and indefensible space-wasters are *due to* (or *in view of*) *the fact that* (= *because*) and *despite the fact that* (= *although*). The simple *the fact that* often is equally superfluous *(the fact that he was ill = his illness)*. Here are some other chunks of dead wood, together with their simple equivalents:

in the matter of (in respect to)	about
a long period of time	a long time
in the capacity of	as
resembling in nature	like
in some instances	sometimes

One especially useless sort of dead wood is that which provides a whole verb phrase where a single verb would do as well, or better:

make an attempt	try
reach a decision	decide
met with the approval of Jones	Jones approved
signed an agreement providing for	agreed to
announced himself to be in favor of	said he favored
it is the belief of	he believes
will be hostess to . . . at a dinner party	will give a dinner for
paid a compliment to	complimented
is in the process of being	is being
exhibits a tendency	tends

Such roundabout expressions seldom cause much confusion their principal offense is that they waste space and the reader' time and eyesight. (We might have said, "Circuitous expres sions of the nature of those cited just above do not cause a grea deal of confusion except on a few occasions; the chief respec in which they are the cause of offense is the way in which the result in the wasting of space and of time and eyesight on th part of the reader." The sense would not have been muc obscured, but your patience would have been tried.) And whe we observe that a writer or speaker habitually clutters up hi discourse with unnecessary words and phrases, we are we justified in concluding two things about him: (1) He is in efficient; zealous though he may be, in other respects, to accon plish things with the utmost dispatch and the least possible waste of motion, his language cries out for the attentions of a so-called time- and motion-study expert; (2) he is a slave to custom; he has absorbed these stereotyped expressions from his associates and from his routine reading—and he has never stopped to examine and criticize them. What an exhilarating experience it would be for him to break with hallowed custom and train himself to say things simply, tersely, directly!

Jargon: (2) Big Words, Stock Words

A more serious enemy of clarity is the jargonist's predilection for big words where shorter ones would do as well. Because so many people are superstitiously afraid of *all* big words, it will not hurt to repeat here what we said on page 75. It is not true that short words are always better than long ones. Many ideas cannot possibly be conveyed in words from the common vocabulary; and in addition, although two words, one short and one long, may seem to be synonymous, practiced readers and writers know that their connotations are substantially different, and therefore that if the longer word conveys the idea more precisely than does the shorter, it must be used. It is a foolish reader indeed who shies away from a book that contains long words because he thinks they are always merely ostentatious. Perhaps they are; but in the use of language, as in the eyes of the law, a man is presumed innocent until he is proved guilty. If the reader resents a writer's use of big words, he must prove that he, the reader, could say the same thing more simply.

The jargon-addict, however, is fatally fascinated by the unnecessary polysyllable. He says *activate* instead of *form* or *establish* (whether he is referring to a new army division or a branch factory), and *inactivate* instead of *disband* or *shut down;* to him, employees are always *personnel;* the business of buying something is *procurement,* and that of hiring new help is *personnel procurement.* (Nowadays, too, in some educational circles, the *personnel counselor* has taken the place of the old-fashioned *student adviser.*) An order is a *directive;* to manage or direct is to *coordinate;* to carry out (an order) is to *imple-ment;* to hurry up is to *expedite;* to attend to is to *process.*

Jargon of this kind, although it became much more preva-lent during and after the Second World War, has clogged communication in business and government for many years. Closely associated with it is a vocabulary of stock words which presumably save the harassed businessman from having to find the exact word he needs to fit each contingency. Such a word is the grossly abused *set-up,* which rushes in to fill the gap when-ever one is too busy (or too lazy) to select *situation, scheme, arrangement,* or *plan.* Another is *picture* ("Do you get the picture?" = "Do you understand?"; "Let me fill you in on the over-all picture" = "Let me give you a summary"; "What's the picture?" = "What's the situation?").

The picture here is that in many organizational set-ups the personnel, particularly on the junior executive level, shows a trend toward acting like automatons when they are contacting other personnel—and to treat those whom they contact as au-tomatons, too. Language like this is language of the machine: it is language as standardized and impersonal as something stamped out by a die. Individuality, freshness, even humanity itself are rigidly excluded from such discourse. It suggests that the human touch has no place in business; that people who write and talk in the course of their duties must be as mecha-nized as a production line. There is as little excuse for robot language in business as there is for a man who, in "contacting" his "junior partner" by telephone late in the afternoon, says "Darling, I regret very much to inform you that the termina-tion of my day's responsibilities will be somewhat delayed. A cutback in the secretarial staff has resulted in unavoidable pyramiding of dictation for Miss Jones, who is therefore unable to process my interoffice communications as per schedule. Will you please convey my best regards to the younger members of our organization, and promise them I will contact them before they are transferred to bed? By the way, was Jackie upgraded in school? And will you please send me information as to whether you have succeeded in procuring a replacement in our kitchen personnel for Lizzie?"

Jargon: (3) *Overworked Nouns*

Another constant element of jargon (as in this sentence) is the overuse of nouns and the accompanying neglect of verbs. In all written and spoken discourse, verbs, and verbs alone, furnish the power by which the sentence moves. They are like truck-tractors: their function is to pull along the nouns (trailers), which have no power unit of their own. But even the strongest tractor stalls if it is given too heavy a load to pull—and that is exactly what happens in jargon. "The EFFECT of the OVERUSE of NOUNS in WRITING *is* the PLACING of too much STRAIN upon the VERBS and the resultant PREVENTION of MOVEMENT of the THOUGHT." One verb—and you can count the nouns for yourself! Forms of the verb *to be* are hard workers, but they cannot possibly do everything that is demanded of them by people who apparently know few other verbs. As in the sentence above, the copulative (*is,* etc.) is too often required to pull a subject loaded down with nouns and noun phrases and at the same time to push a predicate that is also loaded down with them. The result is a sentence that creaks and groans when it moves; and you can hear it groaning, too. For the presence of so many nouns requires one to use many prepositional phrases, especially *of*-phrases, to the detriment of smooth rhythm. Any intelligent writer, if he has committed a sentence like the one quoted, will replace some of the noun phrases with clauses, thus adding verbs which will help share the load: "One who overuses nouns in writing places too much strain upon the verbs and as a result prevents the thought from moving along."

Good judges of English style strongly object to the overuse of nouns in modern writing not merely because their cumulative weight can overtax the single verb or two that the sentence may contain. They also point out that many of the favorite nouns used by businessmen, lawyers, and other kinds of more or less specialized writers end in *-tion, -ity, -ment, -ness,* and

-ance. Words ending with these suffixes are not notably lovely in sound, and if used to excess they grate upon the ear. Listen to this sentence from a professional educators' journal: "Merely to enumerate these five outstanding characteristics of an urban community, namely, chaotic stimulation, mechanization, impersonalization, commercialization, and complexity of organization, suggests many implications for the city school." (It is too bad the last word was not *education*.) Or try this one for sound: "For most Americans, irrespective of party affiliation and predisposition, isolationism is defunct and participation and cooperation commonsensed and essential, in international relations."*

One other abuse is the habit, whose origin seems to have been in headline writers' practice, of piling noun upon noun, sometimes intermixed with adjectives but without even the mortar of prepositions. In educational jargon, for instance, the everyday dilemmas in which one may find himself (to go to class unprepared, or to cut; to run for the bus or wait for the next one) are collectively called the "Policy Determination Problem Question." A news item a few years ago told of a man's being elected to the board of directors of the Perishable Agricultural Products Processing Equipment Manufacturers Institute. Since he was also made a member of the Canning Machinery Manufacturers Industry Advisory Committee of the National Production Authority, he must have had a considerable burden to bear.

---

* Literary men sometimes are guilty of the same fault. Read aloud this sentence by Evelyn Waugh, the well-known contemporary English novelist: "He began to concern himself with the foundation of a literary reputation; considered, and at the last moment rejected, the project of a publication for private circulation; contributed sonnets to the *Fortnightly Review* and to a pamphlet review of the pictures of the year." Pay particular attention to the sound of the middle clause. It would be unfair to conclude from a sentence like this that Mr. Waugh has no ear for music. Still, one of the tests of a good writer is his ability to detect and get rid of unpleasant repetitions of sound, whether they are caused by too many suffixes or by excessive alliteration or assonance. He should not only *see* what he writes; he should hear it, too. The graduate student who wrote this sentence obviously did not reread it aloud: "Thus in 'Andrea del Sarto' the mood of subdued tension precludes the selection of a crucial moment or situation."

"This unpleasant practice is spreading fast," writes a British commentator, "and is corrupting the language"; or, to put it in appropriate terms, the pyramiding attributive substantive policy is a present-day language-decay contributory factor.

Jargon: (4) The Overused Passive

Another prominent aspect of jargon is the overused passive construction. The passive voice is nearly always less effective than the active; that is, it is less vivid to say that "a letter is dictated" than it is to say that "Mr. Barnes dictates a letter." In the first instance, attention is fixed upon the act itself, which is hard to visualize, since apparently no one is around to perform it; the letter is just there, being dictated. But in the second instance, attention is fixed not upon the abstract idea of the act itself but upon the concrete presence of someone who is performing it.

You will recall that we had not finished correcting a sentence upon which we were working on page 77. We had left it in this form: "The redundancy found in so many college students' themes should be eliminated by every means known to the teacher." We now get rid of ("eliminate") the weak passive, and the sentence becomes much more vigorous: "The teacher should use every method he knows to get rid of the redundancy found in so many college students' themes."

Like all legitimate grammatical constructions, the passive voice has its uses. In particular, it allows one to express ideas without attributing them to a specific individual source. That is why it is so widely used in government communications, in which decisions and opinions are presumed to be those of the bureau or agency as a whole and not of individual officials. But legitimate use can easily turn into abuse. While the convention by which governmental edicts come from an impersonal entity can be defended, the indiscriminate use of the passive as a grammatical camouflage can also be a sign of moral weakness. Anyone who does not wish to assume personal responsibility for his statements finds an "out" by writing "it is directed that" instead of "I direct that," or "it is the opinion of the firm" instead of "I think." Readers must distinguish carefully between those writers who use the passive because of well-established convention, as in the armed forces, and those who use it because it is a convenient way out of a tight spot.*

The Uses and Abuses of Technical Language

We are far from wishing to suggest that unnecessary complication of language is a sin confined to businessmen and government employees. We have chosen to speak first of business and "bureaucratic" jargon because it is the most commonly encountered of all types and because, in addition, it can be most easily analyzed to show the folly of overaffection for long, abstract nouns, for circuitous expressions, and for constructions dominated by nouns and *of*. But we must turn now to another vast domain in which jargon flourishes—jargon of a much wilder species. We are speaking of the jargon of the various professions, which many of you will encounter, to your sorrow, in your future careers; but take an oath now that you will do nothing to propagate it!

Here we must inject another word of caution, to reinforce what we said a while ago about the necessity for discriminating between the unavoidable and the superfluous use of oversized and involved language. Since every trade and profession has its own special ideas, methods, materials, and tools, obviously it must have a special vocabulary to designate these things. The medical vocabulary, which may seem completely unintelligible to the layman, is absolutely essential to a doctor, for it enables him to speak concisely and accurately of such things as medicines, surgical procedures, courses of treatment, and clusters of

---

* The sort of language we have been discussing thus far under the name of "jargon" is also familiarly known as "gobbledygook." This expressive word (what does its sound suggest to you?) was coined by the late Congressman Maury Maverick of Texas, who meant it to refer specifically to the prose used by government officials. Now, however, *gobbledygook* is applied to all unnecessarily involved language regardless of its habitat, whether in government, business, or the learned professions.

symptoms which could otherwise be described only by most indirect and time-wasting paragraphs. And similarly with all other men and women who have their own occupational vocabularies—the electronic engineer, the dress designer, the psychologist, the food chemist. Their special vocabularies enable them to think more precisely when they are at work and to communicate with their fellow-workers with the greatest possible ease and exactness. This is, after all, but a logical extension of our earlier principle that men must address their hearers in a language intelligible to both parties.

But by the same token, the use of technical language in addressing a nontechnical audience is not only inappropriate but also inefficient and, it may be, actually dishonest. When a physician speaks to a patient in the scientific terms in which he habitually thinks and in which he speaks to his fellow physicians, he is not achieving rapport with his listener, even though he may not be consciously trying to prevent understanding; but another, less scrupulous, physician may deliberately employ such language to confuse a patient—perhaps to impress him with the magnitude of the miracle he has performed and thus to prepare him for the magnitude of the bill. The willful use of technical double-talk is important to the success of quacks in every field. Every man who sets himself up as a psychologist catering to the emotional ills of newspaper readers and the buyers of popular books, cultivates the glib use of such terms as *complex, neurosis, frustration, sublimation, fixation, compensation, phobia*—terms which have immense prestige value with the public because they are associated with the "mysteries" of the psychological science. Ideally, nobody but a trained psychologist or psychiatrist should use such terms, because they represent complicated ideas which cannot easily be grasped by the layman; but they have become part of the popular vocabulary, even though their meanings are seriously distorted in common usage.

Thus technical language should be kept for times when here is no other way of concise, exact communication. It should

not be used as an elaborate disguise for the simple thoughts
of those who wish to impress the layman, or as an easy escape
for those who are too indolent to express themselves simply.

This is a classic anecdote on the subject:

A foreign-born plumber in New York City wrote to the Federal
Bureau of Standards that he had found hydrochloric acid did a
good job of cleaning out clogged drains.

The bureau wrote: "The efficacy of hydrochloric acid is indisputable, but the corrosive residue is incompatible with metallic
permanence."

The plumber replied he was glad the bureau agreed.

Again the bureau wrote: "We cannot assume responsibility for
the production of toxic and noxious residue with hydrochloric acid
and suggest you use an alternative procedure."

The plumber was happy again at bureau agreement with his idea.

Then the bureau wrote: "Don't use hydrochloric acid. It eats hell
out of the pipes."

Workers in the physical sciences have a crisp, clear professional language which seldom deserves to be described by a
word with the negative connotations of *jargon*. In scientific
writing, certain nouns and verbs which look strange and meaningless to the unpracticed eye actually convey meaning with the
utmost exactness and economy. But the social scientists have
evolved a language bedecked with terminology which often
degenerates into the worst kind of jargon. Of course there are
many specialized terms in these fields as well which are necessary for an adequate expression of meaning. To the sociologist such words as *status, ethnic, mobility, institution, disor-
ganization,* and *culture* are indispensable, because they embody
basic sociological concepts; and while the student may feel
affronted by the constant use of such terms in his textbooks, he
has no alternative but to learn exactly what they mean—otherwise he will know nothing about sociology. But many writers in
these fields go to unwarranted extremes, preferring to describe
the phenomena of human behavior in inhuman language. The
sentence "More and more city people nowadays are moving to

the suburbs" states in plain English the idea which many sociologists would prefer to set forth in these terms: "In recent years there has been discernible in the urban population an accelerating tendency toward decentralization into the adjacent semirural areas."

The following passage might well have appeared in a journal written for sociologists or social workers:

Recent studies have revealed that there exists a large complex of sociological, as distinguished from psycho-physical, sources of marital disharmony. Three factors may be singled out as being especially influential in militating against the optimum adjustment which partners in the marriage relationship should experience. The first is a wide disparity between the two partners in respect to previous socio-economic environment. The second, occurring in marriage situations in which the wife is gainfully employed or is otherwise the recipient of substantial sums of money, is the existence of a broad discrepancy between the income of the wife and the husband, with the former being responsible for a larger proportion of the joint family income than is normally considered acceptable in a cultural pattern in which the female is expected to contribute less in terms of monetary support than the male. The third is a conspicuous divergency between the terminal educational levels attained by the woman and the man respectively. When any or all of these factors are present, the tendency is for one spouse to harbor feelings of resentment and inferiority, which, though initially suppressed, may in time become overt, leading to increasingly sharp conflicts between the two, and, unless the deterioration of the relationship is arrested by attempts at readjustment, especially with the aid of a disinterested outside agent such as a marriage counsellor, the total dissolution of the marriage, either formally, as by divorce, or informally, as by separation, may be the end result.

Rough translation:

When a husband and a wife have radically different backgrounds, one coming from a poor home and the other from a well-to-do one, or when the wife has more money than the husband, or when one of them hasn't had as much schooling as the other, their marriage may go on the rocks. The one who has fewer advantages begins to feel inferior and resentful, and things may get so bad that the couple ends up in the divorce court.

Now try *your* hand at boiling down this further paragraph:

The marriage counsellor's strategy in attempting to effectuate a rehabilitation of the marriage is fairly plainly indicated. He should endeavor to show his clients that the true grounds of a successful marriage relationship are not external considerations such as relative earning power, diverse socio-economic backgrounds, and disparate levels of educational attainment; these, in any event, are largely fortuitous. The primary consideration obviously is that of temperamental compatibility, as exemplified by similarity or identity of spiritual ideals, cultural tastes, recreational interests, etc. Having convinced his clients of this, he should proceed to provide practical guidance. For example, if the woman is employed, he might offer the suggestion that if financially feasible she substitute the role of housewife and mother for that of stenographer or clerk, even though some reduction in respect to the physical comforts of family life might ensue as the result of the termination of her employment; and that the spouse who is deficient in educational accomplishment remedy this defect by attendance at adult education classes or by enrollment at the public library. In such a manner the emotional disequilibrium and dislocation of the present family situation may, in many instances, be transformed into a new and vital realization of the genuine, nonmaterial values upon which the institution of marriage is founded.

The "educationists" are as infatuated with jargon as are the sociologists—if not more so. We have found writers for educational journals speaking of "instructional personnel" when *teachers* would have been just as good a word, and of "homes of low socio-economic status" when *poor homes* would have adequately embodied the meaning. Professional books and articles are filled with such terms as *acceleration, integration, activity, instructional, skill, tool, orientation, relatedness, situation, experience, evaluation, frame of reference.* Use of these words is justified if and when they stand for more or less well-defined concepts—concepts which could not be described in simple language. In many cases, however, the meaning of the term in any given context remains vague at best. Even when an attempt is made to define terms, the results are often less than satisfactory, as in this excerpt:

This article will attempt to point out the part played by personality maladjustment as a causative factor in reading disability. . . . For the purposes of this article "personality maladjustment" will be defined as any behavior that deviates from what is considered the normal behavior of children in the school situation.

Although the emphasis here has been upon the jargon of the social sciences, to be just it must be confessed that people who write about the arts—critics of literature, music, painting, architecture—are by no means guiltless. The books and articles of some contemporary critics are as filled with grandiose terminology and involved sentences, and as lacking in grace, as anything the social scientists turn out. And once the reader has hewed his way through the tangled jungle of words, he often finds that the idea he has labored to expose is simple enough.

––––––––––

EXERCISE 10

What familiar saying is wrapped up in gobbledygook in each of the following sentences?

1. Irrespective of its substandard physical condition and lack of the appurtenances which would place it, and therefore its inhabitants, in a higher socio-economic bracket, the structure in which a family pursues its domestic routine, and which the familial group associates with its mutual emotive attitudes, has a unique status.

2. During the period of the year beginning approximately at the vernal equinox and having a duration of several months thereafter, it is observable that the instinctual drives of the normal adolescent male of the human species are concentrated to an unusual degree upon attracting the attention and favor of persons of the opposite sex.

3. When an operator of any motor vehicle approaches a point on a public highway which is intersected by the right-of-way of a railroad, he is required by law to bring said motor vehicle to a complete standstill, and having done so, to verify by ocular inspection whether or not a train or other factor in a potential collision is approaching from either direction along the afore-mentioned right-of-way, as well as to substantiate the evidence thus obtained by being attentive to the auditory warning of such approach produced by whistle, horn, bell, or other device designed for the purpose of emitting an appropriate signal in such circumstances.

4. In a situation in which there exists the potentiality of further deterioration unless immediate remedial and preventive action is instituted, it is without exception advisable that such steps be taken as are required, before the occurrence of the anticipated additional damage has the opportunity to eventuate.

5. Adopting the practical point of view, it is justifiable to conclude that for every individual the conformity to a standard of be-havior which stresses integrity and lack of dissimulation as the key factor has the optimum probability of producing satisfactory end results.

EXERCISE 11

In the light of the preceding discussion, comment upon the style of this book. Is it *unnecessarily* difficult? Could the author have used simpler language to say the same things? (Apply the rewrite test to any passage you think is *unnecessarily* hard to read.) Does he "talk down" to his audience? (If so, where—and why do you think so?) Does he sometimes use words that are unfamiliar to college students? (If he does, try to explain what his purpose is.)

The whole book is meant to be criticized; at every point you are entitled to ask whether the writer practices what he preaches. But in fairness, you must also consider carefully what his purposes are, and whether you, as a reader, come halfway to meet him.

EXERCISE 12

Examine the writing in the official publications of your college or university—catalogues, bulletins, manuals of rules, and the like. When you find instances of verbosity, jargon, involved sentences, and other faults discussed above, rewrite them in the clearest language possible, though taking care, as always, not to distort the meaning or eliminate any necessary idea.

EXERCISE 13

Read the article by S. T. Williamson, "How to Write Like a Social Scientist," *Saturday Review of Literature,* Oct. 4, 1947.

Circumlocution and Euphemism

One more important way in which diction may obscure truth is the use of circumlocutions and euphemisms. A circumlocution is a roundabout expression which takes one on a pleasant detour around a disagreeable idea; a euphemism is a device, usually consisting of a single word, by which the objectionable idea is given a more attractive appearance as we pass it. Both are based on the interesting psychological principle that an idea can be made less unattractive if it is spoken of in words possessing as pleasant a connotation as possible.

The most obvious examples of such whitewashing devices come to mind immediately: the host of expressions which soften the idea of death (*to pass away, to enter into rest, to expire, to be deceased*—and the less sentimental, more facetious ones, *to kick the bucket, to turn in one's checks, to give up the ghost*); the equally great variety of expressions typified by *rest room* and *powder room;* those which attempt to gloss over the unpleasant truths relating to disease (*mental illness, rest home, malignancy, lung affliction*); and those which attempt to cover up other unlovely phases of life (*halitosis* for *bad breath, ex-*

pectorate for *spit, plant food* for *manure,** *county home* for *poor house, intemperance* for *drunkenness, infidelity* for *adultery, visually handicapped* for *blind, medically indigent person* for one who, while not a pauper, is unable to pay medical and hospital expenses, *public assistance* for *dole*).

Euphemisms are commonly used, also, in referring to occupations, where they serve either to conceal a definite unpleasantness, or to improve social status. There are now relatively few *foremen, bookkeepers, office girls, rat-catchers, undertakers, pawnbrokers, shoemakers, press-agents, hired girls,* or *janitors;* they have become, respectively, *plant superintendents* (or, collectively, *supervisory personnel*), *accountants, secretaries* (or *receptionists*), *exterminators, morticians* (or *funeral directors*), *proprietors of loan offices, shoe-rebuilders, public relations counselors, domestics* and *custodians.* In the school system of at least one large American city, the *head truant officer* is dignified by the title of *director of public personnel.* An example of double promotion (or *upgrading!*) by use of euphemisms is found in the case of *salesman.* To add prestige to the calling, businessmen began to speak instead of *sales* (or *customers'*) *representatives,* or even of *sales engineers.* But the word *salesman* was not thereupon retired, for it then was used to designate the former *milkman (route salesman), door-to-door canvasser (brush salesman),* and even *gas station attendant (service salesman).* Earlier in this chapter, when discussing the inefficiency of business jargon, we referred to "time- and motion-study experts." The term is a euphemism developed to fit a need. Some years ago the *efficiency experts* who were introduced into manufacturing plants to increase production by getting more work out of the employees became, among those employees, the object of ridicule if not of actual indignation. The term *efficiency expert* thus acquired an irretrievably bad connota-

---

* The earlier euphemism for *manure* was *fertilizer.* However, the unpleasant connotations of *manure* eventually caught up with it, too, and when certain manufacturers wished to promote their product for use indoors, with potted plants, they had to find a new, deodorized name for it. *Plant food* was the inspired result.

tion. And so the new terms, *time-study* and *motion-study,* were created. Perhaps in time they too will acquire the negative connotation of the older term.

Business euphemisms and circumlocutions are not limited to names for occupations. *Termination of employment* is a common euphemism for the *firing* or *laying-off* of ordinary workmen. On the white-collar level it is perhaps more frequent to *request one's resignation* (or to point out that *opportunities for advancement are limited*). A similar desire to take maximum advantage of the connotations of words is found in merchandising ("selling"). The *budget* (or *economy*) *shops* of department stores are places for the disposal of cheap goods; the installment plan is *deferred payment;* artificial ("fake") material is *simulated;* a floorwalker is an *aisle manager,* a clerk a *sales person;* a place at which to register complaints, an *adjustment* (or *service*) *desk.* Advertisements, of course, are filled with such attempts to escape the negative connotations of certain familiar words.*

EXERCISE 14

1. Why is the word *institute* used so often to designate establishments devoted neither to education nor to research, as in Good Housekeeping Institute and American Iron and Steel Institute?

2. Why is the word *family* frequently used in the advertisements of great corporations, when referring to their employees or to the subsidiary companies of which the corporation is made up? (And why do some large firms, including department stores, refer to their employees as *associates?*)

3. "Read the fine print" (note all the qualifications and escape clauses) is always useful advice, whether you are signing a contract to buy a car on time, taking out an

---

* See the lively pages on euphemisms in Mencken's *The American Language,* 4th edition, pp. 284-294, and *Supplement One* thereto, pp. 565-595.

insurance policy, or just scanning the ads. What is the difference between the statements in each of the following pairs?

(a) We save our customers 6% for cash.
     We endeavor, with reasonable exceptions which include goods price-controlled by the manufacturer, to save our customers at least 6% for cash.
(b) This shirt needs little or no pressing.
     This shirt needs no pressing.
(c) A skilled neurosurgeon can remove the pituitary without great risk.
     A neurosurgeon can remove the pituitary without risk.

4. Make a list of modern euphemistic synonyms for the old-fashioned *saloon.*

5. What is the difference, if any, between: *grease job* and *lubrication service; foundation garment* and *corset; field underwriter* and *insurance salesman;* (church) *offering* and *collection?*

6. (a) Very often, slang has euphemistic intent (*bump off* for *kill, whopper* for *lie*). How many of the following terms are euphemistic slang? How many are euphemisms without being slang?

    nut house, madhouse, booby hatch, insane asylum, private sanitarium, mental hospital, institution for the treatment of nervous diseases, loony bin, lunatic asylum

    (b) How many euphemisms can you find in Exercise 4 (pp. 61-62)?

7. "And now, a brief message from our sponsor." *Why brief message,* rather than *advertisement, plug,* or *commercial?*

8. A press dispatch not long ago quoted a congressman as observing that "the principals in a controversy sometimes say one thing when they mean another." Among the examples he offered were: "Point of order, Mr. Chairman" (= It's my turn to contribute to the disorder here); "The gentleman" (courtesy title only); "My distinguished friend" (= A worse stinker I never met); "Let's keep politics out

of this" (i.e., your politics). In the same way, can you suggest the "real" meaning of the following phrases?

My friend
My learned friend
I shall be happy to enlighten the gentleman
Would you please repeat the question?
I do not question your integrity
I shall have to refresh my recollection

EXERCISE 15

Comment on the language used in these passages, and rewrite them in the plainest English possible:

1. Because of production cutbacks caused by the termination of government contracts, the management is required to announce that the services of some personnel in this department will be dispensed with beginning September 1.

2. In reviewing our accounts for the past few months we find to our regret that we have not received a remittance from you for a statement payable last April 1, although we have sent you several letters reminding you of that fact. Perhaps these letters have failed to reach your personal attention. If this is the case, we trust you will make remittance immediately. In the absence of word from you, on November 1 we will be forced reluctantly to place the matter in the hands of our attorney.

3. To my great personal regret, I find it necessary to inform you that the conduct of your son Wilmer has once again failed to measure up to the standards set up here at Dotheboys Academy for the common good of all. You will recall that earlier in the term he was counselled several times in this regard. All of us here at Dotheboys had hoped that Wilmer would find it possible to adjust himself to group living. Last Saturday night, however, he was involved in an incident which I am afraid cannot be overlooked, including as it did his having partaken of an intoxicating beverage, which as you know is in disobedience of the rules maintained for the guidance of our students. Accordingly, therefore, we have asked Wilmer to withdraw from the academy.

Clichés

Thus far in this chapter we have seen that we, as readers, can reasonably demand that those who write for us express themselves as clearly as the subject matter warrants. Those who fail to do so lay themselves open to charges of windiness, cloudy thinking, egotism, or deliberate deceitfulness. We have also seen that there is a common characteristic among users of jargon: they are nearly all imitators. Unable or unwilling to clothe their thoughts in their own words, and thus to give individual distinction and force to what they have to say, they blindly adopt the phraseology that others use, regardless of its effectiveness or its aptness. The businessman must write and speak like other businessmen; the sociologist or lawyer must express himself in the language in which his colleagues speak and write, and never give a thought to the possible unloveliness or unnecessary complexity of that language.

The stock expressions we have cited in the preceding pages were preliminary samples of the vast treasury of clichés, to which we must now pay more specific attention. When a printer has occasion to use a certain word very often in the course of setting up type, he may save time and effort by making a single type-block bearing the whole word, which he then inserts each time the word is called for, instead of setting up the word from individual letters. When a writer, likewise, wishes to express a familiar idea, he may save himself time and effort by inserting a block-phrase that has been widely used for that purpose. This is a cliché: a ready-cast expression that saves one the trouble of inventing a fresh new way of saying something.

Superficially it might seem that the cliché is an admirable device; for have we not said that it saves time and effort, and therefore promotes efficiency? But good writing is not merely efficient: it is effective. Effective writing must be fresh. It must impress readers with the sincerity of the author. It must convince them that he is in earnest by showing that he is writing for a special occasion and addressing himself to them in particular. The big drawback of form letters is that they fail to meet these requirements of individuality and freshness; and clichés are nothing but form letters in miniature. One who uses clichés is writing mechanically; his phrases smell of mimeograph ink.

Nor is fondness for the cliché a sign simply of indifference. It may be that a writer's affection for threadbare words is a clue to the quality of his thinking. In the first place, fresh new ideas by their very nature require fresh new language—they cannot be expressed in any other way. Ready-made language can be fitted only to ready-made thoughts. Again, since there is a demonstrable relationship between general intelligence and effective use of language, it is likely that a writer who fails to recognize stale terms when he uses them also fails to recognize stale ideas. Therefore, readers who can quickly detect hackneyed phraseology are forearmed against sloppy thinking. If, for instance, a man begins a letter-to-the-editor or a luncheon-club address in this manner: "The talk about the abolition of the smoke nuisance reminds me of what Mark Twain once said about the weather: everybody talks about it but nobody does anything about it"—the audience is entitled to wonder whether this could possibly be the preface to anything worth listening to. Is the writer or speaker not sufficiently intelligent to realize that the story about Mark Twain and the weather was a chestnut fifty years ago? Similarly with the speaker who must somehow drag in Ole Man River, who just keeps rolling along—and with the one who insists upon involving the hapless Topsy in his description of how a city or a business or a club, instead of developing according to a plan, just grew.

The willful or ignorant use of trite language, then, can expose a writer to suspicion of being intellectually as well as verbally imitative. One does not have to be a perpetual coiner of flamboyantly "original" phrases that might be welcomed in the "Picturesque Speech" department of the *Reader's Digest;* indeed, one can err almost as far in that direction as in the other. But readers have a right to expect that his style will unobtrusively provide traction for their minds rather than allow them to slide and skid on a slippery surface paved with well-worn phrases.

It would be pedantic, not to say useless, to insist that good writers never, never use clichés; let him who has never sinned cast the first stone. But good writers, if they use clichés at all, use them with the utmost caution. In informal discourse, furthermore, clichés are almost indispensable. When we are relaxing with our friends, we do not want to be bothered to find new or at least unhackneyed ways of saying things; we rely upon our ready supply of clichés, and if we do not overdraw our account, no one thinks the worse of us. So long as we succeed in communicating the small, commonplace ideas we have in mind, no harm is done.

When does an expression become cliché? There can be no definite answer, because what is trite to one person may still be fresh to another. But a great many expressions are universally understood to be so threadbare as to be useless except in the most casual discourse. They have been loved not wisely but too well. A good practical test is this: If, when you are listening to a speaker, you can accurately anticipate what he is going to say next, he is pretty certainly using clichés; otherwise he would be constantly surprising you. "Such a precautionary measure would stand us—" ("in good stead," you think—correctly, as it turns out) "—in our time—" ("of need," you think, and you win). "We are gathered here today to mourn" ("the untimely death") "of our beloved leader. Words are inadequate" ("to express the grief that is in our hearts"). Similarly when you read; if one word almost inevitably invites another, if you can read half of the words and know pretty certainly what the other half are, you are reading clichés. "We watched the flames" ("licking") "at the side of the building. A pall" ("of smoke") "hung thick over the neighborhood. Suddenly we heard a dull" ("thud") "which was followed by an ominous" ("silence").

The degree to which a reader is aware of clichés depends

directly upon the scope and sensitivity of his previous reading. If he has read widely, in both good books and bad, and has carefully observed authors' styles, he has probably become quite alert for trite language. Clichés to him are old but exceedingly tiresome friends. But if a reader's experience of books and magazines has been limited, obviously he will not recognize so many overripe expressions; in his eyes most clichés still have the dew on them.

Many (but by no means all) familiar clichés are figures of speech. Now a figure of speech is useful only so long as it makes an idea more vivid, enabling the reader to visualize an abstract concept in concrete terms. If the reader has become so accustomed to it that it no longer stimulates his imagination, it has no more value than a nonfigurative expression. And that is what has happened to many such images, clever and appropriate at first but now almost lifeless. Many are similes (a comparison directly stated): *common as dirt, warm as toast, old as the hills, sell like hot cakes, sleep like a log.* . . . Many more are metaphors (a comparison implied): *a bolt from the blue, politics makes strange bedfellows, blackout of news* (or *the iron curtain of censorship*), *left high and dry, variety is the spice of life, point the finger of suspicion* . . .

The variety of clichés that have sprung from a single source —the desire to suggest a resemblance between some aspect of man's behavior and that of animals—is illustrated by this paragraph from a witty leaflet issued every month by the Columbia University Press. Occasionally we will omit a word to show how automatically the mind supplies the missing element in a cliché:

"Man," says *The Columbia Encyclopedia*, "is distinguished from other animals by his brain and his hands." But there the difference would seem to end because he is chicken-livered, lion-hearted, pigeon-toed. He is treacherous as a snake, sly as a fox, busy as a   , slippery as an   , industrious as an ant, blind as a bat, faithful as a dog, gentle as a lamb. He has clammy hands, the ferocity of the tiger, the manners of a pig, the purpose of a jellyfish. He gets drunk as an owl. He roars like a   ; he coos like a dove.

He is still as a mouse; he hops around like a sparrow. He works like a horse. He is led like a sheep. He can fly like a bird, run like a deer, drink like a   , swim like a duck. He is nervous as a cat. He sticks his head in the sand like an   . He acts like a dog in a manger. He is coltish and kittenish, and stubborn as a   . He plays possum. He gets hungry as a bear, and wolfs his food. He has the memory of an elephant. He is easily cowed. He gets thirsty as a camel. He is as strong as an   . He has a catlike walk, and a mousy manner. He parrots everything he hears. He acts like a puppy, and is as playful as a kitten. He struts like a rooster, and is as vain as a peacock. He is as happy as a   and as sad as an owl. He has a whale of an appetite. He has a beak for a nose, and arms like an ape. He has the eyes of a   and the neck of a bull. He is as slow as a tortoise. He chatters like a magpie. He has raven hair and the shoulders of a buffalo. He's as dumb as an ox, and has the back of an ox—he is even as big as an ox. He's a worm. His   is cooked. He's crazy like a bedbug (or fox or coot). He's a rat. He's a louse. Of course, he is also cool as a cucumber, fresh as a   , red as a beet, etc.—but *The Columbia Encyclopedia* doesn't suggest that he differs in any way from vegetables and other flora, so we won't go into that.

One large category of clichés is composed of those which insist upon associating a particular descriptive adjective with a given noun. Such stereotyped word associations include *clock-work precision, checkered* (or *meteoric*) *career, whirlwind courtship, tight-lipped* (or *stony*) *silence, level best, crushing defeat, intrepid explorer, bumper-to-bumper traffic, skyrocketing costs.* Is there any reason why a formidable task should habitually be described as *Herculean?* None at all, except that people have adopted such phrases as a way of evading their obligation to make their own language.

Other common types of clichés are verb and noun phrases. Outworn verb phrases include *to live to a ripe old age, to grow by leaps and bounds, to withstand the test of time, to let bygones be bygones, to be unable to see the woods for the trees, to eat crow, to upset the applecart.* Noun phrases that have outlasted their freshness include *ace up his sleeve, the full flush of vic-*

tory, the patter of rain, the fly in the ointment, a diamond in
the rough, part and parcel, the old song and dance.

Nowhere is the cliché more to be avoided than in descriptive
and narrative writing, the whole success of which depends upon
the freshness and exactness with which the writer communicates
his impressions to the reader. A virtually certain mark of the
inexperienced writer is his willingness to see his settings and
characters through the eyes of someone else—to wit, the man
who has used his clichés before him. "He walked with catlike
tread" . . . "they were drenched by mountainous waves" . . .
"the child was bubbling over with mirth" . . . "there was a
blinding flash" . . . "he made a convulsive grab for the rope"
. . . "they heard a rustle of leaves" . . . "the flowers nodded in
the gentle breeze" . . . "the shadows were lengthening" . . . "he
looked at her with a glassy stare." The only delight we can find
in such writing is that of seeing old familiar faces. Surely we are
allowed to participate in no new experience; we cannot see
things from any new angle, or receive a fresh interpretation of
their meaning. A "creative" writer who depends upon clichés
is really not creating anything. His stock-in-trade is not genuine experience, and without genuine experience no writer can
succeed. All he has to offer is words—*mere* words, empty shells
incapable of meaning.

Many of our clichés are derived from books that have had
the greatest influence upon the common speech. *To kill the*
fatted calf, his name is legion, covers a multitude of sins, the
spirit is willing but the flesh is weak, the blind leading the
blind, the parting of the way—all have their beginning in the
Bible, even though in most cases their original Biblical connotations have been forgotten. Many sermons are tissues of such
clichés, and their dullness is due to the fact that these phrases,
originally so full of flavor and meaning, have lost their charm
through unremitting use. Few people react to them as deeply as
did those to whom the English Bible was a new and wonderful
book, the phrases shining like coins from the mint. And that is
true, unfortunately, of many of the finest things that have ever
been said in the world. The opening sentences of the Declara-

tion of Independence, Lincoln's Gettysburg Address, certain portions of Gray's "Elegy"—some of the most moving poems and political documents have become hackneyed through constant use.

The alert reader can watch clichés in the very process of being made. For example, in the mid-1950's the "slim margin" which one party possessed over the other in the Senate or the House of Representatives became a *paper-thin* (or *razor-thin*) *majority* —a phrase which, when first used, was reasonably fresh and vivid, but which soon grew intolerably tiresome through repetition. Similarly, words associated with atomic developments have quickly become standard clichés in all sorts of usages. The verb *to mushroom*, admittedly, was a fairly common cliché even before 1945, when it meant "to grow as fast as mushrooms" ("the suburbs of the city mushroomed"). But once the typical ("awe-inspiring") cloud produced by an atomic explosion was designated as mushroom-shaped, the cliché took a new lease on life. Nowadays *mushrooming* is applied to everything from a dam under construction to a sudden burst of public sentiment on some issue. *Chain reaction,* originally a technical term in nuclear physics, now is a handy way of describing a series of events that are (or are supposed to be) causally connected, in the manner of a bowling ball knocking down Pin A, Pin A in turn knocking down Pin B, and so on. And the verb *to trigger,* first applied to the action of an atomic bomb in setting off the far greater explosion of the hydrogen bomb, has already become a tiresome cliché to describe any analogous action, no matter how remote the resemblance may be: "The protest of the home owners' delegation triggered a full-dress investigation by City Council."

EXERCISE 16

Fill in the blanks:

1. First and   , in my search I will leave no stone   .
   It will be a labor of   .

He passed the exam with _____ colors; it was a red-letter
_____ in his life. He could point with _____ to his achievement.
The news spread like _____ .
By prompt action she was _____ from the jaws of _____ ;
otherwise she would have gone to a watery _____ .
After the quarrel she left him, bag and _____ . She said she
wouldn't come back to him for _____ or money. At the party
the next day, she was conspicuous by her _____ .
I was so burned up that I threw caution to the _____ . I should
have known that it doesn't pay to _____ with one's chin.
He did a landoffice _____ the first month he was open, but the
wear and _____ on his health was too great. So he took a
vacation in Florida, saying that the change would either
_____ or cure him. Underneath, though, one could detect
that he was whistling in the _____ .
Last but not _____ , to make a long story _____ , he is caught
between the _____ and the deep blue sea. Such is _____ .

2. As sure as _____ and taxes.
Packed in tight as _____ .
Sharp as a _____ .
Quick as _____ .
Hard as _____ .
Silent as _____ .
Sticks out like a _____ .
Dull as _____ .

EXERCISE 17

1. This is an excerpt from a review of a certain biography. In
what way does the writer unintentionally suggest that people who live in _____ should not throw _____ ?

There is, in a word, more icing than cake. Nor is the icing of the
best quality. Considering the high literary gloss our author tries
for, he is remarkably prone to cliché. Reaction is blind, hope
gnaws, emotions are pent up until they pour forth, increase is by
leaps and bounds, relief sweeps over people in waves, ordeals are
protracted, mobs are roused to frenzy, happiness is idyllic,
candles gutter pale in the light of the dawn, stony hearts are
melted, and patience reaps its reward.

2. The cliché has been discussed above primarily from the
viewpoint of trite language. But since tired language and
tired thoughts generally are inseparable, the term *cliché*
also refers to the statement of an obvious idea. In this sense,
it is roughly synonymous with *commonplace, truism, platitude,* and *bromide.* (For ways in which their connotations
differ, see *Webster's Dictionary of Synonyms,* under *commonplace.*) A great many familiar "sayings"—aphorisms,
proverbs, adages, and so on—are clichés. Whether or not they
have considerable truth in them, they have been so over-
worked as to have lost much of their force: "Still waters run
deep," "It's not what you know that counts, it's the people
you know," "Spare the rod and spoil the child," "Christmas
has become too commercialized," "The artist is lost in
modern society," "There's nothing new under the sun."
How long a list can you make of similar platitudes?

3. Bartlett's *Familiar Quotations* is a rich treasury of oft-re-
peated expressions, a great many of which have become
cliché. With its aid, make a list of familiar phrases which
entered the common speech by way of *Hamlet.*

4. One often reads complaints about "cliché situations" or
"cliché characters" in plays, movies, novels, and television
shows. What do these terms mean? Give examples of plots or
situations that seem to you to be cliché, and describe a few
cliché characters (for example, the "Good Guys" and the
"Bad Guys" in western movies).

EXERCISE 18

Some clichés are enduring; they pass from generation to generation without seeming quite to wear out. Others, the products
of contemporary events and fashions, are short-lived. "Back to
normalcy!" was the great political cliché of the early 1920's,
just as "Two cars in every garage, a chicken in every pot" was
the cliché of the Hoover era. "Prosperity is just around the
corner" was heard from every mouth in the early 1930's; and
then came phrases from Mr. Roosevelt himself—"We have

nothing to fear but fear itself" and the rest. In another realm of American life, clichés spring from popular songs, the comic strips, movies, and television. They have their brief life and then disappear as suddenly as they appeared. Slang clichés and catch-phrases are the froth on the sea of language.

1. What are the new-model clichés most frequently heard at the moment you are reading this book? Where did they originate? What chance have they of becoming established?
2. For those who are interested in recent social history, it would be fun to browse in the several volumes of Mark Sullivan's *Our Times* and in Frederick Lewis Allen's *Only Yesterday* and *Since Yesterday* to discover what were the favorite catch-phrases and clichés in the years between 1900 and 1939.
3. The humorist S. J. Perelman makes great use of current clichés, especially those with a quasi-literary flavor. See his books, *Crazy Like a Fox* and *Swiss Family Perelman*.

"Newspaperese"

The jargon peculiar to newspapers is a combination of the cliché, dead wood, and the weak passive or impersonal construction. The great objection to it, as to all jargon, is that it is machine-made. It is written according to formula, and material written to formula inevitably loses much of its color and interest. Here is a short sampling of newspaper clichés together with their simpler equivalents:

The death toll rose to ten today in the wake of the disastrous fire . . . (*or:* Death today claimed four more victims . . .)	Four more people died as a result of the fire . . .
The mercury soared to a record high for the year . . .	Today was the hottest day of the year
At an early hour this morning the identity of the victim had not yet been established . . .	Early this morning the body was still unidentified . . .
Traffic was snarled (*or* paralyzed, *or* at a standstill, *or* moved at a snail's pace) as snow blanketed the metropolitan area . . .	The snowfall slowed traffic. . . .

State Police, aided by local law enforcement officers, today were combing the area adjacent to Center City in search of clues that might lead to the solution of the mystery of the murder-kidnaping . . .	State and local police were looking for clues to the man who kidnaped and murdered . . .
Three persons suffered injuries when the automobile in which they were riding figured in a collision with a large truck . . .	Three person were hurt when their car hit a big truck. . . .
Preparations for the convention neared completion . . .	Everything was just about ready . . .
As he completed his investigation, the coroner said it was his opinion that death was instantaneous . . .	The coroner said he thought the man had been killed instantly

In addition, there are numerous single words, especially epithets and verbs, which are seemingly indispensable to newspaper reporting. Any better-than-ordinary fire or auto accident is *spectacular;* an accident that is more peculiar than disastrous is *freak;* when public men approve of something they *hail* it, when they disapprove of it they *attack* it, and when they want something they *urge* it; when two factions have a disagreement they *clash;* when anything is announced it is *made public;* and when men accuse others of wrongdoing they *allege* (*assert,* another newspaper warhorse, has a slightly less negative connotation).

The weak passive is used in newspaper writing for the same reason for which it is used in governmental correspondence: to achieve the impersonal note, and thus, in many instances, to disclaim direct responsibility for statements that are based on hearsay. When newspapers send a reporter for an eye-witness story of a disaster or a court trial, or when they quote a press release or statements made during an interview, they can assert positively that this and that are true. But much news cannot be treated in so open and confident a fashion—news based on private information picked up by reporters or on rumors circulating in the city hall or the stock exchange. Although the papers wish to relay this news, they cannot do so on their own authority; the man who gave the reporter his information refuses to be quoted, and the public will be suspicious of anything plainly labeled "rumor." The solution, then, is to use weak passive or impersonal constructions which do not require an agent: "It was revealed (*or* learned *or* reported)" (*not:* the City Commissioner told our reporter but warned him not to use his name); "indications increased" or "a survey today showed" (*not:* our reporter asked several people, and their replies, when put together, suggested). Another device of passing on news without revealing its source (or, it may be, without revealing that it has no source outside the mind of an inventive reporter) is the use of those mysterious oracles, the *officials who asked that their names be withheld, spokesmen, informed quarters, observers,* and *sources usually considered reliable.* Judged from the viewpoint of clear, accurate communication, "newspaperese" has as little to recommend it as does any other kind of roundabout, machine-made language.

One particular brand of newspaper jargon, the language of the sports page, deserves special study. Sports writers, perhaps because they deal with lively, entertaining matters that seldom have dead-serious implications, have greater freedom, and indeed a greater necessity, than do other reporters to invent new ways of saying things. Sports pages are filled with metaphorical language. When first used, such terms add a welcome novelty to the narration of what are, after all, fairly routine events. (One baseball game differs from another only in details, not in general pattern: usually a game has nine innings, each inning is divided into halves, a side is always retired after the third out.) But, like all clichés, sports-page terms soon lose their vividness through overuse. Reporters keep on employing them just the same: *four-bagger* or *circuit clout* for *home run, coveted pasteboards* for *hard-to-get tickets, grid classic* for *big game, thinclads* for *track team, signal-caller* for *quarterback, tankmen* for *swimmers, century* for *100-yard dash, swivel-hipped pigskin toter* for *agile ball-carrier,* and so on.

EXERCISE 19

Here is a news item, written in standard newspaperese. Translate it into simple, direct, unhackneyed English.

Baffled police today were conducting an intensive search for a sailor in connection with the brutal slaying of pretty, dark-haired Rose M———, a night club entertainer, whose battered body was found crumpled in a vacant lot in a remote section of Brooklyn early this morning. The sailor, in whose company the murdered girl was seen at 7 p.m. yesterday, is wanted for questioning in connection with her whereabouts last night. "We know his name," Police Captain S——— declared to newspapermen this afternoon, "and we have reason to believe he had left the girl before she met her death. However, we wish to trace the movements of the pair."

Meanwhile, investigators from the detective bureau were questioning scores of persons acquainted with the slain girl, most of them residents of the neighborhood in which she and her sister, who is employed as a waitress, maintained a small two-room flat. It was reported that they have located a woman who saw Miss M——— engaged in conversation with a tall man on a streetcorner near her home at midnight. However, it was said that the witness was able to furnish police with only a vague description of the man.

Miss M———'s body was discovered at 4 a.m. by Arthur P———, a milk deliveryman who was making his rounds. Crossing the vacant lot as a short-cut between two houses, he noticed a bloody handkerchief caught on some tall weeds, and upon investigation found the fully clothed body of the victim lying face downward. He ran to the nearest house and summoned police who responded in two squad cars. After a preliminary survey, the first police on the scene enlisted the aid of the detective bureau.

Police Surgeon A——— announced after an examination of the body that death had been caused by a crushed skull. Marks on the victim's head indicated that she had been struck several hard blows with a blunt instrument.

Police were at a loss to advance a motive for the crime. The girl had not been criminally assaulted, and her purse was found a few feet away from the body, its contents intact.

EXERCISE 20

1. Comb current newspapers for examples of the coloring of news by newspaperese. Try to find instances of the use of such words as *plot, hit* ("disapprove of"), *fear, flay, decry, assail, menace, smash, deadlock, expose, grave* (adj.), *edict, grill, demand, block, warn, grab, storm* (of disapproval), etc. Substitute words with less dramatic connotation and determine how far such substitution affects the reader's reaction to the news.

2. Frank Sullivan, a veteran connoisseur of clichés, has written two dialogues specifically on newspaper and sports-page language. Look up his "The Cliché Expert Testifies on the Tabloids," *The New Yorker,* October 2, 1948, and "Football Is King," reprinted in several anthologies.

EXERCISE 21

1. Make a collection of sports-writers' jargon from the pages of your local newspaper—and don't neglect your campus paper.

2. Translate the following into sports-page terminology:

made a successful shot (in basketball)
to strike out
touchdown
prevented the other team from scoring by holding firm on the two-yard line
a close finish (in horse racing)
the coach
withdrawn from the game
last place in the league
an outstanding player

EXERCISE 22

This is a review exercise. Discuss the bearing each of the following quotations has upon matters discussed in the present chapter, and then examine it for all the clues it offers to the personality and intention of the author, the time when it was written, and the probable audience to which it was addressed.

1. There is a busybody on your [newspaper] staff who devotes a lot of his time to chasing split infinitives. Every good literary craftsman splits his infinitives when the sense demands it. I call for the immediate dismissal of this pedant. It is of no consequence whether he decides to go quickly or quickly to go or to quickly go. The important thing is that he should go at once.

2. Do but take care to express yourself in a plain, easy manner, in well chosen, significant, and decent terms, and to give an harmonious and pleasing turn to your periods; study to explain your thoughts, and set them in the truest light, labouring, as much as possible, not to leave them dark nor intricate, but clear and intelligible.

3. How can an answer in physics or a translation from the French or an historical statement be called correct if the phrasing is loose or the key word wrong? Students argue that the reader of the paper knows perfectly well what is meant. Probably so, but a written exercise is designed to be read; it is not supposed to be a challenge to clairvoyance. My Italian-born tailor periodically sends me a postcard which runs: "Your clothes is ready and should come down for a fitting." I understand him, but the art I honor him for is cutting cloth, not precision of utterance.

4. As soon as certain topics are raised, the concrete melts into the abstract and no one seems able to think of turns of speech that are not hackneyed: prose consists less and less of *words* chosen for the sake of their meaning, and more and more of *phrases* tacked together like the sections of a prefabricated hen-house

5. *Too* startling words, . . . *too* just images, *too* great displays of cleverness are apt in the long run to be as fatiguing as the most over-used words or the most jog-trot cadences. That a face resembles a Dutch clock has been said too often; to say that it resembles a ham is inexact and conveys nothing; to say that it has the mournfulness of an old smashed-in meat tin, cast away on a waste building lot, would be smart—but too much of that sort of thing would become a nuisance.

6. Every man speaks and writes with intent to be understood; and it can seldom happen but he that understands himself might convey his notions to another, if, content to be understood, he did not seek to be admired; but when once he begins to contrive how his sentiments may be received, not with most ease to his

reader, but with most advantage to himself, he then transfers his consideration from words to sounds, from sentences to periods, and as he grows more elegant becomes less intelligible.

It is difficult to enumerate every species of authors whose labors counteract themselves: the man of exuberance and copiousness, who diffuses every thought through so many diversities of expression, that it is lost like water in a mist; the ponderous dictator of sentences, whose notions are delivered in the lump, and are, like uncoined bullion, of more weight than use; the liberal illustrator, who shows by examples and comparisons what was clearly seen when it was first proposed; and the stately son of demonstration, who proves with mathematical formality what no man has yet pretended to doubt.

There is a mode of style for which I know not that the masters of oratory have yet found a name; a style by which the most evident truths are so obscured that they can no longer be perceived, and the most familiar propositions so disguised that they cannot be known. Every other kind of eloquence is the dress of sense; but this is the mask by which a true master of his art will so effectually conceal it, that a man will as easily mistake his own positions, if he meets them thus transformed, as he may pass in a masquerade his nearest acquaintance. This style may be called the *terrific,* for its chief intention is to terrify and amaze; it may be termed the *repulsive,* for its natural effect is to drive away the reader; or it may be distinguished, in plain English, by the denomination of the *bugbear* style, for it has more terror than danger, and will appear less formidable as it is more nearly approached.

CHAPTER THREE

Patterns of
Clear Thinking

E VEN WHEN LANGUAGE is not colored by connotative words or
by other specially selected devices, people may be misled
into believing what is not true—by failing to detect the faulty
reasoning that lies behind a statement. Our minds, the minds of
even the best of us, are filled with half-truths, superstitions,
falsehoods, and prejudices because we have not taken the time
to search for the errors in logic by which one idea (which may
or may not be true in itself) is falsely assumed to lead to another. In the first part of this chapter, we shall look at some of
the more common types of unsound thinking and some devices
of critical thinking which enable us to discover the hidden
weak link in a simple chain of reasoning. Then we shall devote
some space to the ways in which writers and speakers evade
logic altogether. Finally, we shall briefly consider two other frequent sources of error—the confusion of objectivity and subjectivity, and the failure to evaluate the source of our information.

As we said in the foreword, this book would be of little use
if it led you merely to substitute an attitude of habitual dis-
belief for one of uncritical belief. It is probably just as easy to
believe nothing as it is to believe everything. It is harder, but
in the long run infinitely more satisfying, to separate the true

from the false—to detect opinions masquerading as facts, as well as half-truths and distortions of the truth. The practiced reader, while he always remains alert for these evidences of careless or deliberately abused logic, discovers that plenty of truth remains in the world; there is no dearth of things for him to believe, or to believe in. But he finds an astringent pleasure in his cultivated awareness of deception; the quick detection of error and the equally quick recognition of truth become not only an inexhaustibly rewarding game but also an abiding evidence that he is not so easily deceived as his neighbor. In short, the practice which the ensuing pages will afford you in the art of distinguishing a valid inference from an invalid one, an authoritative statement from a groundless one, can justifiably bolster your confidence in yourself. It can make you consciously more mature, more adult, in your mental processes.

To begin with, there are two kinds of formal reasoning: the inductive and the deductive. When we reason *in*ductively, we begin with particular facts and proceed to larger, general statements. When we reason *de*ductively, we begin with general statements and proceed to particular facts which "logically" follow. To put it in another way, in inductive reasoning we move from the part to the whole, while in deductive reasoning we move from the whole to the part. As we shall see, these two types of thinking are intimately connected.

Inductive Reasoning

Inductive reasoning takes two major forms, each of which we shall look at in turn. One has to do with the gathering of data in an attempt to draw a general conclusion from many bits of related evidence; the other concerns the setting up and testing of hypotheses. Both forms of induction often occur in the course of a single inquiry, especially in the sciences.

1. *The gathering of evidence.* Is the intelligence level of whites higher than that of Negroes? Do business depressions occur every twenty-one years? Do all bluebirds have red breasts? Is there a correlation between the sex of a baby and the month

in which it is born? Are there more automobile accidents at night than in daytime, in proportion to the number of cars on the road? Do guinea pigs multiply faster than any other animals suitable for laboratory purposes? Do college graduates spend more time reading than those who only finished high school? The primary way to settle such questions is to collect and analyze all the available evidence which bears on the point at issue. Sometimes the result may not be clear-cut; a study of birth statistics may not permit the investigator to say that, for example, a baby born in April is twice as likely to be a boy as it is to be a girl. But in other cases the available evidence may overwhelmingly prove that one assumption is correct, while its converse is wrong.

We are forever performing such inductions in our daily lives. Unconsciously, in most cases, our minds formulate questions, and our experience gradually answers them. After a few instructive incidents we learn that an electric light bulb which has been burning for an hour is hot, and that it would be wise for us to wait a little before trying to replace it with another. In a similar way we learn that, unless the power has been off, the contents of a frozen-food locker may be depended upon to be both cold and hard, and that a badly written essay for an English class is not likely to win a good grade. Furthermore, the results of such inductions on the part of other people are constantly being brought to our attention in print or by the spoken word. We are, naturally, expected to believe those generalizations. But should we?

Two dangers are ever-present in generalizations. One is that of unconscious or deliberate exaggeration; the other is that of insufficient or weighted evidence.

When we generalize from our own experience we often go further than we are entitled to. Instead of reminding ourselves of what is actually the truth according to our own observation ("quite often, heavy black clouds in the west mean a thunderstorm is coming"), we prefer a sweeping generalization. "Those black clouds in the west mean we're in for a bad storm," we say, implying that black clouds in the west *invariably* foretell a bad storm. We save ourselves mental exertion when we take the short cut of assuming that a certain generalization always is true, whereas the fact is that it is only usually so. When we make statements of general fact to ourselves or to our friends, we tend to plane off the qualifying words *usually, nearly all, few, seldom* . . . so as to have a shining surface which says (or implies) *always, all, only, never* . . .

If we keep aware of this human shortcoming in ourselves, we shall constantly discover that the sweeping "truths" which others express every day in print or in speech actually are not as all-embracing as they seem. There are comparatively few generalizations which always hold true. Most of those which are incontestably true (so far as all the evidence suggests) are found in the realm of physical science. Men are mammals, trees have roots, steel buildings conduct static electricity, magnesium burns with an intense white flame, human beings have a glandular system, light travels at a speed of 186,300 miles a second, and carbon monoxide gas, if inhaled in a specified quantity, is fatal. In all recorded history, with its billions of individual men, each offering the possibility of an exception, there has been no instance of a human not conforming to the definition of mammal which scientists have set up. Similarly, of all the millions and billions of trees men have actually observed, not one has been discovered that lacked roots. Although theoretically there is always the possibility of an exception, the odds against it are so astronomically large that we are justified in saying that *all* men are mammals and that *every* tree must have roots. There have been fewer steel buildings to observe and draw conclusions from, but the number is still great enough for us to be able to make a sound generalization as to their electrical conductivity.

Hence the confidence with which one may assert that (in the absence of a single known exception) a given statement is *always* true depends on the number of instances observed. For example, any statement which a marine biologist makes about the habits of a certain deep-sea fish must be tentative. While all examples of this fish that have been studied have behaved in the same way, the scientist has not been able to study enough examples to be fairly certain that there are no exceptions.

The first test to apply to a generalization, therefore, is this: If the speaker or writer uses such a sweeping word as *all* or *always* or *never,* is he justified in doing so? Are there really no exceptions to his statement? And if he does not explicitly use *all, always, never* . . . are those words implied? If they are, we must return to the same question: Is he justified in implying that there are, and can be, no exceptions?

But even if the generalization is hedged with what seem to be sufficiently cautious qualifications, its truth is still to be demonstrated. Often a reader is thrown off guard by a writer's willingness to concede the possibility of exceptions, which suggests that he is a careful, sober, scientific-minded person, unwilling to sacrifice truth for the sake of his argument. Granting that such caution may be a good sign, we are still entitled to ask whether his generalization holds true even in as many cases as he claims. Suppose he says "usually": might he really mean only "some of the time"? Suppose he says "very few": might he really mean only "less than half"? The reader has a perfect right to demand more specific language—proportions, percentages rather than elastic terms that may mean one thing to the writer and another to the reader.

Having considered the possibility of exaggeration for rhetorical effect, the critical reader's next job is to find out just what evidence lies behind a general statement. To be sound, a generalization must be based upon a sufficiently large number of pertinent instances, and those instances must provide as accurate a cross section as it is possible to obtain.

Take the question of whether or not fraternity members are better students than men who do not belong to fraternities. A college professor may say that "fraternity members definitely are better students than nonmembers." What he means is that in his necessarily limited experience, and to his perhaps biased mind, fraternity members have proved better "teaching material" (however he may define the term) than nonmembers. Such a judgment must be regarded as an expression solely of personal opinion, being subjective and based on far too few instances. But now let us say that the dean of the institution, which is an engineering college, issues a statistical report which shows that for the year just ended, the fraternity members' average* (on a 4.0 basis) was 2.756, while the nonmembers' average was 2.447. The student body of the college includes 967 fraternity members and 1,082 nonmembers. Such a report is of more value than the professor's, but its value is still limited, because, while it is based on objective statistics, the cases are few in comparison with the total number of men in colleges throughout the country. The dean says only, in effect, that *in his college,* the fraternity members during the past year proved to be somewhat better students than the rest. But this may not be true elsewhere; the experience of a single college cannot be blown up into a generalization covering all the colleges of the country.

Suppose, however, that some ambitious research worker assembled reports from fifty institutions of every description, from small liberal arts colleges to great universities, and geographically scattered from Maine to California. His only aim in selecting those fifty institutions has been to get as wide a sampling as possible of all American colleges which have male students and fraternities. He emerges with a report showing that in these fifty institutions, with a total of 56,980 fraternity members and 47,805 nonmembers, the fraternity men's average in grades for the year was some 15 per cent higher than that of the nonmembers. Now, at last, even though we may question whether those who get higher grades are necessarily better students, we have some justification for the professor's general statement. It is based on a sufficient number of examples, which are widely representative of the country's institutions of higher learning. If the research worker were to analyze the records of

* I.e., arithmetical mean. See below, page 119.

fifty more institutions, the likelihood would be that his new results would closely approximate the first ones.

This principle of statistical caution is further illustrated by the operation of the most responsible of public-opinion polls and surveys to determine consumers' buying habits and brand preferences or the popularity of television programs. Public-opinion surveys in particular go to elaborate lengths to interview a number of persons sufficient, they feel, to permit generalization, and to distribute their interviews among various sections of the country and among various income-groups, occupations, and educational levels, so that they will have a reasonably true cross section of "the American public." A generalization on the state of national feeling on whether the United States should renounce a portion of its national sovereignty in favor of an international federation would be worthless if it were based solely on interviews with, let us say, fifty students at New York University. Obviously the cases are insufficient, and they do not represent a true cross section of the whole country. But a generalization based on interviews with, in addition, fifty Iowa farmers, fifty Atlanta housewives, fifty day laborers in Kansas City, fifty Los Angeles bus drivers, and fifty Chicago bankers, would have more significance. There would be more cases, and those cases would include men and women drawn from various sections of the country and various walks of life. It would be even better to sample various occupations and income groups in each locality, interviewing students, farmers, housewives, laborers, bus drivers, and bankers in Iowa, the same number, similarly distributed, in the vicinity of Atlanta, and so on.

General statements containing or implying such phrases as *tends to, majority, most, as a group* . . . should, therefore, be examined no less critically than those which contain or imply the categorical *all, every, only, never, always.* . . . To assert that something is true in a majority of instances requires as much carefully gathered and evaluated evidence as to say that it is (as far as can be determined) always true.

Another familiar class of generalizations that are booby-traps for the unwary involves terms like *average, normal,* and *typical.* Just what is meant by "the typical homeowner," "the normal American female," "the average rural family"—or by phrases that attempt to generalize about a large group by referring to an imaginary individual like "the French voter" or "the British workingman"? What is meant by "the typical housewife" who is more attracted by one kind of package than by another when she pauses at a certain supermarket shelf? Of *what* is she "typical"? How many housewives do *not* conform to the specified pattern of behavior? Or take "the French voter": we can be sure that he is French and that he votes, but beyond that, any statement concerning his attitudes, motivations, and habits as a voter must be heavily qualified. Some Frenchmen vote for such-and-such a party for such-and-such reasons, but other Frenchmen vote for other parties for other reasons. The pitfall here is the assumption that the large group "represented" by an individual is homogeneous—everybody thinking and acting alike in certain respects—whereas the truth is that it is composed of hundreds or thousands or millions of individuals who can seldom be lumped together in a sweeping generalization.

Like *typical,* the word *average,* so constantly used in asserting the "truth" of a matter, requires precise definition before the statement can be evaluated. It can refer to any of four things: (1) the *arithmetical mean,* which is produced by adding up all the figures in a group and dividing by the number of figures there are; (2) the simple *mean,* which is the halfway point between the extremes; (3) the *median,* which is the middle number in a series; and (4) the *mode,* which is the figure most common in the series. Suppose that in a group of twenty-one candidates, the grades on a civil service examination are 95, 92, 90, 88, 84, 84, 84, 84, 83, 80, 76, 76, 75, 70, 69, 60, 58, 53, 50, 42, and 40. The arithmetical mean is 73, the simple mean is 67.5, the median is 76, and the mode is 84. The "average" of the group therefore may be 73, 67.5, 76, or 84, depending on how you figure—or what you want to prove.

Since statistics are so widely used nowadays to support or clinch an argument, it always pays to be alert not only for insufficient or weighted samplings and elastic terminology but also for hidden qualifications. On each holiday week-end, the National Safety Council gives wide publicity to the "mounting highway death toll." These casualty figures—300, 400, or even more—are misleading, because they silently include deaths that might have occurred, holiday or no holiday. If, say, an average (i.e., arithmetical mean) of 150 people in the United States are killed in automobile accidents on an ordinary week-end, then the much-publicized "Labor Day slaughter" of 450, bad though it may be, is exaggerated. A third of that number may have been marked for death anyway.

Two other common sources of error in the interpretation of statistics are the lack of uniformity between two or more sets offered for comparison and the confusion of absolute figures with rates. Thirty years ago, for instance, each police department had its own pet way of defining and classifying crimes, and some departments contributed their data to a central agency while others did not. Consequently, figures purporting to give the totals and breakdowns for American criminal activity in the 1920's were both inconsistent and incomplete. Later, however, the F.B.I. set up a uniform code for classifying crimes, and most, if not all, state and local law-enforcement agencies now report their data, arranged according to this system, to Washington. Hence a comparison of figures for the past year with those for, say, 1928 can provide only a rough idea of the degree to which crime has increased or decreased in that period. And even if the two sets of statistics were based on the same system and derived from an equal number of sources, one would have to distinguish carefully between absolute figures and rates. Simple totals, especially when used to show trends over a certain period, can be very misleading, because the American population has increased so fast in recent years. An alarmist may "prove" that our national morality is degenerating by pointing to the swelling number of violent crimes, year by year; but in

view of the great growth of population, this is only to be expected—unless the country were suddenly afflicted with con-
tagious virtue. But if it were shown that the number of crimes
per 100,000 population had steeply risen, the argument would
be better supported. Often, therefore, absolute figures can be,
and are, used to distort the actual state of affairs. Statistics showing ratios are, on the whole, safer indications of both trends and
immediate situations. But even they can be manipulated to suit
the purposes of their users, and the reader must examine the
deck carefully for possible jokers.

2. *The testing of hypotheses.* Often it is impossible to collect
a mass of evidence from which a generalization can be made.
Then the investigator attacks his problem in another way. He
sets up a hypothesis: that is, he makes an assumption of whose
truth or falsity he is frankly in doubt. "Supposing, for the sake
of argument," he says, "that such-and-such is true, what would
be the logical consequences of its being true?" Having made a
list of them, he proceeds to see if those consequences do exist.
If they do—*and if there can be no other explanation for them*—
he decides that his hypothesis is correct. This method is used
everywhere in the experimental sciences.

A chemist in a paper mill is asked to find out why a recent
batch of the mill's product has not stood up to routine tests.
Analyzing a sample of the rejected material, he discovers that
it possesses several irregular characteristics, which we shall call
A, B, and C. His training and experience tell him that these
irregularities can be produced by a slip-up somewhere in the
manufacturing process; but he knows also that those same irregularities can be caused by one or more defective ingredients.
In addition, he knows that if he treats the samples with a certain
solution, either no change will occur in their chemical qualities,
which will prove that the manufacturing process is not at fault,
or new characteristics—any or all of D, E, or F—will appear, in
which case the villain will prove to be one of the ingredients.
The chemist suspects that the former is the more likely hy-

pothesis. He treats the samples with the appropriate solution, expecting that nothing will happen. Instead, the samples develop traces of D and E, though not of F. The appearance of D and E eliminates the production method as the source of the trouble and thus forces the chemist to reject his first hypothesis and to focus attention instead upon the ingredients. But which ingredient is defective? Or is more than one defective? He proceeds to another series of tests, with the hypothesis that Ingredient 1 is more probably at fault than Ingredient 2, and in such a manner he steadily narrows down the possibilities until he reaches the only answer consistent with all the facts.

The chemist reasoned out what had to be, in theory, the possible consequences of a hypothesis, and then compared the observable facts with the expected ones. If the facts had all jibed with his first expectation—namely, that the production routine had a bug in it—they would have confirmed the original hypothesis. But since the facts—the results of the second chemical test—were at odds with those required by the hypothesis, it had to be discarded and a new one substituted and duly tested.

It is always essential to remember that plenty of occurrences (a peculiar tint in the sky, insomnia, the failure of an air-conditioning unit, the outbreak of a war) can have more than one cause. This point, as well as the way in which hypotheses can be verified, was memorably illustrated in 1954-55, when Dr. Jonas Salk, building upon the results of many previous experiments, developed a vaccine which proved capable of preventing polio in monkeys. The question was, Would the vaccine work the same way in human beings? To find out, during 1954 hundreds of thousands of school children were given the vaccine, while a comparable number received shots of an inactive substance. Follow-ups showed that the children who got the vaccine were less likely to contract polio than those in the "control" group. The conclusion was that the Salk vaccine was an effective means of preventing polio in a significant majority of cases, and in addition reduced the severity of the disease among those who did contract it.

In 1955, therefore, a program of mass inoculation began among children of the age at which polio is most likely to strike. But within a few weeks, an unexpectedly large number of the newly inoculated children had polio. Why? There were at least three possibilities: (1) Instead of preventing the disease, the vaccine caused it. (2) Because the vaccine was known to be ineffective if a child was already harboring the polio virus, the children who became ill had already had the virus in their systems. (3) Because no vaccine is effective in every single case, the children were simply among the unfortunate minority whose bodies for some reason resisted this particular vaccine.

Possibilities 2 and 3 had been allowed for; it was assumed that they accounted for the small percentage of children who developed polio even after receiving the vaccine during the testing program. The trouble was that in 1955 the incidence of polio among newly vaccinated children was significantly higher than it had been the previous year. Was it possible, therefore, that the vaccine *did* cause polio? The clue to the answer was found in the fact that most of the victims had been inoculated with a vaccine made by one particular company. Investigation showed that, because of inadequate manufacturing and testing procedures, certain batches of that company's vaccine (and, to a smaller extent, the vaccine of other companies) contained live polio virus. Thus possibility 1 accounted for the unexpected number of failures, and immediately more stringent measures were taken to safeguard the manufacture and testing of the vaccine.

During the first weeks of confusion, many uninformed people assumed that Possibility 1 was the *only* way to account for the new polio cases. A child (so their unscientific reasoning went) contracted polio because he had received the vaccine. They thus committed the familiar *post hoc ergo propter hoc* ("after this, therefore because of this") fallacy: because B (the disease) happened after A (the inoculation), B was therefore caused by A. In the case of the vaccine, it is true, the cause-and-effect relationship was established in a certain number of cases, though it was not the vaccine as a whole which was at fault, but only certain defective lots. But much more often, the belief that a given happening caused a later one (contrast the meanings of SUBsequent and CONsequent) is wholly wrong. It springs from neglect of the principle we have been discussing: that a hypothesis can be considered confirmed only if it *alone* can produce the effects noted. "The baby is crying. He must have an open safety pin in his clothing." But all the safety pins prove to be closed, and the cause of the baby's crying is that he is hungry. "The way for any girl to get a high grade from that teacher is to do what June did—sit in the front row with her knees crossed." But, truth to tell, that teacher values brain-work above leg-display, and June was a good student. (Note too the faulty generalization from a single instance.) "No wonder you have a cold today. You didn't change your wet clothes when you came home yesterday." "The accident wouldn't have happened if he hadn't been drinking." "That sudden noise must have been caused by a jet plane breaking the sound barrier." The simple question by which to test all such confident assertions is, "Why do you insist that A alone could cause B? Weren't there any other possible causes?"

These two procedures—the gathering of data and the testing of hypotheses—are the essence of the scientific method. They are used by all who work with verifiable data: mathematicians, physical scientists—biologists, physicists, chemists, and the like—who try to find the principles and "laws" by which the physical universe operates, and social scientists—sociologists, economists, political scientists, etc.—who try to find patterns and tendencies in human conduct and institutions. Because of the very different character of the materials with which these two groups work, the generalizations they reach are of different quality. The physical scientists can verify their hypotheses either by direct laboratory experiment (manipulating their compounds and light-rays and animals as they wish) or by rigidly controlled observation. They can, in other words, virtually create the conditions under which they examine and measure their evidence.

Thus in general their conclusions can be much more positive than can those of the social scientists, who cannot ordinarily create ideal laboratory conditions involving human beings but must, instead, rely on records and observation of human behavior, past and present.

Thus far we have been speaking only of general statements concerned with verifiable data. But obviously there are many general ideas in the world which we cannot hope ever to prove in the scientific sense. Although some of them are backed by considerable evidence, that evidence is insufficient to raise them to the order of verified fact, especially since there may also be much evidence on the other side of the question. Every tenet of religion, for example, ultimately is incapable of objective demonstration. Countless volumes have been written attempting to "prove logically" this or that article of religious doctrine, but every so-called "proof" rests upon some basic assumption the objective proof of which is lacking. Every argument relating to ethics, esthetics, philosophy—any field of human interest except mathematics and the physical and (to a lesser degree) the social sciences—is based ultimately upon such unprovable assumptions. "For the sake of argument let's assume . . ." is the essential, though often unexpressed, prelude to the beginning of any argument on such matters; without an arbitrarily agreed-upon common ground on which to stand, the disputants can get nowhere. "God is immanent in the universe"; "the nature of man is essentially evil"; "there is a life after death"; "democracy is the form of government under which the individual man has the greatest freedom and opportunity"; "common sense is the best guide to conduct"; "wars are unmitigated evils"; "the most important element in artistic creation is sincerity on the part of the artist"; "no society can endure when home ties and family life disintegrate." These statements may be true, or they may not; we simply have no way of finally proving them, however strong and sincere our convictions are. When we use them in our thinking, therefore, we must remember that they are assumed, not proved.

EXERCISE 1

The following statements are based on some form—sound or unsound—of inductive thinking. Examine each statement, with particular attention to these points: (a) Are all the terms satisfactorily defined? (b) If the statement is based on an accumulation of evidence, is the evidence sufficient and of the right kind to justify the generalization? (c) If the statement is a hypothesis, could enough evidence be collected to prove or disprove it? (d) If it is a hypothesis, does it take into account the possibility of more than one cause?

1. The bathtub is the most dangerous place in the home.
2. It's simply not true that if you toss a coin you'll get heads half the time and tails the other half. Out of ten tosses I just made, the coin came up tails eight times.
3. They ought to stop those atomic bomb tests. No wonder we've had such bad weather lately.
4. Last year the grade distribution in this course was 6 A's, 10 B's, 10 C's, 8 D's, and 2 E's. This time the distribution is 3 A's, 6 B's, 15 C's, 10 D's, and 8 E's. College students are getting worse year by year.
5. Now I know that what I suspected is true. There are termites in my garage. I've seen the characteristic mud tunnels they build.
6. The Hope diamond undoubtedly bears a curse. It has brought bad luck to every one of its owners.
7. Racial prejudice is much more pronounced in adolescents and adults than it is in young children.
8. This man was found lying on the sidewalk. He is breathing heavily, he is semiconscious, he can't speak coherently. Must have been drinking canned heat. Put him in a cell until he sobers up.
9. American propaganda efforts, such as the Voice of America and Radio Free Europe, have been failures.
10. Excessive speed is responsible for most fatal automobile accidents.
11. All who were sick had eaten the potato salad, but some other picnickers who had eaten the salad were not sick. Therefore

the potato salad was not the cause of the outbreak of food poisoning.

12. There is some connection between birds' sense of direction and radio waves. The homing instinct of pigeons is dulled or destroyed when they are in the vicinity of radar installations.

13. Politicians are not necessarily dishonest, but they all look out for themselves.

14. The mosquito-killing powers of DDT have been greatly exaggerated, because there are numerous proved cases of mosquitoes flourishing in areas which have been sprayed with DDT.

15. If only a few people who were obviously crackpots reported seeing strange objects in the sky, you could say there weren't any such things. But when the reports mount into the hundreds, there is a strong probability that flying saucers, or whatever you want to call them, exist.

16. The present generation of young men and women is stronger and more capable of physical feats than previous ones. Look at all the athletic records that are being broken.

17. A local minister, who claimed to have much knowledge of "fallen women," asserted that over 50 per cent of them told him their downfall was due to dancing. Dancing obviously is immoral.

18. The meter must be wrong, or else it wasn't read correctly the last time. We couldn't possibly have used that much electricity.

19. Following the use of isotopes, a majority of the cases of early cervical cancer in this hospital were arrested or apparently cured. While it is too early to be positive, it seems likely that the use of isotopes may prove of great importance in the treatment of cancer generally.

20. The steady decline of interest in debating and campus literary magazines shows that the modern college student simply isn't interested in serious intellectual activity.

21. I've read ten Victorian novels, a large anthology of the poetry of the period, and a number of Victorian essays. All I can say is that the Victorians were a dull lot, self-satisfied, humorless, and prudish.

22. America is a land of easy-spending millionaires, sexy blondes, fabulous Park Avenue apartments, and loose morals. How do I know? Monsieur, I see your American movies!

23. Al Smith was defeated for the presidency in 1928 because he was a Roman Catholic.

24. The four men who have most influenced the thinking of mankind in the past century have been Darwin, Marx, Freud, and Einstein.

25. The results of the recent elections show that the American people want their government to follow a middle-of-the-road philosophy.

EXERCISE 2

Specify the kind of evidence you would require to be convinced that the following assertions are true:

1. The *New York Times,* which is owned by Jews, slants its news reports so as to put the Jewish viewpoint in the most favorable light.

2. If a rich man gets picked up for drunken driving, the police quietly forget about it. If a poor man gets picked up, they throw the book at him. So much for justice and "equality."

3. City slum areas breed crime.

4. The best way to bring on a rainstorm is to wash your car.

5. Food should never be left in an open can.

6. We never have the severe winters that our grandparents knew.

7. The increase of suburban shopping centers has seriously affected the business of downtown stores.

8. It is rank superstition for anyone to believe that we can communicate with the dead.

9. The spread of television has sharply reduced the time people devote to reading books.

10. The Marshall Plan was largely successful in rebuilding western European economy.

11. The tendency toward twin births runs in certain families.

12. Her "hay fever" actually is an allergy caused by the face powder she uses.

EXERCISE 3

True or false?:

1. A whale's throat is too narrow to swallow a man (hence the story of Jonah cannot be true).

2. Snakes milk cows.
3. Wolves hunt in packs and eat human beings.
4. Toads can live, sealed in stone or cement, for many years.
5. Rats are gifted with foresight that prompts them to leave a ship that is about to sink.
6. Goats eat tin cans and all kinds of supposedly indigestible junk.
7. Dogs and other animals possess a special instinct that tells them when they are in the presence of death (hence the howling which leads people to the body of the dog's master).
8. If a closely related man and woman marry, their offspring will be degenerate.
9. Feed a cold and starve a fever.
10. If a drowning man goes down for the third time, he is lost.
11. Terror can make one's hair turn white within a few hours.
12. A protruding jaw is a sign of an aggressive disposition.
13. Orientals have slanting eyes.
14. Men of Latin origin are accomplished lovers.
15. There are fully authenticated cases of human infants being adopted and reared by animals.

Look up the answers given in Bergen Evans' *The Natural History of Nonsense* (Knopf, 1946). Reserve your final judgment, however, until you come to Exercise 20, part 5 (page 178).

EXERCISE 4

1. Read Darrell Huff's *How to Lie with Statistics* (Norton, 1954). This is an entertaining little book that can easily be understood by anyone with a knowledge of arithmetic. It contains plenty of good, simple examples of the way statistics can be juggled to "prove" a point.
2. Citing official figures from several states, which show that men are responsible for twice as many fatal automobile accidents as women, someone has concluded that women drivers are twice as safe as men. What vital factors has he failed to take into account?
3. In the nineteenth century, statistics on the literacy rate in England were based on the number of men and women who were able to write their names at the time they were mar-

ried. In 1851, the percentage of bridegrooms who could do so was 69.3; of brides, 54.8. In 1900, the percentages were 97.2 and 96.8 respectively. Can we conclude, therefore, that by 1900 practically everybody in England could read and write?

4. The ten newest houses built in a certain subdivision sold for these prices: $25,000 (two), $21,000, $18,000, $17,000 (two), $15,000, $13,000 (three). What is the "average" price?

5. What questions should you insist on having answered before you will believe the following statement?: "It is simply not true that athletes in this college are poorer students than nonathletes. Official figures in the registrar's office show that the athletes' average is slightly above that of the student body as a whole."

6. What are the fallacies here?: "According to the government's index [based on the prices of rent, clothing, food, and a number of other expenses] the cost of living declined .5 per cent in the past year. Therefore our family spent .5 per cent less on food in the past year."

EXERCISE 5

Probably the best-known recent scientific investigation which has combined the two major techniques of inductive reasoning is the attempt to establish whether or not cigarette-smoking causes cancer of the lung. Scientists have analyzed masses of public-health statistics to find the degree of correlation between heavy smoking and the occurrence of cancer. At the same time, in their laboratories they have painted rodents with various chemicals derived from tobacco to see if the animals would develop cancer. Many questions have arisen, such as: Is it smoking that accounts for the indisputable increase in the rate of lung-cancer victims, or the noxious elements poured into the air by industrial plants? If chemicals from cigarette smoke definitely induce skin cancer in laboratory animals, can it therefore be said that the same chemicals produce cancer in human beings? Look up a few of the many articles on the subject printed in reputable magazines from 1952 onward, to get an idea of the many facets of the problem and the various ways in which scientists have attacked it. What is the present state of medical knowledge and opinion?

Deductive Reasoning

The second great kind of formal reasoning is the deductive, by which one moves from a general truth or assumption to a particular conclusion. The classic way of analyzing this process is the syllogism: a rigidly organized series of three statements, the last of which is the conclusion drawn from the preceding two, which are called the major and minor premises. From the point of view adopted in this book—that of the critical reader —the main importance of the syllogism is that it affords us a quick way of testing and perhaps exposing the incorrectness of a statement that is assumed to follow logically from certain premises.

In our everyday reading we seldom encounter statements ready-made into syllogisms. Instead, the logical antecedents of a statement are usually only implied or half-stated. To understand the reasoning by which a conclusion has been reached, we must, therefore, work backward by reconstructing the syllogism which seems to have been in the author's mind. Beginning with the statement in question, which serves as the conclusion of the syllogism, we build a major and a minor premise which the maker of the statement seems to have assumed to be true. In order to form a syllogism, we must often change the wording of the original statement. There is no harm in doing this, *provided always that we do not change in any way the thought of the author*. The words we select for our syllogism, if different from his own, must be equivalent to them in meaning.

A *major premise* may be derived in any of three ways: (1) It may be the product of an induction, that is, a generalization based on individual instances of verifiable fact, or from the verification of a hypothesis. (This is why inductive and deductive reasoning are intimately connected. The result of an induction serves very often as the major premise of a deduction.) (2) It may be an unverifiable assumption, which may or may not have a considerable body of evidence to suggest its truth, but which in any case is assumed to be true for the purposes of argument. (3) It may be the result of another deductive argument.

In most syllogisms the *minor premise* is a statement that a single individual, or a smaller class, belongs to the larger class mentioned in the major premise. Or it may state that an individual or class has a characteristic which the major premise asserts is possessed by a larger class. The *conclusion,* or *inference,* is based on the relationship of the two premises. If each of the premises is true, and if the syllogism violates none of the rules governing deductive thinking, the conclusion will be true. To be sure, the statement made in a conclusion may be true even though the syllogism is faulty; but in such a case it is true for a reason other than that indicated in the syllogism. In other words, it is in itself a true statement, but not a valid deduction from the premises given. On the other hand, if either of the premises is false, a sound syllogism—one that obeys all the rules of inference—will produce a false conclusion.

Because the "middle term" (the term found in both premises) can occur only in four different positions, syllogisms have four basic forms. We shall, however, confine ourselves to the two most commonly used:

I

(Major premise)   A is B
(Minor premise)   C is A
(Conclusion)   C is B

II

(Major premise)   A is B ⎫ (One of these premises
(Minor premise)   C is B ⎬ must be negative)
(Conclusion)   C is not A [Or: No C is A]

In formal logic, the major premise of each of the above syllogisms must be "universal" *(all, always, none, never)*. But for our purposes we shall modify the rule to allow proportional generalization—that is, statements that such-and-such is true in most cases or few cases. Since, as we have seen, terms like *most, frequently, some, sometimes, seldom, few* . . . are too vague to be useful, a more specific statement of proportion must be given: "half the time," "75 per cent of the cases," "one out of ten instances," and so on.

Now, let us take four ordinary sentences and reshape them into syllogisms. Numbers 1 and 2 illustrate the first form given above, 3 and 4 the second form:

1. "Mr. McGuire's a Catholic, so of course he must go to Mass."

    (Major premise: A is B) All Catholics are obligated to attend Mass.

    (Minor premise: C is A) Mr. McGuire is a Catholic.

    (Conclusion: C is B) Mr. McGuire is obligated to attend Mass.

    [That is, since Mr. McGuire belongs to a class all of whose members have a certain characteristic, Mr. McGuire necessarily shares that characteristic.]

2. "You're likely to find that particular brand in Graham's store, because about 75 per cent of the men's clothing stores in this city carry it in stock."

    (Major premise: A is B) About 75 per cent of the men's clothing stores in this city carry that particular brand.

    (Minor premise: C is A) Graham's store is one of the men's clothing stores in this city.

    (Conclusion: C is B) Graham's store probably carries that brand. (I.e., there's a 75 per cent chance that it does.)

    [That is, while not all stores carry a given brand of merchandise, 75 per cent of them do; therefore, though it is not certain that Graham's store does, it is likely to do so.]

3. "His wife isn't well educated. She doesn't know anything
   about science."

   (Major premise: No A is B)   No well-educated person is ig-
                                 norant of science.
   (Minor premise: C is B)   His wife is ignorant of science.
   (Conclusion: C is not A)   His wife is not well educated.

   [That is, the lady spoken of has a characteristic which is
   asserted not to belong to any member of a given class; possession of that characteristic therefore excludes her from
   that class.]

4. "He doesn't have any excessive thirst, so he can't have a
   fever."

   (Major premise: A is B)   All fever-stricken patients are
                                 excessively thirsty.
   (Minor premise: C is not B)   This patient is not excessively
                                 thirsty.
   (Conclusion: C is not A)   This patient does not have a
                                 fever.

   [That is, the patient does not have a characteristic that is
   said to be universally true of a class, hence he does not
   belong to that class.]

In each of these examples, the conclusion is valid (the product
of a formally correct syllogism), although it may or may not be
true, depending on whether or not both premises are true.

Now for a few of the most frequent errors in deductive thinking. These are *among* the reasons (there are many more) why
statements which seem, at first glance, to be perfectly "logical,"
turn out on analysis to be derived from unsound syllogistic
arguments.

1. *The terms must be accurately and consistently defined.*
No matter how the major premise has been obtained—whether
by induction or deduction, or simply assumed as the first link
in the present chain—the wording must be as exact and clear
as possible. We have seen how ambiguous and misleading are
such words as *normal, typical, average.* In addition, *all* terms
must be defined as precisely as possible. "The intelligence level

of Negroes is higher than that of whites": what, precisely, does that mean? "Intelligence" itself has never really been satisfactorily defined, although probably one may assume that for practical purposes the arbitrary standards of I.Q. tests are meant. But what does the phrase "intelligence level of Negroes" mean? The over-all average I.Q. of southern Negroes tested between 1930 and 1950? The I.Q. of Negroes now in the colleges and universities of six midwestern states? The I.Q. of Negroes enlisting in the United States Army? And what, precisely, does "that of whites" refer to? The generalization is phrased too vaguely, too loosely, for a syllogism to be soundly developed. It needs to be an exact statement which takes into account the limitations of the data upon which it is based.

Again, just what is a "business recession"? What statistical criteria are involved—what is the difference between a recession, a panic, and a slump? What is meant by "the greatest freedom and opportunity" which "democracy" (what is *it*?) is said to afford to the individual? Every such phrase cries out for definition. If it is left undefined, for each party to the argument to interpret according to his own wishes, the argument is worthless, because the parties will not be talking the same language. We pointed out the same thing in connection with "glittering generalities" in Chapter One.

Hence, one of the first things to do in testing the logical validity of a statement is to determine just what the maker of the statement means by the terms he is using, and whether his terms mean the same thing in the conclusion that they were understood to mean in the premises. Shifting definition in the course of an argument invalidates the whole sequence of thought. A recent illustration comes from the field of medicine. At a meeting of the American Psychiatric Association, the drug thorazine was announced as having remarkable powers to relieve "depression." Now in medical usage, *depression* is a technical term referring to a whole group of symptoms, both physical and mental; depression is as much a malfunctioning of certain parts of the nervous system, resulting in bodily ailments, as it is a disturbed state of mind. But in the popular vocabulary, *depression* simply means "the blues." It is not surprising, then, that when a newspaper columnist read of the report, she translated *depression* into laymen's language and announced "the invention of a new pill that chases the blues away. . . . Obviously, the world is going to heck in a hack and as far as aspirin is concerned, we have reached the point of no return. But just as mankind was about to be permanently marooned in its misery, presto! A new kind of pink pill for pale people who, emotionally, are lower than a snake's abdomen." Medical men who read that column must have shuddered at the misrepresentation of what the "new mood-lifter pill" accomplished—all because the term *depression* changed meaning in its trip from the psychiatrists' meeting to the pages of a newspaper. (The uncritical reader would have responded this way: "People who suffer from depression will be helped by this drug. I suffer from depression. Therefore this drug will help me." But the term in the major premise does not mean the same thing that it does in the minor premise.)

2. *Any qualification in a premise must be faithfully retained in the conclusion.* This is, in effect, an extension of what has just been said. Here the vital point is that if a premise allows for no exception (*all, none, every, always, never . . .*), the conclusion must retain the same idea; and similarly, if a premise contains a proportional generalization of the *some-many-few-often . . .* variety, the conclusion must contain it too. In Example 2 above, the categorical conclusion that "Graham's store *will* have that particular brand" would have been unwarranted. The major premise said that 75 per cent of the stores in town carried the brand, hence there is only a 75 per cent chance that Graham's did.

It may not be really necessary, in ordinary writing, to be so careful to qualify one's statements. In practice, the writer tacitly allows for exceptions: "The rate of fire alarms [in most cities] is highest in the slums"; "the efficiency of stenographers [in nine cases out of ten] is improved if they work in air-conditioned offices"; "the children of divorced parents [as a rule] have two strikes against them in life." The danger remains, however, that the uncritical reader, not realizing that such exceptions are implied, will follow the reasoning through to an unjustified conclusion. "Psychologists," says a magazine article, "show that boys' minds mature more slowly than girls'." "Bob and Mary are both sixteen," thinks a parent, "therefore Mary's mind is more mature than Bob's." The writer means that *as a rule* his generalization holds true. The reader instead thinks that it is always true, hence necessarily applicable to Mary and Bob in particular.

This almost universal human habit of reducing things to the simplest possible terms is the weakness on which the unscrupulous writer thrives. Clever persuaders deliberately omit such words as *always, never, only, none but, every, all* . . . because if they appear, they signal the reader to take a second, more critical look at what is being said. Without them, a statement is more likely to be accepted at its face value. If we keep always in mind the fact that a statement can be positive and sweeping only to the degree to which its implied premises are positive and sweeping, we are well equipped to expose the false dogmatism of writers and speakers.

When we first read the adventures of Sherlock Holmes, we are impressed by the uncanny accuracy of his split-second deductions. But our admiration is somewhat tempered when we realize that much of it is due to the unwarranted positiveness with which the deductions were phrased. In "The Case of the Norwood Builder," for example, Holmes welcomed John Hector McFarlane to his Baker Street rooms with these words: "I assure you that, beyond the obvious facts that you are a bachelor, a solicitor, a Freemason, and an asthmatic, I know nothing whatever about you."

"Familiar as I was with my friend's method," writes Dr. Watson, "it was not difficult for me to follow his deductions, and to observe the untidiness of attire, the sheaf of legal papers, the

watch-charm, and the breathing which had prompted them."*
The implication is that Holmes reasoned in this fashion:

> Men who dress untidily are bachelors.
> This man is dressed untidily.
> This man is a bachelor.

—and so on with the other three deductions. On that basis, we
are prone to assume that there could be no question whatsoever
that McFarlane was everything Holmes deduced he was. But
let us phrase the syllogism more strictly:

> *All* men who dress untidily are bachelors.
> This man is dressed untidily.
> This man *must* be a bachelor.

Or: A man who dresses untidily *can only* be a bachelor.
> This man is one who dresses untidily.
> This man *can only* be a bachelor.

Now we have brought the vital idea of *all* or *only* (which was
hidden in the syllogism as previously stated) into the open, and
the weakness of the major premise is exposed. Obviously it is
untrue that *all* men who dress untidily are bachelors; there
must be some untidy men who have loving wives at home.
Therefore the conclusion—that this man *must* be a bachelor—is
invalid. Maybe he is a bachelor, but the proof does not lie in
the syllogism.

Actually, of course, what Holmes did, though his manner
concealed the fact, was to count on the probabilities. A somewhat sounder syllogism—though still unsatisfactory, because
most is too vague a word and it would be hard to prove the
major premise—would be:

> *Most* men who dress untidily are bachelors.
> This man is dressed untidily.
> This man *probably* is a bachelor.

Thus it appears that even though the odds may have been in

* Sherlock Holmes materials are used in this chapter by special permission of
the executors of the late Sir Arthur Conan Doyle.

favor of McFarlane's being a bachelor, it was quite possible that Holmes could have been mistaken. The degree of probability in the conclusion depended, as always in such reasoning, on the degree expressed in the major premise.

To sum up this important point:

(correct) *All* Congressmen are United States citizens.

Mr. Benton is a Congressman.

Mr. Benton *must* be a United States citizen.

(wrong) Sixteen of the twenty Congressmen from this state are Republicans.

Mr. Morgan is a Congressman from this state.

Mr. Morgan *must* be a Republican.

[What is the correct conclusion?]

(correct) *Only 10 per cent* of the towns in this county have over 5,000 population.

The town in which I live is in this county.

My town *probably* has less than 5,000 population. [I.e., there's only a 10 per cent chance that it has a population of over 5,000.]

(wrong) March *usually* is a stormy month.

This month is March.

This month is *bound* to be stormy.

[How many flaws can you find in this argument?]

(correct) *All* the rivers on the western side of this watershed flow into the Gulf of Mexico.

Two-thirds of the rivers I'm talking about are on the western side of this watershed.

At least two-thirds of the rivers flow into the Gulf of Mexico.

[Why say "at least"?]

(wrong) *All* Quakers refuse to take oath.

Ten of the twenty witnesses in this case are Quakers.

Most of the witnesses in this case will refuse to take oath.

3. *The conclusion of a syllogism must not be identical with a premise.* This is the fallacy known as "begging the question." Since the whole purpose of deductive reasoning is to progress from one point (the premises) to another (the conclusion), an argument in which the two points are identical gets nowhere; it doubles back on itself, and is therefore sterile. "Begging the question" usually occurs in a statement which makes the same assertion in two different ways: "The reason why Sally is so mischievous is that she has just a little of the devil in her." Which is to say, A equals A. "This ordinance will certainly reduce juvenile delinquency, because it provides for steps which will prevent crimes on the part of teen-agers." "Because it will stir up the frictions between us and our potential enemy which will eventually ignite the powder keg, this diplomatic policy will bring us closer to war." By assuming as true the very point he ostensibly is trying to prove, the arguer changes roles: he ceases to be a counselor at the bar, presenting the evidence that supports his case, and becomes the judge, who hands down a verdict before the trial starts. (In what way are the devices of name-calling and the glittering generality related to begging the question?)

EXERCISE 6

Here are several syllogisms with one statement missing. From the information given in the other two statements, reconstruct the missing one:

1. (Major premise)   More than half of the members of this class have read some American literature in high school.

   (Minor premise)   Carol is a member of this class.
   (Conclusion)

2. (Major premise)
   (Minor premise)   Captain Turner is a pilot.
   (Conclusion)   Captain Turner does not have defective eyesight.

3. (Major premise)   All families threatened by the flood waters
                      were safely evacuated.
   (Minor premise)
   (Conclusion)   Our uncle and his family were safely evac-
                      uated.
4. (Major premise)
   (Minor premise)   The proposal to share atomic information
                      with other governments is part of our offi-
                      cial policy.
   (Conclusion)   The proposal to share atomic information
                      with other governments is motivated solely
                      by self-interest.
5. (Major premise)   There was rain on twenty-two of last July's
                      thirty-one days.
   (Minor premise)   The day I'm speaking of was last July 15.
   (Conclusion)

EXERCISE 7

Using a syllogism wherever necessary (sometimes more than one
may be needed in a single case), analyze the soundness of the
reasoning in each of the following statements. Are the premises
correct? Does the conclusion necessarily follow from the premises? (When you recast a statement into syllogistic form, omit
rhetorical flourishes like "everyone agrees," "obviously," etc.
As will be pointed out later [page 173] they are often used
to conceal the lack of logic.)

1. The large increase in church membership in recent years shows
   that the American people are becoming more religious.
2. We can go on our trip as we planned. The weather man says
   there won't be any snow for at least forty-eight hours.
3. The revolt in that South American country was caused by the
   antigovernmental factions that have long been plotting to over-
   throw the government.
4. Let's not go to the orchestra concert tonight. It's bound to be
   pretty bad—most of the program is devoted to contemporary
   music.
5. The solution is an acid. It turned the litmus paper red.
6. If you're old enough to fight you're old enough to vote.

7. I don't deny that I copied most of the theme from a magazine article. What's the matter with that? Everybody does it.

8. Anyone who refuses to testify before an investigating committee by invoking the Fifth Amendment automatically proves that he is guilty of something.

9. The Communist party is the most democratic party because it is the most uncompromising enemy of Fascism, and everybody admits that the real test of a party's democratic principles is the intensity of its opposition to Fascism.

10. This book contains only advice that is based on scientific evidence; if you follow its rules on how to write, you can be certain that people will understand you better.

11. To beg the question is to take an argument for granted before it is proved. This is one of the most insidious of fallacies, hence one of the most prevalent.

12. Boy, look at that red hair! I'll bet she has a temper.

13. The fact that there is no direct evidence that William Shakespeare, a minor Elizabethan actor, was capable of writing the great plays attributed to him proves that he didn't write them.

14. It is degrading to a man to live on a dole or any payment made to him without his being required to render some service in return. The reason is that he thus becomes, from an economic standpoint, a parasite upon the community as a whole, a position which is inconsistent with the maintenance of an individual's self-respect.

15. There are a few typographical errors in the answers in the back of this math book, so even though my answer doesn't agree with the one in the book, it's probably correct.

16. Last year Foam detergent outsold the next three brands combined. It's the best you can buy! There's no flakes like Foam!

17. Don't hurry. The train is due now, but you know how that railroad is. We have plenty of time.

18. My daughter Desdemona has always been innocent, modest, retiring. She had no interest in men. If she actually has eloped with Othello, he must have drugged her with some sort of magic potion. And since Othello is a foreigner, of a different race from ours, that is undoubtedly what he did. Those people know all about casting evil spells.

19. I never did trust him. He always had that sneaky look on his face.
20. If you prohibit the taking of pictures while the court is in session, you are interfering with the freedom of the press, which is a fundamental right guaranteed by the Constitution.

Other Obstacles to Clear Thinking

In addition to the pitfalls awaiting the unwary in formal inductive and deductive thinking, there are a number of common errors which perhaps can be called "abuses of logic" only by courtesy. Some of them, at least, may best be described as sheer avoidances of logic. For the sake of convenience, we may classify these errors as:

1. Introducing emotion in place of evidence.
2. Attacking a person instead of a principle.
3. Introducing irrelevant or unproved evidence.
4. Oversimplifying the issue or the evidence.
5. Suppressing evidence.
6. Distorting evidence.

These categories constantly overlap. Unlike a flower or a moth, which can be mounted and given a label that clearly assigns it to a particular genus and species, many specimens of unfair argumentation and cloudy thinking fall into several classifications simultaneously.

We have already looked at the first kind of obstacles to clear thinking—the substitution of emotion for facts—in Chapter One. The effectiveness of *name-calling* and the *glittering generality* depends on stock responses. Just as the scientist Pavlov, in a classic experiment, conditioned dogs to step up their production of saliva every time he rang a bell, so the shrewd persuader expects his reader to react automatically—without thought—to language that stirs his prejudices.

The dividing line between name-calling and the *smear* or *mud-slinging* technique is almost invisible, and in common usage the terms are virtually interchangeable. But the mudslinger makes personal attacks on his opponent, not merely by hurling a few choice epithets, but (often) by presenting an array of supposedly damaging evidence against his opponent's motives, character, and private life. Thus the audience's attention is diverted from the argument itself to a subject which is more likely to stir up prejudices. If, for example, in denouncing his opponent's position on the reduction of the national debt, a candidate refers to Mr. X's intimate connection with certain well-known gamblers, he ceases to argue his case on its objective merits and casts doubt upon his opponent's personal character. His object is not primarily to hurt Mr. X's feelings, but to arouse bias against Mr. X in his hearer's mind. Every critical reader or listener must train himself to detect and reject these irrelevant aspersions. It may be, indeed, that Mr. X *has* shady connections with the underworld. But that has nothing to do with the abstract rights or wrongs of his position on a national issue. Although, as the history of American politics shows, it is a hard thing to do, issues should be discussed apart from character and motives. The latter are also important, since obviously they bear upon a candidate's fitness for public office, but they call for a separate discussion.

A somewhat more subtle kind of personal attack is the *innuendo,* which differs from the direct accusation roughly as a hint differs from a plain statement. It is chiefly useful where there are no facts to give even a semblance of support to a forthright charge. The writer or speaker therefore slyly plants seeds of doubt or suspicion in the reader's or listener's mind without saying anything that he could be forced to retract later. Innuendo is a trick that is safe, effective, and dirty. It is a favorite weapon of the gossip. "They were parked for an hour with the lights out." The statement, in itself, may be entirely true; but what counts is the implication it is meant to convey. The unfairness is compounded when the doubts that the innuendo raises concern matters that have nothing to do with the issue anyway. An example of the irrelevant innuendo is found in the writings of the historian Charles A. Beard. In assailing the ideas of another historian, Admiral Alfred T. Mahan, Beard referred to him as "the son of a professor and swivel-chair tactician at West Point" who "served respectably, but without distinction, for a time in the navy," and "found an easy berth at the Naval War College." Actually, the occupation of Mahan's father has nothing to do with the validity of the son's arguments; but observe the sneer—which is meant to be transferred from father to son—in "professor" and "swivel-chair tactician." Beard's reference to Mahan's naval record is a good elementary instance of damning with faint praise. And whether or not Mahan's was "an easy berth" at the Naval War College (that is a matter of opinion), it too has no place in a discussion of the man's ideas.

Another instance of the way in which emotionally loaded language can be combined with irrelevant or unproved evidence to stir prejudice may be taken from the field of art. A modern critic condemned certain pictures as "a conventional rehash of cubist patterns born among the wastrels of Paris forty years ago." In so doing, he attacked the art through the artist. Actually, the worth of pictures has nothing to do with the private lives of the people who painted them. The painters referred to may well have been wastrels, but that fact—if it is a fact—has no bearing on the point at issue. The assumed connection between the personal virtues or shortcomings of an artist and the aesthetic value of his productions has resulted in a great deal of confused thinking about literature, music, and the other arts.

Another diversionary tactic is the *red herring*. This is an irrelevant issue introduced into a controversy when one side feels its case, argued strictly on merit, is too weak, or when, the opposition having demolished its previous arguments, it wants to change the subject. The red herring technique may involve shifting attention from principles to personalities, but without necessarily smearing. Since neither golf-playing nor having fairly elevated intellectual interests is yet counted sinful or criminal, a political party slings no mud (though it may arouse prejudice) when it constantly alludes to the other party's candidate as a golf addict or a highbrow. Still, such matters are largely irrelevant to the main argument, which is whether one candidate and what he stands for, or the other candidate and *his* platform, will better serve the interests of the nation. The red herring device need not involve personalities at all; it may take the form simply of substituting one impersonal issue for another. If a large corporation is under fire for alleged monopolistic practices, its public-relations men may start an elaborate advertising campaign to show how well the company's workers are treated. Thus, if the campaign succeeds, the bad publicity suffered because of the assertions that the company has been trying to corner the market may be counteracted by the public's approval of its fine labor policy.

Several of the techniques mentioned so far depend on the principle of association, by which one idea receives emotional coloration from another close by. The *transfer* device also exploits the reader's willingness to link one idea with another, even though the two may not be logically connected. On the positive side, it is an attempt to clothe the subject of one's praise in borrowed raiment that gives it a dignity, an attractiveness it may not possess by itself.

Here is an advertisement that illustrates how transfer works:

THE TELEPHONE POLE THAT BECAME A MEMORIAL

The cottage on Lincoln Street in Portland, Oregon, is shaded by graceful trees and covered with ivy.

Many years ago, A. H. Feldman and his wife remodeled the house to fit their dreams . . . and set out strips of ivy around it. And when their son, Danny, came along, he, too, liked to watch things grow. One day, when he was only nine, he took a handful of ivy slips and planted them at the base of the telephone pole in front of the house.

Time passed . . . and the ivy grew, climbing to the top of the pole. Like the ivy, Danny grew too. He finished high school, went to college. The war came along before he finished—and Danny went overseas. And there he gave his life for his country.

Not very long ago the overhead telephone lines were being removed from the poles on Lincoln Street. The ivy-covered telephone pole in front of the Feldman home was about to be taken down. Its work was done.

But, when the telephone crew arrived, Mrs. Feldman came out to meet them. "Couldn't it be left standing?" she asked. And then she told them about her son.

So the pole, although no longer needed, wasn't touched at all. At the request of the telephone company, the Portland City Council passed a special ordinance permitting the company to leave it standing. And there it is today, mantled in ivy, a living memorial to Sergeant Danny Feldman.

What did the telephone company wish to accomplish by this ad? The reader is not urged to install a telephone, or to equip his house with extra telephones, or to use any of the various new services the company has developed; nor is he told how inexpensive and efficient those services are. Instead, this is what is known as an "institutional" advertisement: one whose purpose is to inspire public esteem, even affection, for the company.

How is it done? Simply by telling a little anecdote, without a word to point the moral. Every detail is meticulously chosen for its emotional appeal: the cottage ("home, sweet home" theme); the ivy (symbol of endurance through the years; often combined, as here, with the idea of the family homestead); the little boy (evoking all the feelings associated with childhood); the young man dying in the war (evoking patriotic sentiment). Thus at least four symbols are combined—all of them with great power to touch the heartstrings. Then the climax: Will the company cut down the ivy-covered pole? *Company* to many people has a connotation of hardheartedness, impersonality, coldness, which is the very impression this particular company, one of the biggest in the world, wants to erase. So, with no hint of a boast—indeed, with almost excessive modesty—the company reports that it went to the trouble of getting special permission to leave this one pole standing, "mantled in ivy, a living memorial."

The writer of the advertisement has, in effect, urged his readers to transfer to the telephone company the sympathies aroused by his story. The ivy-covered telephone pole aptly symbolizes what he wanted to do—to "mantle" the prosaic pole (symbolizing the company) with the ivy that is associated with home, childhood, and heroic death. If it is possible to make one feel sentimental about a giant corporation, an advertisement like this—arousing certain feelings by means of one set of objects and then deftly transferring those feelings to another object—will do it. But the story, while true enough, is after all only one incident, and a sound generalization about the character of a vast company cannot be formed from a single anecdote. The company may well be as "human" as the advertisement implies, but it is through an appeal to our emotions, not our reason, that we are led to that belief.

A second extremely common form of "transfer" is the *borrowing of prestige* from a highly respected institution (country, religion, education) or individual (statesman, philosopher, scientist), for the sake of adorning something else. Political orators like to work into their speeches quotations from Scripture or from the secular "sacred writings" (the Declaration of Independence, the Preamble to the Constitution, the Gettysburg Address). Such quotations are depended upon to arouse favorable emotions in the breasts of the auditors, emotions which are then transferred to the orator's pet policy. Much of William Jennings Bryan's success as a public figure was due to the way in which he transformed an ordinary political campaign into a quasi-religious crusade by his "Cross of Gold" speech: "You shall not press down upon the brow of labor this crown of thorns; you shall not crucify mankind upon a cross of gold!" Actually, although the underlying idea, that the national monetary policy at the end of the nineteenth century worked to the serious disadvantage of the "common man," was entirely valid, the metaphor in which it was expressed was not. There is no connection between economics and the passion and crucifixion of Jesus. But the metaphor succeeded admirably in rallying to

Bryan's cause millions of Americans to whom Biblical allusion had the most powerful of connotations. In the presidential campaign of 1912 Theodore Roosevelt capitalized upon the same emotions with his cry, "We stand at Armageddon, and we battle for the Lord!" The First World War was often spoken of as "the great crusade," and even though the phrase went sour during the disillusionment of the 1920's and '30's, the idea of "crusade" regained enough potency to recommend itself to the Republican strategists in 1952. On the whole, however, as the influence of the Bible and religious symbols generally upon men's emotional responses declines, these devices are losing favor with persuaders. Similarly, mention of Valley Forge, the Founding Fathers, and other familiar patriotic symbols is not as inevitable in political appeals as it used to be; they have worn too thin to be of much use. But Republicans still seize on Lincoln's birthday as an annual occasion for dinners and speechmaking, just as Democrats use Jefferson's birthday for the same purpose.

When analyzing an appeal that uses quotations from men and women who have achieved renown in one field or another, the crucial question is whether the quotation is appropriate here. Does it have real relevance to the point at issue? It is all very well to quote Washington or Jefferson or Lincoln in support of one's political stand—but it must be remembered that circumstances have changed immensely since those quotations were first uttered, and their applicability to a new situation may be dubious indeed. The implication is, This man, who we agree *was* great and wise, said certain things which "prove" the justice of my own stand; therefore it behooves you to believe I am right. But to have a valid argument, the writer must prove that the word of the authorities whom he cites has a logical bearing on the present issue. If that is true, then he is borrowing not so much their popular prestige as their wisdom—which is perfectly permissible.

In essence, what the writer who invokes august authority for his point of view does is to imply that if the great men of the past were living today, they would write testimonials in behalf of his position. The familiar *testimonials* of present-day advertising are another instance of the transfer device. In some cases, the "authority" who testifies has some connection with the type of product advertised. The problem to settle here is, When we try to decide which brand of surgical cotton is best, how much weight may we reasonably attach to the enthusiastic statements of certain nurses (who, in addition to being quoted, are pictured in their starched, antiseptic prettiness)? When we are thinking of buying a tennis racket, should we accept the say-so of a champion, who, after all, is well paid for telling us that he considers a certain make to be the best of all possible rackets? In other cases, the testifying authority may have no formal, professional connection with the product he recommends. An actor, who may very well be a master of his particular art, praises a whisky, an after-shaving lotion, or a new convertible. He likes it, he says; but, we may ask, does the fact that he is a successful actor make him better qualified than any person who is *not* an actor to judge a whisky, a lotion, or a car? Competence in one field does not necessarily imply competence in another.

Furthermore, in recent times it has been increasingly customary for advertisers to borrow the prestige of science and medicine to enhance the reputation of their products. The American people have come to feel for the laboratory scientist and the physician an awe once reserved for bishops and statesmen. The alleged approval of such men thus carries great weight when it is a question of selling something, or (which amounts to the same thing) inducing someone to believe something. Phrases such as "leading medical authorities say . . ." or "independent laboratory tests show . . ." are designed simply to transfer the prestige of science, which presumably is incapable of either error or corruption, to a toothpaste or a cereal. Seldom are the precise "medical authorities" or "independent laboratories" named. But the mere phrases have vast weight with the uncritical. Similarly too the honorific "Dr." or "professor" implies that the person quoted speaks with all the authority of which learned men are capable—when as a matter of fact "doctorates" can be bought from mail-order colleges. Whenever, therefore, an attempt is made to convince by appeal to the prestige that surrounds the learned, the reader should demand full credentials. Just *what* medical authorities say this? Can they be trusted? *What* independent laboratories made the test—and what, actually, did the tests reveal? Who is this man that speaks as a qualified educator or psychologist or economist? Regardless of the fact that he is called "doctor," does he know what he is talking about?

In all cases where the power of reputation and authority is invoked in behalf of a policy or a product, it is well to remember that before he can testify in a court of law, a man about to provide specialized evidence, which may have an important bearing on the jury's decision, must establish his competence in his field. A pathologist, a psychiatrist, an engineer, is asked to outline briefly the nature of his special training and experience. It would not hurt if, when we encounter the appeal to authority in any type of persuasive writing, we adopted the strategy of the opposing lawyer and probed more deeply into the witness' genuine competence to speak on the particular issue that is before us. A few pages later on, we shall suggest some pertinent questions in this respect.

At many places in the present chapter we have been dealing with various kinds of *oversimplification,* though not usually identifying them as such. We have said that no hypothesis is sound unless it takes into account all the factors that are related to it; and when we touched on the syllogism, we warned against the error of drawing a universal conclusion *(all, always, never, none)* from a qualified premise *(most, some, few).* Unfortunately, with our natural human indolence, to say nothing of our intellectual limitations, we are always eager to view questions in their simplest terms and to make our decisions on the basis of only a few of the many aspects which the problem involves. If that is true of problems of a practical nature, such as those we cited to illustrate the use of the hypothesis, how much more true it is of those involving a problem of human conduct, or a grave decision facing the voters or the statesmen of a nation! The problem of the so-called minority groups in America, for instance, is not simply one of abstract justice, as many would like to think it; it involves deeply complex questions of economics, sociology, and politics. Nor can one say with easy assurance: "The federal government should guarantee every farmer a decent income, even if the money comes from the pocketbooks of the citizens who are the farmer's own customers"—or "It is the obligation of every educational institution to purge its faculty of everyone who holds leftist sympathies." Perhaps each of these propositions is sound, perhaps neither is; but before it is adopted as a settled conviction, the intelligent man or woman must canvass its full implications, just as he should do with any hypothesis. After the implications have been explored, it may be found that there is more evidence against the proposition than there is supporting it; in which case it should be abandoned.

Countless false generalizations concerning parties, races, religions, and nations—to say nothing of individuals—are the result of the deep-seated human desire to reduce a complex idea to its simplest terms. Democrats tend to think of all Republicans as progress-obstructing conservatives, when in fact many Republicans are more "liberal" than many Democrats. Some Protestants regard Catholics as bigoted and superstitious, even though the views they regard as "bigoted" and the practices they regard as "superstitious" may have their roots deep in the philosophical grounds of the Catholic religion. Similarly some Catholics regard Protestants as infidels or atheists, although there may be as much philosophical justification for Protestant doctrine as there is for Catholic. It is easier to condemn than to understand. But every man and woman has a pressing moral as well as intellectual, obligation to analyze the basis of every judgment he or she makes: "Am I examining every aspect of the issue that needs to be examined—do I understand the prob lem sufficiently to be able to make a fair decision—or am I taking the easiest way out?"

A particularly dangerous form of oversimplification is the *either-or assumption,* which denies the possibility of any middle ground, or of shadings or variations between two extremes. It insists, on the contrary, that something is either A or Z, and that between the two there is not B, C . . . X, Y, but only a vacuum; that in the spectrums of politics, ethics, religion there are only absolute blacks and absolute whites. But everywhere we turn in life, we know that this is not the case. Instead of two positions between which we must choose, there may be three, or there may be a dozen. To divide all people into two classes, the "sane" and the "insane," is to neglect the fact that there are innumerable gradations of sanity, and only by an artificial definition do medical men and jurists decide that one person is sane and another insane. There are not merely "good" writers and "bad" writers, but all degrees of competence in between; not merely "godly" people and "atheists," but all shades of religious faith. The law, though often arbitrary, as in its insistence on a choice between "guilty" and "not guilty," equally often recognizes the existence of shades of guilt, as in its allowing any one of several different charges to be brought against a man accused of killing another, its enabling a jury to accompany a verdict of guilty with a recommendation of mercy, and its giving judges wide discretion as to the severity of the sentence imposed.

The either-or assumption is the prime weapon of the intolerant. It is the means by which one group, which flatters itself that it, and it alone, basks in the light of truth, denounces all others as children of darkness. All too familiar in recent times has been the conflict represented in this dialogue:

"We have all the right on our side (A). We are militantly opposed to the evil which is Z. Therefore you must come out in favor of A and help us fight it."

"But I don't think the issue is absolutely clear-cut. There's something to be said for and against *both* A and Z. And isn't there at least one alternative—M?"

"No, there isn't. You've got to make your choice between A and Z. A is wholly right, Z is wholly wrong. If you're not pro-A, heart and soul, then you must be pro-Z. If you're pro-Z, obviously you're dedicated to evil."

This dialogue, it need hardly be said, is wholly imaginary. It never takes place because, by describing his position in such bald terms, the partisan of the all-good A would expose the weakness of his stand. Arrogance based on the either-or assumption is a poor substitute for open-mindedness based on the realization that most issues in life are not as simple as people make them out to be.

False analogy is another kind of oversimplification. Analogy itself is based on a resemblance, in one or more particulars, between two situations, objects, or persons. It is usually employed in an attempt to simplify and make more vivid a complex idea. Newspaper political cartoons are often nothing more than pictorial analogies. Often such analogies serve admirably to point up, dramatically and colorfully, the crux of a problem. The analogy of a governmental agency in the role of the legendary Dutch boy, trying desperately to stop a leak in the dike ("national economy") while the waves of the sea ("inflation") are already spilling over the top of the dike, is plainly very useful. But the ever-present danger is that the analogy will assume a nonexistent resemblance between the two objects of comparison. "Don't change horses in the middle of a stream" is a familiar cry in political campaigns when, pleading a national emergency, the partisans of the incumbent in office declare he cannot be superseded without grave danger to the country. There is, of course, a superficial similarity between the two situations: changing horses in the middle of a swift stream is dangerous, and so too may be changing public officials at certain junctures in national affairs. But riding horseback is not much like being president of the United States, and while there may be only one or two reasons why one should or should not change horses, there may be many reasons, none of them having anything to do with horseback riding, why one man should be elected president and not another. Equally dangerous is any attempt to prove a point which is based on the fancy that the nations of the world are like school-children, and that when one nation does not have its way it goes into a corner and sulks; or that two opponents, labor and capital, for example, may be likened to two prize-fighters squaring off in the ring, with some government official or agency as referee. Such analogies are, we repeat, useful in dramatizing a situation; but it is always perilous to maintain that because two situations are alike in one or two respects, anything that is true of one is necessarily true of the other.

In one way or another, the various techniques of oversimplification distort the truth: they fail to "give the whole picture." *Wrenching from context* is one other device that accomplishes the same end. A sentence or a phrase can easily mean one thing when it is quoted alone, and a quite different thing if it is read against the background of the whole discussion to which it belongs. An extreme example is a sentence from a newspaper review of a new movie: "For about five minutes 'Fruits of Desire' is a top-notch show, brilliantly acted and magnificently photographed. After that it degenerates into a dismal spectacle of Hollywood hokum." It would not be surprising to see the subsequent advertisements of the movie flaunting this headline: " 'A top-notch show, brilliantly acted and magnificently photographed . . . a spectacle'—Smith, *Daily News*." The familiar "avoid foreign entanglements" advice in Washington's farewell address, when read in full context, means something very different from what it means when quoted separately. And probably no public figure whose statements are quoted in the newspapers or on the radio has ever escaped the chagrin that comes from seeing prominence given to one or two paragraphs of his latest speech which, thus isolated, completely distort his argument. Listening to a speech or reading an advance copy, a reporter will quickly select a passage or two which he thinks will make the best (i.e., most interesting) story and, if the speech is a controversial one, will fit in best with his paper's policy. The sentences thus selected for quotation may be relatively unimportant—a mere aside in the speaker's main discourse; and, when wrenched from context, they may represent the speaker as saying something entirely different from what he meant. The truly critical reader will never base an opinion upon the exceedingly fragmentary press report of someone's public utterance. He will withhold opinion until he can see the full text as printed in, for example, the *New York Times*.

Although in everyday usage it is quotations alone that are said to be "wrenched from their context," the meaning of events themselves is often exaggerated and otherwise distorted when they are separated from their background. (In its wider sense, *context* means "the whole background or situation against which an occurrence is to be viewed.") This is one of the chief faults of daily journalism. Although some attempt is made, especially in syndicated columns, to fill in the background of the news, by and large the content of the news columns themselves is determined by several considerations, all of which tend to isolate the individual event from the context against which it must be viewed if its true importance (or lack of importance) is to be understood. One is the necessity the journalist faces of finding a "news angle"—something he can write about excitedly, something that a copy editor can put a dramatic headline over. No matter if the "angle" seizes upon some trivial or irrelevant occurrence, an insignificant side-issue; the "story" is the thing. In an international conference, a brief "clash" of tempers between two diplomats will provide fine headlines for the evening papers. The "clash" may be over in two minutes and someone else may make a speech of top importance an hour later; the momentary flaring of tempers nevertheless remains the news of the day. Similarly, the day-to-day reporting of the work of Congress is a relatively dull affair; somehow it must be livened up. Hence every congressman who "hurls a charge" at someone else, however unfounded the charge, is sure of ample newspaper coverage.

Because most newspapers are preoccupied with whatever is controversial and dramatic, much important news goes unreported. What really determines the course of events goes on quietly, in the unpublicized routine of the United Nations and the various departments of government, in the highly private correspondence and talks between the President and his experts, in the offices of great corporations and laboratories and research libraries. Wherever policy is being determined, wherever knowledge is being applied to the solution of contemporary problems—there the future of men is truly being shaped. But until these proceedings result in a public statement or provoke a sharp controversy, as a rule (with the notable exception of "inside dope stories") they go unheeded in the press. What one reads in the newspapers is only the most superficial, though momentarily exciting, manifestation of the vast movements beneath the surface.

From the distortion of truth, it is but a step to the outright suppression of truth. A common name for this final, crowning device of deception is *card stacking,* which means the playing up of evidence favorable to one's cause and the concealing of evidence that weakens one's position. Newspaper practice again furnishes a convenient illustration. Virtually all papers are biased one way or another, and while some may make an honest attempt to present a balanced account of what has been going on, others deliberately give prominence to news that helps support their editorial position, especially in respect to politics, and play down or simply fail to print news that is more favorable to the other side. If, for example, a congressman makes a speech attacking a proposal for a Missouri Valley project similar to the TVA, a paper which opposes public ownership of utilities will probably find room for the dispatch. But if, the next day, another congressman defends the proposal and points out several serious errors in the first speaker's facts, the paper may suddenly become too full to permit inclusion of the rebuttal.

In a Republican paper, the utterances of orthodox Republicans always will be featured, and those of Democrats neglected or at least played down, except when the paper expects they will invite Republican rejoinders. And the converse is true, of course, of a Democratic paper. It is seldom possible to discover what both sides are saying without reading two papers, one from each side of the fence.

Similarly with political parties themselves, and with advertisers. A state administration, running for re-election, may devote all its propaganda to boasting about the reduction in taxes which it has effected in an "economy program"—and it will fail to mention the way in which state services have deteriorated as a result of the "slashed budget." This same practice is evident in virtually every advertisement one reads. The attractive points of a product are dwelt upon unceasingly; the less attractive ones, never. An automobile may be streamlined and easy-riding, it may have fast pickup in traffic, it may have a wealth of gadgets—these facts will be proclaimed from every newspaper, magazine, billboard, and television screen; but that the car eats up gasoline and oil, has a poorly made engine block, and costs $200 more than other cars in the same price-class—these facts are religiously suppressed. But, as you will no doubt agree, they are worth knowing about.

EXERCISE 8

1. Comment on the following advertisements as examples of the "transfer" device:

(a) In all the world, only four Monks at the Monastery of La Grande Chartreuse in France know the secret formula of Chartreuse Liqueur. Since 1605, no one has ever duplicated this rare recipe combining more than 130 different herbs, gathered by the Monks on the hillsides near their Monastery. Try Chartreuse yourself, and you will discover why it is known as the "Queen of Liqueurs."

(b) Those who have that special awareness of what constitutes a really fine Scotch invariably turn to House of Lords. They share a tradition with members of the House of Lords, often called "the most exclusive club in the world," who serve and enjoy this rare Scotch.

(c) This is the Whisky that made Kentucky whiskies famous. From this land of bourbon comes legendary Early Times, a great name in whisky since 1860, all whisky, fine whisky, its famous flavor hearty but never heavy. Bottled at the peak of perfection, enjoyed at the peak of flavor, Early Times is truly every ounce a man's whisky.*

2. Examine the use of various "transfer" techniques in the advertisement quoted on pages 64-65.

3. Make a collection of current advertisements that borrow the prestige of science to help sell cosmetics, toothpaste, food, drugs, etc. Try to determine just what the scientific terms they use mean ("homogenized lanolin," "vitamin-fortified emollient," "estrogenic hormones"). Is the product really any better for their presence? How many terms can you find that may be suspected of originating in the advertising writer's inventive brain ("Bacteria-Destroyer WD-9," "Formula 56")?

EXERCISE 9

Look up Mark Antony's funeral oration in Shakespeare's *Julius Caesar* (Act III, Scene 2) and enumerate the ways in which Mark Antony arouses the emotions of his listeners. How does this speech differ from a calm appeal to reason?

EXERCISE 10

Choose a controversial national or international topic of great importance at the moment, preferably one on which you have already formed an opinion. Make a list of all the arguments you can think of (or collect from current printed discussions of the subject) *on both sides* of the issue. Also, try to deduce the probable consequences of each of the proposed courses of

* Courtesy of Early Times Distillery Company.

action. Is the evidence overwhelmingly in favor of one alternative or the other? Has your own opinion been changed as a
result of examining the subject more closely? (This exercise
would have additional value if the lists compiled by all members of the class were pooled, compared, and debated.)

EXERCISE 11

The advertisements of books in the weekly book sections of
the large metropolitan papers or the *Saturday Review* usually
quote enthusiastic comments from newspaper or magazine reviews. Copy a handful of such quotations from current book
ads and, using the *Book Review Digest,* look up the reviews
from which they were taken. Were the critics really as enthusiastic about the books as the brief fragments quoted in the ads
suggest they were?

EXERCISE 12

Make a collection of current newspaper cartoons as examples
of possibly false or misleading analogies. What is the basis of
the implied resemblance between the two situations? What
does the cartoonist imply by selecting that particular analogy?
How far can the analogy be logically extended?

EXERCISE 13

Make a collection of "letters to the editor" in the local newspapers and analyze them intensively for examples of the various types of error discussed in this chapter.

EXERCISE 14

Comment on the reasoning displayed in each of the following
statements:

1. Extra-curricular activities are very important because they
   teach you how to get along with people, and that's just about
   the most valuable preparation you can have for your future
   life.

2. The local barbers' union today announced that the price of haircuts was raised from $1.50 to $1.75. In explanation of the rise, the head of the union pointed out that this is the only large city in the state in which haircuts have not previously cost $1.75.

3. [From the news letter of Phi Beta Kappa, noting that a grandmother had won high honors on graduating from the School of General Studies at Columbia University] "The adult mind," said Dean Louis M. Hacker, of the School of General Studies, "is as good as the youthful mind, if not better. It's time we stopped underestimating the potential mental growth of our adult men and women." Mrs. Stanley's record proves his point.

4. Modern art is communistic because it is distorted and ugly, because it does not glorify our beautiful country, our cheerful and smiling people and our great material progress. Art which does not portray our beautiful country in plain, simple terms that everyone can understand breeds dissatisfaction. It is therefore opposed to our government, and those who create and promote it are our enemies.

5. [A series of advertisements captioned "The Disaster of Government Intervention"]

    The Hammurabi Code, written before 2000 B.C., imposed controls over wages, prices, production, consumption and all the rest of the economy. It was thus that Babylonia was wrecked.

    ———

    Governmental extravagance and bloated bureaucracy killed individual initiative and led to the fall of ancient Greece.

    ———

    A planned economy of state maintenance of the lazy, plus excessive taxation, brought about the collapse of the Roman Empire, and plunged civilization into the Dark Ages.

    ———

    The welfare state of the Incas became so oppressive as to become easy prey for Pizzarro and his "Conquistadores."

    ———

    The great Spanish Empire collapsed when the throne so regimented every activity that no one could earn a living except by being a public employee, a priest, or a sailor. For the same reasons, the British Empire is dissolving before our eyes right now.

6. Ohio health commissioners approved the fluoridation of water by city water departments, which the State Health Department considers effective in reducing tooth decay.

Will the people of Ohio allow a deadly poison to be put into their drinking water? Do the people know what sodium fluoride is, and for what other purpose it is used?

Sodium fluoride is used in rat poison, and is the lethal element in insect powers! A fine thing to put into the hands of water-works employes for "treatment" of tooth decay!

It is reported that sodium fluoride is only beneficial to children up to six and one-half years old, but dentists will paint it on their teeth, if you insist, so why should we all be forced to drink the filthy stuff?

It will be interesting to hear from our local medical profession on the pros and cons of fluoridation; let's have both sides of the matter, and then let the people decide whether or not we shall have a lethal potion added to our water.

7. Ever since the days of Horatio Alger, people have been led to believe that newsboys gained experience that would help them become successful businessmen. However, former Warden Lawes of Sing Sing Prison exploded this myth when he compiled statistics showing that of the 2,300 inmates in the prison, over 69 per cent had sold papers when they were boys.

8. I've known Vicki since she was a little girl, and up till now I've always considered her a sweet, charming, and intelligent girl, with a spotless reputation. But to think that she belongs to that sorority! Everybody knows the sort of things those girls do. They are notorious. You may say that Vicki hasn't been corrupted by them, but nobody can handle a barrel of tar and not get some of it on his own hands.

9. Certainly I don't want to cast any aspersions on his integrity as a bank cashier. I have no reason for believing he isn't 100 per cent honest. I'm merely saying that he seems to have a pretty keen interest in horses. I've seen him at the races several times in the last couple of months.

10.   "All Nature is but Art, unknown to thee;
          All Chance, Direction, which thou canst not see;

OTHER OBSTACLES TO CLEAR THINKING

> All Discord, Harmony not understood;
> All partial Evil, universal Good:
> And, spite of Pride, in erring Reason's spite,
> One truth is clear, WHATEVER IS, IS RIGHT."

These famous lines, from Pope's "Essay on Man," admirably illustrate not only the fatuous optimism of the poet himself, willfully closing his eyes to the evil rampant in the world, but also the complacency of the whole age in which he lived. Pope and his fellow-men in the first half of the eighteenth century deliberately lived in a fool's paradise, deluding themselves by the simple process of refusing to look reality in the face.

11. There's no question that the car we looked at is the best value for the money. Nothing else we've seen can compare with it. Still and all, I don't think we should buy it. I don't like the high pressure methods the salesman used, and I think he drinks.

12. Make this simple test to *prove* to yourself that Nurp is the best anti-acid remedy on the market! Drop a single handy tablet in water! See how quickly it dissolves! It gets to work faster in your stomach! Give it a trial this very day!

13. The unfitness of this man to teach impressionable youth, especially in a tax-supported institution, is amply proved by the following facts: He was investigated by the F.B.I. when he applied for a leave of absence to do research under a government grant; on his shelves at home he has many highly questionable books, among them volumes by authors who are well known in left-wing circles; his wife is active in so-called "liberal" political activities, including the League of Women Voters, which meddles in every election by issuing factual analyses of the various candidates' records and platforms; his brother is a longtime official in the garment workers' union. The teaching of botany obviously is a front to conceal his true activities.

14. The superficial brilliance of his poetry, its enticing rhythms, its arresting images, should not lead us to overvalue it, as many allegedly bright young critics have done. Basically, it is unhealthy and corrupt. Like an overripe mackerel in the moonlight, it shines—and stinks.

15. "He that is not with me is against me." Thus spoke Jesus Christ (*Luke* xi:23). No phrase could better describe the present situation. Every man, every woman who fails to join the crusade

against re-zoning this residential area for light industry is, whether he will admit it or not, an unpaid agent of the powerful forces that are out to ruin our suburb for the sake of further enriching their already overflowing private coffers.

EXERCISE 15

Merely by being a little dishonest, anyone could use the following quotations to "prove" that the author of this book made certain untrue or half-true assertions or held certain views which, in fact, are not his own opinions. Look up each quotation in its original context and show precisely how the excerpt given below oversimplifies or misrepresents the author's actual meaning, or attributes to him opinions that may not be his at all.

1. "The Democratic party is riddled with second-generation New Dealers and radicals." (page 21)
2. "Again, what is labor? A clique of racketeering union bosses, with criminal convictions in their past and no doubt in their future." (page 26)
3. "The G.O.P. still lives in the horse-and-buggy days, even though it rides around in Cadillacs." (page 27)
4. "The use of technical language . . . is not only inappropriate but also inefficient and . . . dishonest." (page 85)
5. "The cliché is an admirable device; for have we not said that it saves time and effort, and therefore promotes efficiency?" (page 96)
6. "The contents of a frozen-food locker may be depended upon to be both cold and hard." (page 114)
7. "A writer's willingness to concede the possibility of exceptions . . . suggests that he is a careful, sober, scientific-minded person." (page 116)
8. "To be sound, a generalization must be based upon a sufficiently large number of pertinent instances." (page 116)
9. "The *New York Times,* which is owned by Jews, slants its news reports so as to put the Jewish viewpoint in the most favorable light." (page 128)
10. "Cigarette smoking causes cancer of the lung." (page 130)

EXERCISE 16

Select two or three current news stories of political significance (for example, a foreign-policy issue or a controversial national issue) and compare the treatment they have received, or are receiving, in several newspapers, among them a local paper; a paper of the stature of the *New York Times,* the *St. Louis Post-Dispatch,* or the *Christian Science Monitor;* a strongly Republican paper; and an equally strong Democratic one. In what ways, if any, are the various accounts "slanted"? How do they differ in selection and emphasis of details? What reasons can you suggest for these differences? Compare the treatment of the same stories in *Time* or *Newsweek.* Do these news magazines give any broader perspective on the events and the personalities involved? Does their treatment reflect editorial bias or the policy of dramatizing news? How close to the actual "truth" of the matter do you think such a study has brought you?

Objectivity and Subjectivity

When we distinguished between the various kinds of general statements, we noted that there are some statements of universal application which can be verified by our senses—by observation or experimentation, or both. Other sweeping assertions cannot be verified by this means. Even though a substantial body of evidence may appear to support such "truths," that evidence often is capable of different interpretations, depending on who does the interpreting. One man will believe a certain "truth" because his personal background, his tastes and temperament—everything that makes him an individual distinct from other men—incline him to do so. Another man will reject that same assumption because he has a different background, different tastes and a different temperament. In assessing the validity of any judgment, therefore, it is essential that we always be aware of the way in which individual differences affect the understanding and interpreting of human experience.

All our experience, all our knowledge of the world, is made up of two sorts, objective and subjective. Objective data are data which everyone will agree upon: Columbus made a voyage to America in 1492, giraffes are found in Africa, this book has certain dimensions. Subjective data are data which depend upon one's personal feelings or opinions: General Eisenhower was the greatest military man that the Second World War produced, Roquefort cheese is repellent, Anne's new hairdo is much less attractive than her old one.

For the first group, one can adduce "proof" that will be acceptable to all reasonable persons. We have not only Columbus' own journal of his voyage to America in a year that is designated by common agreement as 1492 A.D., but also much independent supporting evidence; although four and a half centuries have passed, we can be very sure that Columbus did make the voyage, just as the historical documents say he did. We know that giraffes are found in Africa because many trustworthy explorers have brought them back from there. We know that this book has certain dimensions because a hundred people can measure it with an accurately calibrated ruler (a universally agreed-upon standard of measurement) and give the same answer.

But there can be no such agreement concerning the second group of assertions. Many people may agree that General Eisenhower was the greatest military leader in the Second World War, but many others will violently disagree; in the nature of things there can be no agreement, because, in the first place, we have not defined what we mean by "greatest," and, in the second place, even if we could arrive at a universally acceptable set of standards for "greatness," not everyone would concede that Eisenhower most adequately fulfilled those requirements. Roquefort cheese may be repellent to some of us, but to others it may be irresistibly delicious; it is a matter, as we say, of "personal taste." Anne's new hairdo may be less attractive to half of our number, but to the other half, and probably to Anne herself, it is a great improvement over the old one. Who can say which party is right? Such matters can never be decided one way or the other.

Just as there is no sharp distinguishing line between denotation and connotation, so there is no plain division between the realm of the objective and the realm of the subjective. What is the color of the walls of a classroom? Some may call it buff, some cream, some eggshell, some "an off shade of white," some yellowish; there is no community of opinion because our common names for colors are based upon more or less personal standards. Yet a pigments expert or an optical physicist could say authoritatively that the walls are painted one specific color, and one color alone. That is because experts have agreed upon a system of designations based on scientific measurements; using a colorimeter, they can easily reach a conclusion which no one who accepts their standards will dispute. In other words, where there is no commonly accepted measure of truth, there can be no objective fact; everything that is judged by the individual, on the basis of his own personal standard, is subjective. But what are subjective data in one aspect, as for example the measurement of a table by eye alone, are turned into objective data when measured by agreed-upon standards and procedures.*

The degree to which we must be aware of the distinction between objectivity and subjectivity depends upon the reason why we are reading at any given moment. If we are reading a newspaper, we want *facts* about the day's happenings; if we are reading a textbook on economics, we want *facts,* or at least well worked-out theories (themselves supported by facts) of economic phenomena; if we are listening to a radio commentator's report on international developments, we want (primarily) the *facts* of what has taken place.

But we may also want someone's interpretation of facts. Thus we may be interested in getting not only a straight news summary from our commentator, but also his own viewpoint, and

* Of course, there are plenty of sensory impressions that cannot be measured. Are there any "agreed-upon standards and procedures" which justify the assertion, in an advertisement, that "Science has proved that freshly ground coffee *tastes better* than coffee ground weeks and months before you buy"?

the opinions of other people he has spoken to. In a lecture on history, a magazine article on contemporary music, or a book on political science, we normally do not wish the lecturer or writer to confine himself to a statement of bare facts; we also want his opinion of what they mean. Was the disaster of Pearl Harbor the result of a conspiracy in high governmental circles to get us into war? Is contemporary music running out of things to say and ways to say them? Do present-day conditions make the electoral college obsolete? In such cases, where both objective and subjective data are involved, we must keep alert to distinguish between the fact and the interpretive comment. Both may be valuable, but for different reasons.

When we read imaginative writing, however, we can relax our vigilance. Most of the great literature of the world is essentially subjective: it is the account, in one form or another, of private, personal experience—of the inner feelings and moods of a highly sensitive man or woman, of the way in which the external world impinges upon that person's senses and spirit. A personal essay, an autobiography, a love lyric, an appreciation of the art of Shakespeare, a bit of nature-writing, a philosophical meditation—each is intensely subjective. The objective facts contained in such pieces, we can easily obtain from encyclopedias; but the impressions and reactions reported in them are unique to that writer. And that, indeed, constitutes one of the chief values of literature: the opportunity we are thus afforded to view life and people through the spirit of someone else, someone peculiarly gifted both in experience and in the ability to recapture and communicate that experience to us.

The Question of Authority

When we are dealing with writing that makes no pretense of objectivity, writing in which the author frankly acknowledges that he is spinning material out of his own substance, there is no question of authority. On matters that go on inside his own self, every man is best qualified to speak. We do not question the truth *so far as the writer alone is concerned* of a statement

made by Charles Lamb, let us say, or Max Beerbohm, or Henry
Thoreau, or E. B. White, or anyone else who reports on himself. There is no means of checking up on him, anyway.

But when we return to objective fact, the case is quite different. Here we are obliged constantly to decide whether or not
to believe what we hear or read. Who is writing or speaking?
Does he know what he is talking about? Are his opinions based
upon study and observation and experience, or have they been
formed hastily and carelessly? Is he in a position to know more
about the subject than we do? Is he shrewder, more sensitive,
more analytical than the majority of people, so that his personal
judgments carry more than ordinary weight? Why is he saying
what he does: because he sincerely believes it, or because he has
some ulterior motive? These are a few of the questions that
should constantly hover in your head when you read, for they
will help you pierce to the basic truth or falseness of any piece
of writing.

It is a mistake to assume that only men who are qualified to
speak with authority on a certain subject have access to the
public eye and ear. Actually, the greater part of what we hear
and read on a given topic comes from persons who have no
special right to make pronouncements on it but who, for one
reason or another, assume the privilege just the same. Members
of the House of Representatives and the Senate are constantly
expressing their views on every topic of current discussion in
Washington. Sometimes they must be listened to with attention
and respect, because they may have made a special study of their
subject and may actually know much more about it than most
people. But on the other hand they may know nothing at all
about the issue they are pronouncing upon, apart from what
they read in the newspapers or in pressure-group publicity
handouts, or hear by word of mouth from their colleagues. Part
of our responsibility as citizens is to follow the activities of
congressmen and government officials, so that we may know
whose utterances should normally be discounted, as based upon
nothing but casual opinion, or prejudice, or political strategy.

"Says who?" is an invaluable watchword. Who tells us about a new scientific discovery? If it is an ordinary newspaper reporter, covering a meeting of scientists, not understanding a tithe of what he hears and yet obliged to return to his office with an "interesting" story, what he writes is scarcely worth reading except for amusement; certainly it can never be taken seriously as a piece of scientific information. But if it is a man like W. L. Laurence of the *New York Times,* who specializes in science, reads the scientific journals and knows leading scientists, his report should be read at least with respect. And if it is a professional scientist who has been personally involved in the scientific experimentation of which he writes, we should give him our full attention. He knows what he is talking about.

In every field of information and opinion there are charlatans as well as honest, reliable writers. It always pays to find out which writers belong to which category. Obviously the most reliable authorities on any subject are those who specialize in it and therefore know the most about it: professional historians, literary scholars, pathologists, geneticists, physical chemists, economists, musicologists. Human capability being a variable quality, there are many shades of competence even among the experts, Historian A being more dependable than Historian B, and so forth. More than a few writers whom laymen look up to as authorities in their respective fields are known to fellow-specialists as careless and uncritical in their use of materials and overhasty in jumping to conclusions.

Unfortunately, many genuine experts have neither the ability nor the inclination to write for the layman. To cull the most essential information from their scholarly treatises and put it into a form that is agreeable to the layman, there exists the so-called "popularizer," whose indispensable qualification is that he can write simply and interestingly about complex matters. There are good popularizers and bad popularizers, and it is often useful to know which are which, because reading an article by the bad kind is a waste of time. Good popularizers have sufficient knowledge of the subject about which they are

writing and sufficient scholarly sense to be able to report accurately to their audience. They may simplify their material—
indeed, they have to do so; but in simplifying they guard so far
as they can against distortion or misinformation. Bad popularizers, on the other hand, fail to understand their subject in
the first place, but they nevertheless proceed to give their readers a badly twisted account of it, filled with misstatements,
exaggerations, and fancies.

"Does the man know what he is talking about?" is, then, a
question that must remain uppermost in our minds as we read
anything that purports to give information or to offer an opinion. Again and again we must conclude that the writer knows
no more about his subject than do we, who also read the newspapers, and that therefore his data and opinions may be ignored
without loss.

"What is his motive in saying what he does?" is a second,
equally important question. In many cases the motive is easily
apparent: the writer of a magazine article on the outlook for
interplanetary travel, for example, probably wants to make
some money. But what of those numerous articles and books on
more controversial subjects, such as politics, economics, religion, social affairs, education? Although the superficial reader
may seldom be aware of it, nearly all of them are written from
a particular viewpoint. Few are impartial or disinterested; the
great majority are biased, if only because the subjects with
which they deal can scarcely be discussed at all without taking
sides.

Take for example the columnists who discuss national affairs. They usually develop their discussions from a hard kernel
of indisputable fact: the President has actually made this statement, Congress has actually taken that stand on a current issue.
But their interpretations of these facts differ tremendously, for
two reasons. One is that every columnist has a bias for or against
certain persons, parties, and principles. Westbrook Pegler, Walter Lippmann, James Reston, Arthur Krock, Marquis Childs,
the Alsop brothers, David Lawrence, and George Sokolsky rep-

resent different shades of opinion, and when we read their columns we must remember that each of them construes an event or situation in terms of what he personally judges to be right and wrong. Their comments are largely subjective, even though, with the notable exception of Mr. Lippmann's articles, the qualifying "I think" or "I believe" or "it seems to me" is nearly always missing.

Some columnists have a high sense of public responsibility; they write with no other thought than to inform their readers of the significance of events *as they see it*. They are aware, of course, of their prejudices, but such prejudices are the result of honest study and analysis. Every man, after all, must take his stand somewhere. But other columnists are sensation-mongers. Their only aim is to gain attention, and they achieve it by digging up scandal (an occupation which, it is true, sometimes serves a useful end), by reporting rumors (which they often fail to identify as such), and by making confident "predictions" (which can seldom stand the scrutiny of hindsight). At their best, political commentators are the most intelligent means by which the public can be informed of what the government is doing and should do; at their worst, they spread vicious mis-information and groundless rumor, and encourage people to political action based upon irrational bias rather than upon intelligent grasp of issues.

Just as it is necessary to know what allegiance a so-called "Washington observer" holds before we can evaluate what he says, so is it necessary in every discussion of controversial matters to discover the bias of the writer, particularly, if possible, his connection with a party or organization. When we know that the author of a book on recent American foreign policy was for many years a high official in the Department of State, we must remember that his analysis of our foreign policy is written from a certain point of view. It may be a thoroughly able and honest book, but it is still colored by a desire to justify the author's own position. Thus it cannot be regarded as a wholly dispassionate analysis. Similarly, when we know that a new book on the shortcomings of American education is from the pen of a fervent believer in the "Great Books" scheme, we must make allowance for a definite bias in his advice as to what should constitute a truly liberal education. A disciple of John Dewey probably would discover a great many flaws in the assumptions and the arguments.

In this chapter we may seem occasionally to have wandered rather far from the principal theme of the book, which is the use of language as such; but surely it has become obvious how intimately and inextricably language and logic are associated. A word remains to be said as to how the essential weakness of many ideas can be concealed from the unwary by plausible language.

The more confident the manner of a writer or speaker is, the more necessary it is to inquire what makes him so confident. His forthright assertion that "every right-thinking man will agree . . ." or "there can be no question that . . ." or "it has been proved time and again that . . ." may or may not be justified; certainly it should not be accepted on his mere say-so. Dogmatism—which is what this fault really amounts to—has no place in genuinely intelligent discussion. The dogmatic writer or speaker is using devices of style to forestall doubt. "This man knows what he's talking about!" . . . Does he?

Rhetorical questions also serve to hypnotize the uncritical. "Has this party not served the state faithfully for twelve critical years? Has it not increased the state's industrial capacity? Has it not completed a highway system that is the envy of the nation? Has it not set up a fine system of social benefits for the unfortunate and helpless? Can the people of this state therefore *afford* not to return this party for another four years?" Rhetorical questions always take the answer for granted: disagreement is not provided for. But it should be. The expected answers are not necessarily the right ones. And in any event, the questions have been carefully chosen for the purpose. The opposition might with equal propriety ask another set relating to the past twelve years of state government—and get very different answers.

The use of proverbs, axioms, and other "folk truths" also has its narcotic effect upon the critical intelligence. Because we have lived so long with such generalizations, few of which we have ever bothered to examine, and because they came to us from sources whose authority and wisdom we revere—Scripture or parents or teacher—we accept them on sight. "To the victor belong the spoils"—"the gods help them that help themselves"—"a soft answer turneth away wrath"—these are observations which may contain much truth, springing as they do from the long experience of the race. But they can never be used to "prove" anything. A man defending a certain governmental policy of expediency says succinctly that "the end justifies the means"; but does it *in this case?* Might not the means that are employed result in more harm than failure to achieve the end? Merely because we have grown up accustomed to believing such a thing, are we obliged therefore to accept it as justification for a deed which, if we were to come right down to it, could not be justified on any logical or moral grounds? Familiar gems of popular wisdom, then, have only limited usefulness in intelligent discussion. Their truth may never be taken on faith.

EXERCISE 17

1. Here are four selections which combine subjective and objective materials in various proportions. Analyze each one. In the case of every bit of objective data, decide how the writer's statement can be verified to the satisfaction of any reasonable person; in the case of subjective data, decide to what degree each item is purely a matter of private opinion or impression or is, on the other hand, an opinion or impression likely to be shared by many people though not capable of objective proof.

(a) Near the centre of the State of New York lies an extensive district of country, whose surface is a succession of hills and dales, or, to speak with greater deference to geographical definitions, of mountains and valleys. It is among these hills that the Delaware takes its rise; and flowing from the limpid lakes and thousand springs of this region, the numerous sources of the Susquehanna meander through the valleys, until, uniting their streams, they form one of the proudest rivers of the United States. The mountains are generally arable to the tops, although instances are not wanting where the sides are jutted with rocks, that aid greatly in giving to the country that romantic and picturesque character which it so eminently possesses. The vales are narrow, rich, and cultivated; with a stream uniformly winding through each. Beautiful and thriving villages are found interspersed along the margins of the small lakes, or situated at those points of the streams which are favorable to manufacturing; and neat and comfortable farms, with every indication of wealth about them, are scattered profusely through the vales, and even to the mountain tops. Roads diverge in every direction, from the even and graceful bottoms of the valleys, to the most rugged and intricate passes of the hills.

(b)
> Riches I hold in light esteem,
>   And Love I laugh to scorn;
> And lust of fame was but a dream,
>   That vanished with the morn:
>
> And if I pray, the only prayer
>   That moves my lips for me
> Is, "Leave the heart that now I bear,
>   And give me liberty!"
>
> Yes, as my swift days near their goal,
>   'Tis all that I implore;—
> In life and death a chainless soul,
>   With courage to endure.

(c) If the most fashionable parts of the capital could be placed before us such as they then were [i.e., in 1685], we should be disgusted by their squalid appearance, and poisoned by their noisome atmosphere. In Covent Garden a filthy and noisy market was held close to the dwellings of the great. Fruit women screamed, carters fought, cabbage stalks and rotten apples accumulated in heaps at the thresholds of the Countess of Berkshire and of the Bishop of Durham.

The centre of Lincoln's Inn Fields was an open space where the rabble congregated every evening, within a few yards of

Cardigan House and Winchester House, to hear mountebanks harangue, to see bears dance, and to set dogs at oxen. Rubbish was shot in every part of the area. Horses were exercised there. The beggars were as noisy and importunate as in the worst governed cities of the Continent. A Lincoln's Inn mumper was a proverb. The whole fraternity knew the arms and liveries of every charitably disposed grandee in the neighborhood, and, as soon as his lordship's coach and six appeared, came hopping and crawling in crowds to persecute him. These disorders lasted, in spite of many accidents, and of some legal proceedings, till, in the reign of George the Second, Sir Joseph Jekyll, Master of the Rolls, was knocked down and nearly killed in the middle of the square. Then at length palisades were set up, and a pleasant garden laid out.

(d) Throughout his brief life—he was born in Asheville, N. C., in 1900, and died in 1938—Thomas Wolfe, as a man, made legend, and as a novelist, made literature. Physically a giant, he had a gigantic appetite for all the experiences, sensory, intellectual, emotional, that life affords. He lived and wrote in superlatives. When he was a student at Harvard, he tried literally to read through the whole vast library, consisting of millions of volumes. People who knew him then recall that he was in the practice of moving down the long aisles of the stacks, grabbing one book after another from the shelves and devouring its contents as if he were a starving man suddenly let loose in an immense storehouse of food. He wrote with the same abandon, turning out incredible quantities of manuscript, filling whole packing cases with the product of his frenzied pen. It took a gifted and superhumanly patient publisher's editor, Maxwell Perkins of Scribner's, to put this chaos into some sort of order. From it he quarried two novels (*Look Homeward, Angel*, 1929; *Of Time and the River*, 1935) which took the critical world by storm. Though overvalued at first, they still are well worth reading and not merely as monuments to a prolific but undisciplined talent.

2. Examine in the same way the selections quoted in Chapter One, especially the advertisements; or analyze a group of advertisements found in current magazines.

EXERCISE 18

From the current *Reader's Digest,* select five or six articles which seem to you to call for specialized knowledge of certain topics—aviation, science, diplomacy, etc. Then, using reliable reference works, such as *Who's Who in America, American Men of Science,* and *Living Authors,* try to determine how well qualified was the author of each article.

Try the same experiment with the current issue of *Harper's.*

EXERCISE 19

The following persons are well known as "popularizers" in various fields. Try to find out from an expert in each field—the most learned professor you know, for example—how each popularizer is regarded by the experts, and why.

Rachel Carson (marine biology), Frances Winwar (literary biography), Hendrik Willem Van Loon (history and art), John Gunther (contemporary history and world affairs), Stuart Chase (economics), Paul DeKruif (bacteriology and medicine), Marchette Chute (literary biography), Lewis Browne (comparative religions), Stewart Holbrook (American history), Will Durant (history and philosophy).

EXERCISE 20

1. In recent years the verb *report* and the noun *reporter* have acquired great popularity in communication media. A president or other government official will label his radio-television speech "A Report to the Nation." A news commentator will introduce himself as "Bill Jones reporting." A new book by a journalist will be entitled *Report from Murmansk, Report on the Senegambians,* or whatever. A magazine concerned primarily with political affairs is called *The Reporter.* What are the connotations of *report* that account for its vogue?

2. Among the oracles whose pronouncements are customarily given wide publicity are the so-called "elder statesmen." What does the phrase imply? Who are the "elder statesmen" of the present moment? Does their "counsel" (how does it differ from "opinion"?) have special authority?

3. There are over 500 members in the two houses of Congress. Of these, only a small fraction are known, even by name, to most Americans. Who are the best-known senators and representatives, and for what reasons do these few receive the bulk of publicity? How can you account for the fact that every time an important event occurs in Washington or on the international scene, and the newspapers seek "congressional reaction," the same few men are quoted? Are their opinions necessarily the most authoritative or representative?

4. In John Gunther's best-seller, *Inside U.S.A.*, published in 1947, occurred this sentence: "Such a fracas over academic freedom as occurred in the University of Texas would be inconceivable in California; its university is by most standards one of the six or eight best in the country; it has no regent trouble." Note the dogmatism of Gunther's statement; then look up two or three of the articles, with "loyalty oath" in the title, listed under "California. University" in the *Reader's Guide to Periodical Literature* for 1949-51. How accurate a prophet was Mr. Gunther? Can you think of any other instances of a confident public statement by a well-regarded writer being belied by events?

5. In Exercise 3 (page 129) you were asked to consult Bergen Evans' *The Natural History of Nonsense* for information on various "folk beliefs." Mr. Evans is a professor of English and a veteran master of ceremonies on television quiz programs, not a scientist. His book, designed for laymen, includes footnotes giving "authority" for his statements; thus it has at least the appearance of being a reliable study. How can you determine whether or not it is?

EXERCISE 21

How much attention should be paid to the pronouncements of the following writers on the stated subjects? Why?

1. A sports expert, writing in the September 14 issue of a maga-

zine, on what will be "the nation's ten top teams" in the coming football season.

2. A probation officer with thirty years' experience, on the causes of juvenile delinquency.

3. A retired admiral, on the proper course the Department of State should follow in dealing with a current international problem.

4. The English physician William Harvey (1578-1657), on the circulation of the blood.

5. A good-looking New York "socialite," on the cold cream that is best for your hands.

6. The president of the National Association of Manufacturers, on a proposed law to curb union activity in politics.

7. The president of the United Automobile Workers, on the same subject.

8. Your family doctor, on the type of vitamin tablet you should take to regain your strength after an illness.

9. A Hollywood columnist, on the soundness of the federal government's financial policies.

10. The same writer, on the inside reasons why the much-publicized marriage of two popular stars went on the rocks after a year.

11. A young mother, in a short article in a happy-parenthood magazine, on ways of keeping children entertained during a rainy spell.

12. The author of the standard biography of Robert Browning, reviewing a newly published book on the life of Browning.

13. Jean Henri Fabre (1823-1915), French entomologist, on the social behavior of ants.

14. A Harvard economist, on the long-range prospects of a uranium-mine stock you are thinking of buying.

15. Three friends of yours, on whether or not you should elect a certain course next year.

EXERCISE 22

In the above discussion (page 171) a number of popular American political commentators were named. What can be said of the bias of each one? Are some more independent than others? Give a detailed report on the "line" taken by each columnist syndicated in the local newspapers.

CHAPTER FOUR

Sentences and Paragraphs

WE HAVE SEEN how it is possible to "read between the lines" by analyzing the implications of a writer's choice of words and examining his habits of thought. We turn now to still another way of discovering more than appears on the surface of any example of communication: the analysis of form.

The sentence is a basic unit of communication. Individual words, to be sure, have meanings in and of themselves: nouns stand for persons, places, objects, ideas; verbs stand for actions or states of being; and so on. But only a sentence can express the relationship between the various ideas represented by the individual words. Babies begin by uttering single words. Often they succeed in communicating important ideas to their parents, but that is only because the parents are able to infer from single words the sentences that the baby is as yet unable to put together. Later the child begins to speak simple sentences; and when he does, we know that he has reached the stage where he understands elementary relationships between ideas. As he progresses toward adulthood, his sentences become more and more complex: a sign that he is gradually extending his command of ideas to include more complicated relationships. To his college instructor, his ability to write good sentences is at least as valuable a measure of his ability to think as is a whole battery of intelligence tests. The student who knows how to use the devices of grammar and rhetoric to clarify and sharpen his meaning, and for whom such things as subordination hold no terrors, cannot fail to impress his teacher with his ability to put ideas together and to discriminate between the essential and the auxiliary parts of what he has to say.

Therefore, the length and structure of sentences, as well as of paragraphs (the unit of composition next in size), can sometimes be significant clues to the mental ability of the writer or speaker. They may also throw light on his sincerity of purpose and upon his skill in judging the capabilities and expectations of his audience. In this chapter, also, we shall examine the closely connected subject of sentence-rhythm. In the end we shall have put another string to the bow by which we can pierce to the heart of meaning.

At the outset, it must be emphasized that throughout this chapter no sweeping generalizations are intended. If, sometimes, our remarks about the length, arrangement, and rhythm of sentences and paragraphs seem unwarrantedly dogmatic, it is only because space does not allow our going into the many *ifs* and *buts* that undoubtedly will occur to you. Our sole purpose is to suggest some things that are worth looking out for in your reading—not, in any sense, to lay down inflexible rules.

(At this point, if you have any doubt at all as to what is meant by "subordination," look up the subject in your handbook of composition and study it thoroughly. The following discussion assumes a sound elementary knowledge of the principles of subordination and sentence construction from the writer's viewpoint.)

Sentence Length

Sentence length depends, for one thing, on the complexity of the idea to be expressed. A simple, unqualified statement requires only a very short sentence; a statement of an idea that is more subtle, or set forth in some detail, or hedged about with modifications and restrictions, requires a longer sentence. In our time, the average length of sentences written for a wide middle-class audience—say, the audience to whom the *Reader's Digest, Newsweek,* or a best-selling novel is addressed—is somewhere between twenty and thirty words. This means, in effect, that the average sentence is longer and more complex than that of a fourth grader ("George Washington was born in 1732. His father was a wealthy plantation owner. The story about the cherry tree is not true.") but that it is shorter and less intricate than that of a writer addressing himself to an audience of superior education and intelligence ("Whatever the event may be, the difficult but essential task which confronts all democratic societies today may be formulated as follows: how in practice to curtail the freedom of the individual in economic enterprise sufficiently to effect that equality of opportunity and of possessions without which democracy is an empty form, and at the same time to preserve that measure of individual freedom in intellectual and political life without which it cannot exist").

Fashions in sentence-length change. Although there never has been a time when very long or very short sentences were overwhelmingly predominant in literary practice, it is true that past generations were more hospitable to the long sentence than we are. Whenever we read in older books—Shakespeare or Milton or Boswell or Scott or Melville—we are struck by their authors' frequent use of what seem to us, with our present-day standards, to be extremely long sentences. Milton's poems contain sentences running to thirty or more lines of verse, and prose writers sometimes produced sentences two or three hundred words long. They are often fine sentences, too; though their thought is complex, and they can hardly be skimmed through, they are themselves works of art. For a single example, look at this summary-sentence from Sidney's *Defence of Poesy,* which is here arranged so as to make its component parts more easily discernible:

Since, then, poetry is of all human learnings the most ancient, and
of most fatherly antiquity, as from whence other learnings have
taken their beginnings;

since it is so universal that no learned nation doth despise it, nor
barbarous nation is without it;

since both Roman and Greek gave such divine names unto it, the
one of prophesying, the other of making, and that indeed that
name of making is fit for him, considering that where all other
arts retain themselves within their subject, and receive, as it
were, their being from it, the poet only, only bringeth his own
stuff, and doth not learn a conceit out of a matter, but maketh
matter for a conceit;

since neither his description nor end containeth any evil, the thing
described cannot be evil;

since his effects be so good as to teach goodness, and delight the
learners of it;

since therein (namely in moral doctrine, the chief of all knowledges)
he doth not only far pass the historian, but, for instructing, is
well nigh comparable to the philosopher, for moving, leaveth
him behind him;

since the Holy Scripture (wherein there is no uncleanness) hath
whole parts in it poetical, and that even our Saviour Jesus
Christ vouchsafed to use the flowers of it;

since all his kinds are not only in their united forms but in their
severed dissections fully commendable;

I think, and think I think rightly, the laurel crown appointed for
triumphant captains doth worthily, of all other learnings,
honour the poet's triumph.

That, you will agree, is a *long* sentence. But the mere length of
sentences sometimes found in older writing should never dis-
courage you. Because you are not used to them, you will often
have to shift into low gear when reading them. Taking them
slowly, and analyzing them into their components, you will find
that they are really not as formidable as they look on the printed
page (when the eye is searching desperately for a period), and,
in addition, that in the hands of a master-writer they have an
unmistakable architectural beauty, massive and yet graceful.

In the past century or so, the tendency in writing that is

specifically designed for a large audience has been toward shorter, easier-to-grasp-at-one-glance sentences. The spread of literacy among the masses of people (America was considerably ahead of England in this respect), the development of cheap books, magazines, and newspapers to satisfy the consequent demand for "something easy and interesting to read," and the increase in the tempo of living all combined to make the shorter sentence desirable and indeed necessary. Since as a rule the millions who formed a popular market for reading matter had had only a few years of schooling, everything they read had to be in simple English, the vocabulary confined to everyday words and the sentences brief and uncomplicated. In time, this tendency toward simple expression spread from large-circulation magazines and newspapers into many fields of writing, so that nowadays books and periodicals designed for a relatively small, well-educated audience also are written in shorter sentences. Finally, the pace of living has become so much faster that the man who runs while he reads has become virtually the symbol of modern civilization; and the long sentence cannot be read and comprehended by those who are in a hurry. Reading matter must be fitted to the needs of those who manage to read only in the odd moments of their lives, between business and social duties, household chores, and television programs. Thus the existence of an audience ill-equipped to grasp the complexities of longer sentences, and, in the face of so many other claims upon time, the absence of leisure and inclination to do so, virtually requires that sentences be fairly short.

Now, what can sometimes be inferred from the length of the sentence a writer uses? When we find a modern writer employing sentences whose *average* (i.e., mean) length is about "normal," there is nothing especially significant to infer concerning him or his motives. He is simply following the custom of the day. (The length of his individual sentences may, of course, vary widely.) But when present-day writers deviate habitually from the norm, we may profitably ask why.

In the first place, we have already noted that the extremely brief, uncomplicated sentence is characteristic of the child. It is also characteristic of the mind which remains immature beyond the years of physical immaturity. Suppose, for example, a grown woman wrote in a personal letter:

Henry came to see us today. He brought his new bride with him. We were glad to see them. We hadn't seen Henry for at least a year. Of course we had been wondering what sort of girl he was going to marry. She is rather tall. She has light hair and looks much younger than he is. She seemed a little shy. I suppose that will wear off in time. She probably sensed she was being looked over. They stayed only an hour. Henry seems very much wrapped up in her.

There writes someone who must handle her thoughts one at a time, in separate and distinct units, without any regard for their relationship one to another or for their relative importance. A mature mind would have instinctively seen that the information to be conveyed could be grouped conveniently about two or three main ideas, to which the remaining details should be attached as explanatory pendants:

Henry and his new bride spent an hour with us today. We were glad to see them, because we had not seen Henry for at least a year and of course we had been wondering what sort of girl he was going to marry. She is a light-haired girl, rather tall and seemingly much younger than he is. We thought she was a little shy, but she probably sensed that she was being looked over; I suppose her shyness will wear off in time. Henry seems very much wrapped up in her.

Secondly, because there is no room in a very short sentence for anything but one unelaborated thought, it follows that an idea set forth in such a sentence will receive a degree of emphasis impossible if some of the reader's attention is claimed by details. The writer or speaker who wishes to persuade an audience of average or less-than-average education knows that he will succeed best when the argument is couched in brief, almost staccato sentences.

Our city is on the threshold of a great era. Of this we can be sure. But in order to fulfill the promise of the future, we must be willing to work—and to spend. We need a larger police force for public protection. We need a modernized fire department. We need an enlarged library. We need to increase the pay-scale of teachers in the public schools. We need to improve our water supply. For all these needs there is but one solution. We must see that the bond issue is approved by the voters at the November election.

By the use of such brief sentences the successive ideas are hammered into one's consciousness, separately and emphatically. The same material could easily have been incorporated into three sentences of fairly "normal" length; but much of their force would have been lost.

From the point of view of the reader, the danger in a writer's use of brief, sharp sentences is that it can make the ideas appear much more important and unqualified than they really are. Anyone can write in short sentences, but not everyone has something to say that deserves the prominence and emphasis of short sentences. In most readers' minds, the short sentence carries an unmistakable connotation of wisdom, because down through the ages it has acted as the setting for all the familiar gems of "truth"—"people who make no noise are dangerous"—"he that spareth his rod hateth his son"—"the reward of a thing well done, is to have done it." And so when a writer wishes to convince his audience of the deep truth of his ideas, he takes care to couch them in the language which people habitually associate with proverbs and axioms and the sayings of philosophers.

Our nation has always taken the middle road. Its motto is, Nothing to excess. On the one hand, it spurns the advice of the Cassandras that change means disaster. On the other hand, it rejects the proposals of those who would create Utopia overnight. Nothing is more profoundly characteristic of Americans than their reverence for the golden mean. It follows, then, that progressivism is the true American philosophy. Neither conservative nor radical, it believes in gradual, well-considered, above all *sound* evolution.

In essence, what we have here is simply another manifestation of the "transfer" device—the borrowing of prestige. Here the prestige is obtained, not so much from the words themselves, with whatever affective connotations they may have, as from the manner of the sentences—short, dignified, reminiscent of the style of popular philosophers. But the result is the same. The questionings of the mind tend to be stilled, and the reader is swayed by devices of rhetoric rather than by reason.

Finally, the short sentence is used for special dramatic effects, such as suspense and excitement. Often such use is perfectly legitimate and honest. What would a crime thriller be like without the terse, clipped sentences that portend a crisis or describe a tense episode? The very absence of elaboration, the concentration upon a few bare, simple facts, add a peculiar sense of horror to the narrative. But often the short sentence is used to work up dramatic effects that are not justified by the facts involved. Sometimes, indeed, the shortest possible sentence is itself too long, and the writer falls back on single phrases. This produces what may be called the slam-bang-zowie style, as in the following excerpt from a self-help book on "how to write":

Sweat wins. Never rely on inspiration. Never put your trust in bright ideas. Never sink into deep thought, hoping that at the bottom of the well you'll find treasure.

Sit at your desk. Take up pen or pencil—better yet, start thumping at the typewriter keys. Set yourself a task. Go at it. This morning. This afternoon. Tomorrow morning. Tomorrow afternoon. And so on, forever and ever, amen.

Warming up will carry you further than any other single procedure. Writing is like a Marathon. No. It is a Marathon. Over hill and dale you go. Under trees, over brooks, on and on until you pant and puff, drip and shine. It's a rough game, this business of writing.

Sweat wins. Drip, drip, drip. Win, win, win. It's as simple as that. It's as hard as that.*

The book from which those paragraphs are quoted obviously was not written for the same people for whom *Preface to Critical Reading* is intended. Try to describe the sort of person

* From Walter B. Pitkin's *The Art of Useful Writing*. By permission of the McGraw-Hill Book Company, Inc., publishers.

who would be influenced by such writing; and then put the same advice (which is not necessarily endorsed by the present author) into a style more suited to your own tastes.

Little need be said here of extremely long sentences. We have already noted that their presence should never deter you from reading older literature. In modern writing for a general audience, they are relatively infrequent; if they occur in an author's manuscript, usually they are broken up by his editor, before the manuscript goes to the printer. They do, however, occur in some kinds of specialized writing, such as those discussed in Chapter Two; in legal writing, where they can sometimes be defended, sometimes not; and in governmental correspondence, records, and other documents. A satirical commentary on sprawling, formless sentences that run on and on—as well as upon the kind of writing we discussed on pages 76-89—is found in the following excerpt from a government publication:

The present movement toward simplification of language and directness of statement in government writing and the elimination of jargon and unnecessary wordiness as well as the use of short, direct statements instead of long sentences which are difficult to understand because the reader is apt to get lost before he arrives, if he ever does, at the meaning intended by the writer, is a valuable attempt to achieve economy and intelligibility, for many pamphlets, instruction sheets, ordinary memoranda and assorted missives circulated through the War Department fail of their primary purpose through befogging their contents by use of pseudo-official phraseology which only the initiated can hope to understand and of which even they cannot be certain without reference either to the key works needed for translating them or to their own garbled and confused memories of dealing, usually without much success and always after a long period of time and travail, with similar kinds of wording in similar situations, so, though don't be too hopeful, for someone with unusual gifts and energy in applying them will manage triumphantly to misunderstand you no matter what you say or how you say it, try saying what you have to say as simply and as briefly as you can, and then after you've said it, stop saying it and don't say it any more.

EXERCISE 1

1. Since this book is intended for readers with at least an "average" education (high school graduates), its sentences should come fairly close to the "norm" described on page 182. To check this, count the words in a sufficient number of sentences to permit a sound generalization and then find the arithmetical mean. If the average sentence turns out to be longer than you expected, can you attribute it to any special intention on the part of the author? (At the same time, in anticipation of later pages in which the topic of paragraph-length is discussed, determine the average number of sentences contained in a paragraph of this book.)

2. In the same manner, study the sentences and paragraphs in a copy of each of the following: *Life,* the *Reader's Digest,* the *Atlantic Monthly, Foreign Affairs,* a pulp magazine of the true-romance, western, or detective variety, a textbook used in some other course you are taking, and a recently published book written for a fairly wide audience of intelligent adults. Are there any significant differences in sentence- and paragraph-length? How can you account for them?

EXERCISE 2

The following sentences were written between 1800 and 1850. What changes would have to be made if they were to be printed in a contemporary magazine? Try your hand at rewriting each of them in modern prose.

1. Her mighty lakes, like oceans of liquid silver; her mountains, with their bright aerial tints; her valleys, teeming with wild fertility; her tremendous cataracts, thundering in their solitudes; her boundless plains, waving with spontaneous verdure; her broad deep rivers, rolling in solemn silence to the ocean; her trackless forests, where vegetation puts forth all its magnificence; her skies, kindling with the magic of summer clouds and glorious sunshine;—no, never need an American look beyond his own country for the sublime and beautiful of natural scenery.

2. I made a study of the ancient and indispensable art of bread-making, consulting such authorities as offered, going back to the primitive days and first invention of the unleavened kind, when from the wildness of nuts and meats men first reached the mildness and refinement of this diet, and travelling gradually down in my studies through that accidental souring of the dough which, it is supposed, taught the leavening process, and through the various fermentations thereafter, till I came to "good, sweet, wholesome bread," the staff of life.

3. If the reader has ever been present in a vast metropolis on the day when some great national idol was carried in funeral pomp to his grave, and, chancing to walk near the course through which it passed, has felt powerfully, in the silence and desertion of the streets, and in the stagnation of ordinary business, the deep interest which at that moment was possessing the heart of man—if all at once he should hear the death-like stillness broken up by the sound of wheels rattling away from the scene, and making known that the transitory vision was dissolved, he will be aware that at no moment was his sense of the complete suspension and pause in ordinary human concerns so full and affecting as at that moment when the suspension ceases, and the goings-on of human life are suddenly resumed.

EXERCISE 3

Comment on the appropriateness of the style to the subject-matter and the probable effect the author desired to achieve:

He lighted a match and held it up to the number on the door. It flickered and went out. He cursed under his breath. Somebody was coming down the pavement. A cop? Wait and see. Took his good old time coming, too. As if this was a balmy night in June instead of gusty March. No, not a cop. Just a fellow smoking a cigarette. Wonder if he saw anybody in the shadow of the doorway. Now back to the number. This must be the place. Devil to pay if it isn't. Another match: cup it with the hands. There—first number both two's. Out goes the match. Not many more left. Not much more time, either.

Sentence Arrangement

The precise order in which the various elements of a sentence are arranged determines the emphasis and clarity with which a writer's ideas are communicated to his reader. Why is this so? What happens in the reader's mind as it meets sentences of various types? What clues to the author's competence and intention may be found in his choice of one kind of sentence rather than another?

If we were to examine in slow-motion the process by which a sentence impresses itself upon the mind, we should see first of all that between each sentence there is a definite break in the reading function. The mind, signaled by the full-stop punctuation (period, exclamation point, or question mark), pauses for an instant before proceeding with the next sentence, just as there is a short lapse between sentences in the electric signs that spell out news items and advertisements in large cities. As we read, we are of course completely unaware of this pause, but it occurs nevertheless. In it, our mind is momentarily refreshed and made ready to absorb the next idea. Therefore, since the mind is particularly receptive to the idea contained in the first few words of the next sentence, a writer is well advised to place an important idea in that intial position. The portion of the sentence which follows (i.e., the middle) is a less favorable position for important ideas, because the mind is busy with that first thought, and though it takes in these following ideas, it does not give them the same degree of attention. But then the mind reaches the end of the sentence; the punctuation signals another pause; and what happens? The last words of the sentence are not obscured by anything following, the mind has a chance to echo them; they "sink in."

Thus, of the three main positions in a sentence of normal or greater-than-normal length, the end is the most desirable for the placing of the idea which the writer wishes to impress upon his reader's mind. This is the principle underlying the so-called "periodic" sentence—a sentence which either wholly postpones the most important idea, or else delays its completion, until the very end. The periodic sentence is effective for three reasons: (1) It keeps the reader's mind alert throughout the sentence, waiting for what is to come. (If the reader is satisfied that he has received the main idea at the very outset of the sentence, his mind will relax, even doze, for the remainder of the sentence.) (2) Having thus stimulated the mind to alertness, the technique will make the main idea, when it does finally appear, the more impressive. (3) It enables the mind, in its brief pause between sentences, to register the final words more vividly.

In the light of this discussion of how the mind works when reading a sentence, compare these two sentences:

The girl somehow suggested a Chinese princess, with her jet-black hair, her singularly high cheekbones, her slanting eyes, her hands with their long, tapered fingers.

With her jet-black hair, her singularly high cheekbones, her slanting eyes, her hands with their long, tapered fingers, the girl somehow suggested a Chinese princess.

There is nothing the matter with the first sentence: it covers all the details, systematically and clearly. But if the writer wished above all to impress his reader with the fact that the girl resembled a Chinese princess, he would have done better to keep that fact for the last. In the first sentence, though the Chinese-princess idea is presented to a mind refreshed by its pause between sentences, that general idea is immediately pushed into the background by the details of the girl's appearance, and the item upon which the mind dwells, when it completes its course through the sentence, is the fact that she had long, tapered fingers—which may be the least significant of all the details. The emphasis is corrected in the second version, which presents a series of details that merge in the mind and then are effectively summarized by the core of the sentence—the subject, verb, and object.

The following sentences all follow the same scheme:

With all their faults, and they were many, it is safe to say that such WPA projects as the Federal Theatre and the Federal Writers' Project were the most significant cultural developments of the middle 1930's.

Staring into space, absently twirling the silver keychain attached to his belt, he realized for the first time the ambiguity of his position.

If there is no change in his condition by tomorrow noon, and if, as I hope, I can get a reservation, I shall fly back to Chicago.

Those are instances of the *complete* delaying of the principal idea. (Another instance is the monumental sentence quoted on page 183.) A second common means of maintaining reader-interest throughout the sentence is that of beginning the clause containing the main idea and then postponing its completion by inserting modifiers or other interrupting (but always relevant) material. "A few minutes after noon the police, who had been awaiting the arrival of reinforcements from several other precincts, rushed into the barricaded house." "The nations of the world, because another world war would result in complete and unthinkable annihilation, have no alternative but to find some means of coexisting." There is, however, the danger that such sentences may defeat their purpose if the interruption between subject and predicate is too long. The intervening matter may completely erase the subject of the main clause from one's mind: "A fresh approach to the problem, free of partisan bias, motivated by a realization of the disaster that would result from neglect or unintelligent handling of the complex factors involved, utilizing the information amassed by the experts who have been studying the question for many months—" (at this point the mind suddenly realizes that it has completely forgotten what all these phrases were supposed to modify, and must go back to the beginning) "is needed." And the end, when it comes, is so brief and, in comparison with the important-sounding phrases that preceded it, so flat, that the mind may feel cheated of its labor.

(Now criticize in turn that last sentence. It is a periodic sentence; the two *so's* force the mind to look forward to some completing thought, which comes only in the final clause. Is it effective? Or are there too many interruptions; is the development of the idea too piecemeal? Notice that the two elements *when it comes* and *in comparison . . . preceded it,* break up the sentence into small chunks.)

There are many degrees of periodicity in sentence structure. At the opposite end of the scale is the "loose" sentence, which gives away its secret at the very outset, or else sandwiches it between subordinate ideas. The loose sentence is not grammatically wrong, and good writers use it frequently. To use nothing but periodic sentences, indeed, would be desperately monotonous. But excessive devotion to loose sentences produces writing that is just as monotonous—and it may be added that this is one of the chief weaknesses of undergraduate themes.

The best writers mix sentences of all degrees of periodicity and looseness in their paragraphs, though never forgetting that the most important ideas naturally deserve the most prominent positions. But they also never forget that clumsy use of the loose sentence can spoil the effect they strive for. "The supreme spot of the performance was Miss Anderson's sleep-walking scene, I think." Here the tacking of "I think" onto what had purported to be a positive, forthright statement erases any pretense of authority which the author wished to make. Presumably the reader was disposed to believe him—he seemed sure of himself. And then the cautious "I think"! Or take this sentence: "The coolest, most restful spot on the campus, nestling as it did in the bend of the river, was the area called Seniors' Solace, which boasted also a few worn green benches." Here the logic of the sentence leads steadily forward to "the area called Seniors' Solace"; but then there is a sudden descent into the unimportant, and when the sentence ends, the mind is left contemplating the worn green benches instead of Seniors' Solace. In a word, the inexpert use of loose sentences is very likely to take the edge off any piece of writing.

Which brings us to the matter of climax. If we define a climax as the peak of interest or importance, we can see that any periodic sentence is built with an eye to climax: most important thing (or completion of the main idea) last. One especially effective kind of periodic sentence arranges several ideas in order of increasing importance, so that the one that the author wishes to emphasize above the rest will occur at the end:

Whatever the defects of American universities may be, they disseminate no prejudices; rear no bigots; dig up the buried ashes of no old superstitions; never interpose between the people and their improvement; exclude no man because of his religious opinions; above all, in their whole course of study and instruction, recognize a world, and a broad one too, lying beyond the college walls.

It was good for me to live under sharp discipline; to be down on the realities of existence by living on bare necessaries; to find out how extremely well worth living life seemed to be when one woke up from a night's rest on a soft plank, with the sky for canopy and cocoa and weevilly biscuit the sole prospect for breakfast; and, more especially, to learn to work for the sake of what I got for myself out of it, even if it all went to the bottom and I along with it.

The delayed-payoff, or climactic, sentence is also used for surprise. The sequence of subject-verb-object is so common in English sentences that our minds early adopt it as a habit-pattern. ("The cat caught a mouse." "The women who went shopping found nothing to suit them." "The President, while admitting that some of the criticism might have been justified, defended the general policy of the cabinet member.") Almost as if by instinct, when we read or listen, we expect the same order: subject (and modifiers), verb (and modifiers), object or complement (and modifiers). Therefore, when a writer wants to bring his reader to sudden attention, he unexpectedly varies his sentence sequence, from normal order to an inversion of the normal order: "The car sped on. [Subject-verb.] Jack's foot pressed the accelerator almost to the floor. [Subject-verb-object.] Then suddenly the foot lifted and jammed down on the brake pedal instead. [Subject-verb-object.] Looming dead ahead, its black mass lying inert directly across the concrete highway, was an overturned truck." [Surprise! Modifiers, verb—*then* subject.] Here the established pattern, under whose familiar impetus the reader's eye has been traveling swiftly through the narrative, suddenly is broken. The author has achieved a dramatic effect by reversing his sentence order.

This same principle of climax-for-surprise may also be used for the sake of humor. If the general context of a passage is serious, the mind naturally expects to be fed only serious ideas; hence any sudden descent into the trivial or incongruous, which is called *anti*climax, is bound to arrest attention. Sometimes a writer creates an anticlimax without intending to do so, as in this sentence from a freshman theme: "Some of the other points of interest in the Finger Lakes region are Keuka Lake, which is shaped like a huge Y, the Robert H. Treman State Park, with a waterfall higher than Niagara, Ithaca, the home of Cornell University, and Phelps, the home of the largest sauerkraut canning factory in the world." One who writes such a sentence in all seriousness lacks a sense of relative values. On the other hand, the use of the anticlimax may be a sign of wit of a high order—of a mind which instinctively perceives the ridiculous side-by-side with the solemn. Byron's poetry, for example, is filled with anticlimaxes, in which, after sustaining a high, serious tone for perhaps many lines, he deliberately destroys it with a stroke of humor:

> They looked up to the sky, whose floating glow
> > Spread like a rosy Ocean, vast and bright;
> They gazed upon the glittering sea below,
> > Whence the broad Moon rose circling into sight;
> They heard the waves splash, and the wind so low,
> > And saw each other's dark eyes darting light
> Into each other—and, beholding this,
> Their lips drew near, and clung into a kiss;
>
> A long, long kiss, a kiss of Youth, and Love,
> > And Beauty, all concentrating like rays

Into one focus, kindled from above;
Such kisses as belong to early days,
Where Heart, and Soul, and Sense, in concert move,
And the blood's lava, and the pulse a blaze,
Each kiss a heart-quake—for a kiss's strength,
I think, it must be reckoned by its length.

EXERCISE 4

Here is a group of sentences illustrating the various principles of arrangement discussed in the preceding pages. In each instance, decide what point the author wished to emphasize; whether he was successful in doing so; and if not, how he might have revised the sentence.

1. One of the things that the general public perpetually fails to understand about the life of a creative writer is that he is hard at work when he appears to be loafing, for sitting about and staring into space in pursuit of an idea or a good way of expressing it is just as much a part of the writing process as pecking furiously away at a typewriter, and indeed takes up much more of an author's days—and nights.

2. That the American theatre today lacks original talent both in playwrights and performers is a frequently-heard complaint, even if, in the opinion of some (among whom I include myself), this situation is over-emphasized, considering the number of really first-rate new plays which have appeared briefly on the stage and then disappeared because of the indifference of the critics and the public, who seem to fail to recognize new talent when it does show up.

3. There are few more obvious, natural, apparent, ostensible, plain, intelligible, literal, and downright objects on this earth than a boiled potato.

4. Inverted every sentence is: heaped-up are the prepositional and appositive phrases within them, making reading the book seem like a fast trip over a road full of glacial detritus. Never does the man know what to do with his odd adjectives and adverbs; they turn up here and there, wherever they will. Alternately spasmodic and colloquial his sentences are. A fatal affinity for frag-

mentary sentences, too. His mother frightened by a telegraph operator? Compare the almost unexampled confusion inherent in this six-word gem: "Almost wholly today is he unread."

5. There were no foreclosures of mortgages, no protested notes, no notes payable, no debts of honor in Typee; no unreasonable tailors and shoemakers, perversely bent on being paid; no duns of any description; no assault and battery attorneys, to foment discord, backing their clients up to a quarrel, and then knocking their heads together; no poor relations, everlastingly occupying the spare bed-chamber, and diminishing the elbow-room at the family table; no destitute widows with their children starving on the cold charities of the world; no beggars; no debtors' prisons; no proud and hard-hearted nabobs in Typee; or to sum up all in one word—no Money!

6. The history of *Sister Carrie* is a case of uxorious publishers. The first edition of 1900 was already in print when the wife of the publisher read it and refused to allow her husband to have anything to do with it, it is reported.

7. We are told by a contemporary that many of Lord Halifax's reflections occurred to him suddenly in conversation with his friends; we cannot but ask ourselves, however, who of his contemporaries were worthy to be the friends and intellectual companions of this spiritual son of Montaigne, who was nourished on his essays, and who appears to us a somewhat lonely figure amid the gay and shallow world of the Restoration, in the politics of which, nevertheless, he played a part of immense importance, although, both as a statesman and as an author, his name is barely remembered now.

8. The group, of which our house was the quarter, consisted of two precisely similar partner-couples of houses, gardens and all to match; still the two highest blocks of buildings seen from Norwood on the crest of the ridge; so that the house itself, three storied, with garrets above, commanded, in those comparatively smokeless days, a very notable view from its garret windows, of the Norwood hills on one side, and the winter sunrise over them and of the valley of the Thames on the other, with Windsor telescopically clear in the distance, and Harrow, conspicuous always in fine weather to open vision against the summer sunset

Sentence Rhythm

The human voice, and, in imitation of it, the mind itself when silently reading, lays most stress upon those sentence elements whose meaning is most important. Substantives and verbs receive the most emphasis, modifying words (adjectives and adverbs) less, connectives (prepositions and conjunctions) least. However, if a modifier or a connective has an unusually vital role in the total idea that the sentence contains, it is stressed more than it would be ordinarily: "I was going to wear my *black* dress, but Jim wanted me to wear my *blue* one"; "I'm going to take advantage of this sale and buy the St. Matthew Passion *and* the six Brandenburg concertos."

In prose (as well as in poetry) there are all degrees of stress. Any scheme that tries to mark off each syllable as being unstressed, lightly stressed, or heavily stressed, is a mere approximation. The voice, reading a passage without attempting any more than ordinary "expression," rises and falls, emphasizes and modulates, in ways far too subtle for precise analysis or notation. Yet we often speak of "bad rhythm" and "good rhythm" in sentences. If we cannot measure such rhythm, except by the roughest of standards, how can we distinguish between the bad and the good?

With all his knowledge, a music critic still must depend on his cultivated ear for a final verdict on the quality of the music he hears. In exactly the same way, a reader who would judge the rhythm of a passage he reads or hears must first teach his ear to be sensitive. There are elaborate treatises on English prose rhythm, but one cannot go to them for much practical advice on the quality of the rhythms typical of the material he reads. All that is possible in a short book on reading is to make several very broad observations on an extremely complex subject.

In the first place, prose lacks something which verse possesses: namely, meter. Underlying most verse is a regular rhythmic pattern, made up of a constantly recurring combination of accented and unaccented syllables. In prose, however, there is no such pattern, iambic, trochaic, or any other. Indeed, one of the earmarks of bad prose is a tendency to suggest the regular rhythms of verse. English prose rhythms have their own charms, but metronome-like regularity is not one of them. You will recall that one of our counts against jargon in Chapter Two was that a long string of prepositional phrases, for example, gives an unpleasant recurring beat to the sentence. "The observation of the construction of the portion of the road between Mifford Center and the county line is incorrect in nature, inasmuch as the road is actually rough in character." Read that aloud (which you should do whenever testing for rhythmic quality) and you will understand what we mean. It is true that there have been writers, such as Sir Thomas Browne, Thomas De Quincey, and Walter Pater, whose prose came close to the border-line of verse. But if a writer is not a highly skilled word-musician, he is well advised to avoid any suggestion of meter in his prose.

Secondly, unless it is written by an expert craftsman, an over-long sentence is usually unrhythmical. Compare, in this respect, the sentences quoted on pages 183 and 188: the former has a graceful yet dignified rhythm, the latter has little rhythm at all. If you have studied music, you know that the twin essences of rhythm are phrasing and accent—the grouping of notes (= words) into an agreeable accentual pattern, and the shrewd distribution of rests (= punctuation: commas, semicolons, colons, dashes, periods). The most important of these rests are the long ones, which correspond to the intervals between sentences, the intermissions during which the reader has a chance to pause momentarily and let what he has just read sink in. If those all-important full stops are long delayed, the reader will become fatigued and lose the continuity of the thought. In addition, the successive thought units within the sentence must be given just the right grammatical length, and greater or less pauses must be inserted to set off the units. We freely admit that such a phrase as "just the right grammatical length" is not very helpful, because we have not defined our terms—but in the nature of things we cannot do so. "Rightness" varies from sentence to sentence, idea to idea, writer to writer. Everyone probably would agree, however, that a long sentence written without any stops at all is unrhythmical, and that on the other hand a sentence excessively interrupted by punctuation—which means that the thought is chopped into little pieces—is no better. We can suggest what we mean by two examples:

The period of reappraisal of Western policy inaugurated by the repudiation of the European Defense Community in the French Assembly presents one of those rare moments in which private persons can enter into the discussion of delicate matters of high policy without fear of bringing into question existing decisions or of embarrassing their own Government in its undertakings.

Sentences just as long as this, and as innocent of punctuation, are found all around us in everyday life. Yet the eye cannot comprehend in a single sweep, nor the voice utter in a single breath, a sentence as unbroken as this. There is no rhythm because there is no phrasing.

On the other hand:

Society, through every fibre, was rent asunder: all things, it was then becoming visible, but could not then be understood, were moving onwards, with an impulse received ages before, yet now first with a decisive rapidity, towards that great chaotic gulf, where, whether in the shape of French Revolutions, Reform Bills, or what shape soever, bloody or bloodless, the descent and engulfment assume, we now see them weltering and boiling.

In this sentence there is too much phrasing. The fault lies primarily in the author's insistence upon qualifying phrases and clauses. Putting aside the first independent clause (down to the colon), we see that the remainder of the sentence is based upon the simple predication "all things . . . were moving onwards . . . towards that great chaotic gulf, where . . . we now see them weltering and boiling." All the rest is a sort of spasmodic parenthesis. Not only is the mind led, with justifiable reluctance, through a tortuous labyrinth of subordinate ideas; there are too many jerky stops and starts.

A third requirement for good sentence rhythm is only superficially in conflict with the first. Although an approach to regular meter in prose is usually undesirable, regularity in the larger
design of the sentence can often be a most attractive and effective rhetorical device. A sentence that sounds like a record with
a deep scratch across its surface (click, click, click) is disagreeable; but one whose larger elements recognizably match, like
the three arches in the façade of a cathedral, gives pleasure.
This is the principle that appears in handbooks of composition
under the topics "balance" and "parallelism." The matching of
phrase against phrase, clause against clause, lends an unmistakable eloquence to prose. That, indeed, is one of the principal
glories of the King James Bible:

> Behold, the day of the Lord cometh, cruel both with wrath and
> fierce anger, to lay the land desolate; and he shall destroy the
> sinners thereof out of it.
> For the stars of heaven and the constellations thereof shall not give
> their light: the sun shall be darkened in his going forth, and the
> moon shall not cause her light to shine.
> And I will punish the world for their evil, and the wicked for their
> iniquity; and I will cause the arrogancy of the proud to cease,
> and will lay low the haughtiness of the terrible.
> I will make a man more precious than fine gold; even a man than
> the golden wedge of ophir.
> Therefore I will shake the heavens, and the earth shall remove ou
> of her place, in the wrath of the Lord of hosts, and in the day o
> his fierce anger.*

And, to some extent in reminiscence and imitation of the Bible
English prose all the way down to our own time has tende
toward balanced structure for the sake of contrast or antithesi
or climax:

> What he attempted, he performed; he is never feeble, and he di
> not wish to be energetic; he is never rapid, and he never stagnate

---

* On the subject of the rhythms of the King James Bible, as well as oth
aspects of Biblical prose which illuminate points made in the course of th
book, see John Livingston Lowes's fine essay, "The Noblest Monument of Engli
Prose," in his *Essays in Appreciation*.

His sentences have neither studied amplitude, nor affected brevity; his periods, though not diligently rounded, are voluble and easy. Whoever wishes to attain an English style, familiar but not coarse, and elegant but not ostentatious, must give his days and nights to the volumes of Addison.

Study hard; divert yourself heartily; distinguish carefully between the pleasures of a man of fashion, and the vices of a scoundrel; pursue the former, and abhor the latter, like a man of sense.

It is the addition of strangeness to beauty, that constitutes the romantic character in art; and the desire of beauty being a fixed element in every artistic organization, it is the addition of curiosity to this desire of beauty, that constitutes the romantic temper.

In the past several decades many important literary experimentalists have renounced the very principles of rhythmic language which we have been emphasizing in these pages. Writers like James Joyce, E. E. Cummings, John Dos Passos, and William Faulkner, to name only a few, have often deliberately abandoned punctuation and the other usual devices by which thought-units are marked off and rhythmic pleasure communicated. One main reason why they have done so is that many of them are deeply interested in representing the "stream of consciousness"—the uncontrolled, vagrant, fragmentary thoughts and moods that course continuously through the human mind. Since in their raw state such thoughts and moods have nothing of the neat packaged quality which sentence and paragraph organization suggests, these writers argue that their chaotic nature should be suggested by a chaotic style. Perhaps the most famous example of this manner is the representation of the flow of Mrs. Bloom's thoughts in the last section of Joyce's *Ulysses*—forty-five closely printed pages without a punctuation mark!

A cultivated awareness of rhythm inevitably increases the reader's pleasure, heightening an emotional experience whose other principal element is the suggestiveness of the words themselves. One great requirement for prose rhythm, as has been remarked, is that it avoid metrical regularity. Another is that it be appropriate to the context; for a passage of quiet imaginative beauty demands a slow, even (though never monotonous) rhythm, a passage of exciting narrative a rapid rhythm, a passage intended to sway patriotic emotions a measured but vigorous rhythm, and so on. Readers come to associate certain rhythmic effects with certain intentions on the part of the writer or speaker. Rhythm, in other words, has its own connotative value. And just as word connotations may be employed to affect emotions rather than reason, so too may rhythm connotations.

Consider first these grave sentences:

If, perchance, you have seen a copy of the first issue of *Gentry* in the home of a discerning friend, then you know why we say that only those of an unusual turn of mind can fully appreciate this quarterly magazine. *Gentry* is edited for the rather rare individual whose mind is ever open to new ideas, new forms; for the individual who respects the best of the thinking and art which has endured over the years; who feels that there is much, much more to living than merely making a living; and therefore seeks constantly to gain more from his hourly association with people, objects, and ideas.

Among your friends there may be one, possibly three or four such people; and since you wish to present them with a Christmas gift of an especial nature, which is attuned to their high level of thinking, we suggest a year's subscription to *Gentry* (4 issues) as a suitable gift. Here, for example, is a brief description of just a few out of the long list of editorial features which will appear in the next issue of *Gentry;* you can judge from them how intrigued and enthralled your discerning friends will be when they receive this fine magazine

In this discussion we will not pause to analyze the implications of the language itself, although you should do so on your own for the sake of reviewing what you have learned in Chapters One and Two. Here, however, we are concerned only with rhythm Contrast the above paragraphs with this version:

Have you seen the first issue of *Gentry?* Perhaps your most cultured, intelligent friend has a copy. Look at it—then you'll know why *Gentry* is for a very special sort of person. The person who keeps up with things. The person who is well-read, unusually well-educated, with broad interests in the old as well as the new. The person who wants to live, not just make a living. The person who's always alert to learn more about life, art, philosophy.

People like that are pretty rare. You may know one, two, three—hardly more. Naturally, they deserve the most unusual type of Christmas present you can find. Why not a year's subscription to *Gentry?* Look at this brief list of some of the features in the next issue. Judge for yourself how happy those special friends of yours will be to receive *Gentry*—as a gift from you!

The question here is, which advertisement would persuade you to pay a relatively high price ($8 a year) for a magazine subscription? (Despite the Christmas-gift angle of this particular ad, the writer naturally wanted you to subscribe for yourself as well as for your friends.) Quite probably the first version would be the more impressive. It has the more elegant "sound." It suggests that here is something precious and rare, something that can be appreciated only by the discriminating, not by the hoi polloi. If it costs $2 a copy, it is worth it; high quality never comes cheap. In brief, a conspicuously dignified rhythm, along with well-chosen connotative words, has been used to convey the idea of a magazine appealing to the cultured few—a select group to which you, as the reader of the ad, are assumed to belong.

Again:

Who can say at what point the revelations come? A man falls in love . . . or suddenly sees the growing character of his son . . . or knows the quick pride of being needed, although no longer young. Each has his discoveries . . . a series, making up the sharp core of life. From birth and being . . . through youth, maturity, and lengthening years . . . each follows his own way, and hopes to find it good. We believe that this is as it should be . . . we believe, too, that we can help you plan to make your way a little easier, whatever it may be.*

* Courtesy of Security Mutual Life Insurance Company, Binghamton, New York.

Here too the key to the effect of the advertisement is the carefully wrought rhythm of the sentences. Many of the devices of the prose-poet-turned-advertising-writer are here, such as the balanced clauses *(A man falls in love . . . or sees . . . or knows— each follows . . . and hopes—we believe . . . we believe)*, the repetition of sound to give the effect of alliteration or internal rhyme *(suddenly sees—son/young—discoveries/series—birth and being—should be/may be)*, as well as the selection of words weighted with a certain kind of connotation *(falls in love—quick pride of being needed—sharp core of life—youth, maturity, and lengthening years—find it good)*. Only the signature, and perhaps a hint in the last sentence, identifies the passage as a commercial appeal. Up to that point, it appears to be an extract from a book of meditations. And that is just what the writer desires. The reader is put into a meditative frame of mind; he is asked to meditate, that is, on whether he has enough insurance.

But when the appeal is to the active, fun-loving side of one's nature, rather than to one's concern for protecting his family another type of rhythm is needed—perhaps the most familiar in modern advertising. Turn back to the Chevrolet ad quoted on pages 70-71. Apart from the breezy, slangy vocabulary, which contrasts so strongly with the grave diction of the insurance advertisement, the effect of this "message" lies in its rhythm short, snappy, lively, suggesting (indeed actually saying) that this is a car for people who are young at heart—wanting to g places and do things, and enjoy themselves on the way. How i that rhythmic effect obtained? By short, direct questions; by ex clamations; by fragmentary sentences; by contractions. Th writer is talking directly, excitedly, to you (note the use of *yo* throughout) rather than uttering thoughts about someone *man* in the insurance ad) who turns out to be yourself.

In contemporary advertising, one of the most-used devices the points of suspension (. . .). In imaginative writing a gener tion ago, especially in certain types of verse, the dots were popular rhetorical method of suggesting continuation thought or mood even after the actual words had stopped. The reader was expected to imagine more than the words themselves conveyed:

> A shadowy glade,
> The murmur of a hidden brook,
> Your white hand in mine . . .
> Candlelight through the wine glass,
> Oblivious of the snow without,
> Silence binding us into one . . .
> A Beethoven sonata,
> The Gauguins at the Metropolitan,
> The skyscrapers' sharp upward tilt.
> And you . . . always you . . .

Nowadays, as is shown both in the insurance advertisement and in other ads quoted earlier, the dots are used liberally, not only where the purpose is to evoke a dreamy, complaisant mood in the reader, but even in ads with a jauntier tone.

EXERCISE 5

Comment on the rhythm of the following sentences:

1. Here you shall find emphasized true hospitality and history so intertwined that upon departure, all ideas you have encountered shall have become blended into a decision that Washington surely has been emerging as a typical expression of American civilization which has surmounted all problems as they appeared and here we have proven a wholesome, sturdy pioneer philosophy which has strengthened your belief in your mission in coming to the Capitol City to give your measure of effort for the stabilization and survival of sound government which "under God" shall operate upon the premise "that the value of history lies in the perspective it gives us as we take up the problems of the present" with a common faith in "liberty and justice for all."

2. Dickens shows lamentable taste in his treatment of the Smallweed family, not especially palatable at best, almost revolting in the scenes in which, for the sake, I am afraid, of comic relief, he has old Smallweed, a paralytic, amuse himself by repeatedly

crowning his senile consort, who crouches in the chimney corner across from him, with a cushion or two.

EXERCISE 6

Analyze in detail the rhythmic devices used in the following excerpt from the *Autobiography* of Edward Gibbon, a writer famous for his rhythmic prose:

The proportion of a part to the whole is the only standard by which we can measure the length of our existence. At the age of twenty, one year is a tenth, perhaps, of the time which has elapsed within our consciousness and memory; at the age of fifty it is no more than the fortieth, and this relative value continues to decrease till the last sands are shaken by the hand of death. This reasoning may seem metaphysical; but on a trial it will be found satisfactory and just. The warm desires, the long expectations of youth, are founded on the ignorance of themselves and the world; they are gradually damped by time and experience, by disappointment and possession; and after the middle season the crowd must be content to remain at the foot of the mountain; while the few who have climbed the summit aspire to descend or expect to fall. In old age, the consolation of hope is reserved for the tenderness of parents, who commence a new life in their children; the faith of enthusiasts who sing hallelujahs above the clouds; and the vanity of authors who presume the immortality of their name and writings.

EXERCISE 7

Here are two versions of the same paragraph. From the standpoint of rhythmic effectiveness, which is the better?

1. In Maryland in the summertime, dawn is an almost timeless process. It has neither beginning nor end; but it endures, endures so long, and so without apparent progress, that the wakeful and suffering and troubled in the valley between the ridges always fall to wondering if the ageless routine of the day has been arrested, and despair of ever seeing the universal grayness lifted from the hills and fields. The concord of sounds which since twilight had made the night seem lively and cheerful has died away; the musicless rasping of the tree frogs, the perpetual

echoing of katydids, the simple young noise of the crickets, have disappeared one by one; and there are left for the sleepless listener only the low liquid rippling of the brook-water over the slippery stones, and the mysterious, unassignable pops and rustles the vegetation utters as it grows and expands. In the moonless sky the rigid pattern of the stars continues its journey to the tops of the trees on the very summit of the western ridge; but one by one, the easternmost and less bright ones first, the pinpoints falter, until all that remains above the valley is one solitary star. When that one falls behind the ridge, there is only a dark grayness left in the sky. And below, in this, one of the colossal furrows that were left, long ages ago, when an agrarian Paul Bunyan drove his plow southward from Pennsylvania to Tennessee, a soft mist hides even the dimmest outlines of forest and clearing.

2. Dawn, in Maryland, is an almost timeless process in the summertime. It has neither beginning nor end. But it endures long, and without apparent progress. Therefore the wakeful, the suffering, the troubled in the valley between the ridges always fall to wondering. They wonder if the ageless routine of the day has been arrested. They despair of ever seeing the universal grayness lifted from the hills and fields. Since twilight, a concord of sounds had made the night seem lively and cheerful. Now, however, the musicless rasping of the tree frogs has disappeared, as have the perpetual echoing of the katydids and the simple young noise of the crickets. For the sleepless listener are left only the low liquid rippling of the brook-water over the slippery stones, together with the vegetation's pops and rustles, mysterious and unassignable, uttered as it grows and expands. The rigid pattern of the stars continues, in the moonless sky, its journey to the treetops on the summit of the ridge to the west. One by one, nevertheless, first the easternmost and less bright ones, the pinpoints falter, until one solitary star is all that remains above the valley. With the fall of that one behind the ridge, in the sky there is only a dark grayness. And below, even the dimmest outlines of forest and clearing are hidden by a soft mist, in this, one of the colossal furrows left when an agrarian Paul Bunyan long ages ago drove his plow southward from Pennsylvania to Tennessee.

EXERCISE 8

For examples of the way in which, for various purposes, contemporary authors have abandoned the conventional ideas of punctuation and sentence organization, see the following: James Joyce's *Ulysses;* the "Camera-Eye" sequences in John Dos Passos' *U.S.A.;* T. S. Eliot's "Ash Wednesday"; Archibald MacLeish's "You, Andrew Marvell" and "Immortal Autumn"; E. E. Cummings' "Impression: IV" and "Chanson Innocent"; William Faulkner's *The Sound and the Fury* and *Intruder in the Dust.*

EXERCISE 9

Comment on the use of rhythm, the connotation of words, and the sentence arrangement of each of the following excerpts from advertisements:

1. Yes, I'm marrying the finest girl in the world. That's why I want to *know* that the diamond ring she'll wear forever is also the *finest.* For more than half a century, this kind of reasoning has inspired men everywhere to choose Keepsake Diamond Engagement Rings.

   Now, how can you *know* that a Keepsake Diamond is the finest quality? Simple! . . . because the famous Keepsake Certificate signed by your jeweler, permanently registers and *guarantees* a perfect diamond . . . regardless of price or carat weight. The name "Keepsake" is in the ring and on the tag.

   So . . . when you choose *her* diamond ring, make it a Keepsake. She will remember always that you gave her the finest . . that you gave her *perfection.*

2. On an anniversary . . . how fitting it is that a man may express his pride and devotion brilliantly enscribed in diamond light . . . For the diamond gift that marks an anniversary, or other great moment . . . an important birthday, the birth of a child a daughter's debut . . . or a specially meaningful event . . . will recall the occasion always. A trusted jeweler should, of course be consulted.*

3. Across the river, the lights were beginning to glimmer through the winter mist. From far below, came the faint hum of home

   * Courtesy of DeBeers Consolidated Mines, Ltd.

ward-bound traffic, punctuated now and then by the hoarse notes of passing ships.

Here, in his own apartment, the world's greatest violinist had just put aside his Stradivarius and turned to his Magnavox radio-phonograph. Now he sat listening as the instrument poured forth an ecstasy of sound. Full-throated it was; crystalline in clarity . . . music that had been immaculately conceived in the hope that it could thus be so perfectly reproduced.

4. They have an inconspicuous seam down the center—that's the only reason under the sun why they're priced so low. Otherwise, they are absolutely top quality blankets. All wool, of course—beautifully finished—in three lovely colors. You'll want to stock up—winter will soon be here! Come down tomorrow, early. We don't have too many of these blankets—and we won't keep them long!

EXERCISE 10

Reread the three versions of the Gettysburg Address printed on pages 67-69. Explain the differences in sentence rhythm in terms of the assumed writer of each version, the audience he addressed, and his probable purpose.

Paragraphs

The paragraph, the next largest unit of communication, is in a way merely a larger, more complicated sentence. Many of the observations we have made about the length, organization, and rhythm of sentences also apply to the paragraph.

The ability to construct good paragraphs is even more significant an indication of a writer's intelligence than is his ability to write good sentences. While most college freshmen can write acceptable individual sentences, only the superior student, at least at the beginning of his course in English composition, can write whole paragraphs that "hang together."

The first fundamental thing to remember about the paragraph, as about the sentence, is that it is a *unit,* concerned not with a group of topics but with one topic only. The paragraph differs from the sentence in that it can tell more about that topic than an ordinary sentence has space to do. It expands a definition, it offers examples and analogies, it breaks down a main argument into subheads, it presents a chronological narrative; but it nevertheless sticks to one main point. In handbooks of composition much stress is laid upon the so-called "topic sentence" of a paragraph—the sentence that contains the essence of what the paragraph is about, and to which every other sentence bears some relation. Sometimes the topic sentence is implied rather than expressed; but the other sentences must be bound to it nonetheless.

The second thing to remember is that a paragraph must take the reader somewhere, and take him by a fairly direct route. No piece of writing is worth much if it does not move along, leading the reader into some new region of information or argument. Hence each paragraph must somehow contribute to the total effect of progress. The reader must come out with more than he took in with him. Furthermore, he must be given his new ideas systematically, not haphazardly. He must be enabled to follow the writer's line of thought. There must be no by-paths or detours, unless they are plainly marked as such and their presence can be completely justified.

This is the substance of what is said in the textbooks of writing. What, then, are the rewards in store for the close reader, who remains always alert to the writer's obligation to produce unified, progressive paragraphs?

The most obvious clue an analysis of paragraph structure can offer is to the orderliness of a writer's mind. If the organization of a paragraph is clear, if the sentences are arranged in a logical pattern with each leading directly into the next, it is reasonable to assume that the writer has his material under control, knows just what he wishes to say about it, and is able to present it to his reader as systematically as he has arranged it in his own mind. Only inexperienced writers usually are conscious of the process by which they organize their material; to practiced writers it is an instinctive, automatic occurrence. When we wrote the next-to-last paragraph above, for example, we did not say to ourself, this sentence should go so far, and the next sen tence should serve such-and-such a purpose, and the two should be tied together by a connective. Yet it can illustrate the way in which sound paragraphs are built.

Sentence 1 is the theme, saying that "the second thing to remember" ("second" ties in with the preceding paragraph, which began with "first") has two aspects. This division of the idea into two parts does not violate the principle of unity because, as the reader will be aware when he has finished the paragraph, the two aspects are closely related. Unless each requires an exposition which would make the paragraph too unwieldy, both can legitimately be included in a single paragraph.

Sentence 2 relates the idea being discussed to the larger topic of writing in general. But unity remains: "leading the reader . . ." parallels "take the reader somewhere" in Sentence 1.

Sentence 3 binds together the ideas of Sentences 1 and 2 as the conclusion to an implied syllogism: What is true of writing in general is true of paragraphs in particular: they must progress.

Sentence 4 develops and completes the preceding idea of "progress": compare the verbs in Sentences 1, 2, and 4.

Sentence 5 turns the reader's attention to the second aspect spoken of in Sentence 1. "Furthermore" is the signal that an additional idea is to be presented.

Sentences 6 and 7 both amplify Sentence 5: Sentence 7 by stating the idea of Sentence 6 in a negative way.

The whole paragraph has been unified by constant reference to "the reader," who is alluded to in five of the seven sentences. The "point of view," as the textbooks call it, has been kept constant. Frequent and unjustified shifting of the point of view leads only to confusion.

We shall go a step further and show how the two-sentence paragraph following the one we have just analyzed is connected with it. "This is the substance": a sign that this sentence refers back to what has just been said. "What, then" is a phrase designed, like "furthermore," to guide the reader's mind to the next topic. This paragraph is a transitional one; though it adds nothing to the reader's knowledge, it contributes to the progress of the argument in the sense that it clinches the point previously made and then directs the reader's attention to a new topic which, the writer implies, logically derives from the one already developed. The generous use of such signposts, whether they be single words or phrases (*therefore, however, first of all, on the contrary, in conclusion, as we have seen, another example* . . .) or whole little paragraphs, is a mark of the writer who is careful to keep his reader in touch with his argument. (Query: Are there enough signposts in this book?)

Now examine for yourself this paragraph, on which we shall not comment:

There hasn't been as much publicity about the laying of a telephone cable across the Atlantic as there should be. I was reading about it the other night. It reminded me of something else I read recently, about the troubles they had when they laid the first telegraph cable across the Atlantic back in the 1860's. It was a ship called the *Great Eastern* which was used for the purpose, and that ship had gone through all kinds of misfortunes since she was first built, as the biggest iron ship constructed up to that time. It was a seven days' wonder, and everything seemed to go wrong, even before she was actually launched. On the day she was launched, there was a big stampede among the mobs who had gathered to witness the event, and many people were hurt. A regular telephone cable across the Atlantic has been badly needed, because radio service never has been too satisfactory. Atmospheric conditions just couldn't be licked, even with the best tools of modern science. The new cable lies on the ocean floor, sometimes two or three mile down, and the pressure of the water per square inch is something terrific. Water-tight amplifiers, or boosters, are installed every so often so as to step up the electrical impulses. This is a great age we are living in.

The same influences that have shortened sentences in th past century have also reduced the length of paragraphs. Th reduction has been due partly to the necessity for makin printed matter *look* easier to read. In deference to the requir ments of the hasty reader, material that once would have constituted one large paragraph is now broken up into smaller units. The "normal" modern paragraph contains anywhere from three to eight sentences. The shortest paragraphs are those in newspapers, popular magazines, and advertisements—the sort of writing that will not be read at all if it cannot be read with minimum effort. Serious books, however, as well as magazines intended for a more or less restricted group, have longer paragraphs.

Because the paragraph, like the sentence, is designed to show the relationships between ideas, it follows that the shorter the paragraph is, the less complicated the subject-matter has to be. Just as short sentences can only state an idea, barely, directly, without qualifications, so short paragraphs can show only the most elementary relationships between two or three ideas.

The following passage from a novel illustrates one of the commonest uses the curt, one- or two-sentence paragraph has in modern writing:

She spent the early part of the night in studying her defence. Then she laid it quite aside and prayed long and fervently.

Towards morning she fell asleep from exhaustion.

When she awoke, Mrs. Houseman was sitting by her bedside, looking at her, and crying.

They were soon clasped in each other's arms, condoling.

But presently Houseman came, and took his wife away rather angrily.

Mrs. Gaunt was prevailed on to eat a little toast and drink a glass of wine, and then she sat waiting her dreadful summons.

She waited, and waited, until she became impatient to face her danger.

But there were two petty larcenies on before her. She had to wait.

At last, about noon, came a message to say that the grand jury had found a true bill against her.

"Then may God forgive them!" said she.

Soon afterwards she was informed her time drew very near.

She made her toilet carefully, and passed with her attendant into a small room under the court.

Here she had to endure another chilling wait, and in a sombre room.

Presently she heard a voice above her cry out, "The King versus Catherine Gaunt."

Then she was beckoned to.

The author is concerned only to present a bare sequence of events. Each sentence tells, in the plainest language possible, of one happening. There is no attempt at the painting in of details or at interpretation. This is narration reduced to its simplest terms and presented so that the eye can skim quickly down the page. Another writer, using the same events, could have devoted several times as much space to making the reader see the characters and the physical environment, to bring out the emotional significance of the situation. This writer, however, assumed that his readers wanted only to learn, as quickly and easily as possible, *what* happened, not what the happenings meant in terms of the characters, the situation, or the whole theme of the novel. Where the reader's interest is so limited or casual, the miniature paragraph is a legitimate enough device. It does not say much, but it says all that is needed to satisfy the reader's curiosity.

The extremely short paragraph has various other legitimate functions, such as the one illustrated in Carl Sandburg's description of the people's reaction to the first news of Lincoln's death:

Men tried to talk about it and the words failed and they came back to silence.

To say nothing was best.

Lincoln was dead.

Was there anything more to say?

Yes, they would go through the motions of grief and they would take their part in a national funeral and a ceremony of humiliation and abasement and tears.

But words were no help.

Lincoln was dead.

Nothing more than that could be said.

He was gone.
He would never speak again to the American people.
A great friend of man had suddenly vanished.
Nothing could be done about it.
Death is terribly final.*

Here Sandburg evidently wishes to suggest the dazed state of
the people, the incoherence brought on by shock. The tiny
sentences—hardly more than fragmentary phrases—illustrate the
first statement, that "Men tried to talk about it and the words
failed." Such few ideas as are expressed are utterly commonplace; when they are stunned almost into silence, men are
capable of only the most obvious thoughts ("He was gone. He
would never speak again to the American people"). And the
stunned mind thinks the same thoughts over and over: "Lincoln was dead . . . Lincoln was dead." The bereaved people of
1865, Sandburg suggests, were too choked up to speak. When
they did manage a few words, the phrases they uttered were
like sobs. And the phrases Sandburg *writes* are like sobs. (Why,
by the way, did he not combine the thirteen sentences into a
single paragraph? Why would the effect have been spoiled?)

Short paragraphs can be put to unscrupulous uses, too. They
are especially tricky in that they may persuade the reader that
the ideas they present are as uncomplicated as they sound.
Terse, single-sentence paragraphs are a rhetorical device that
often aids and abets the fallacy of oversimplification. Like short
sentences, short paragraphs have a connotation of solemnity and
overwhelming authority. Thus newspaper "philosophers," advertising men, and others who wish to infuse their writing with
these qualities are partial to brief paragraphs.

It is hardly necessary to say anything of the overlong paragraph because it is seldom encountered except in legal and
governmental writing, whose shortcomings we have already examined. It is the sign of the man who seems unwilling to give
his reader a break, in both the standard and slang senses of the

* From Carl Sandburg's *Abraham Lincoln: The War Years.* By permission of
Harcourt, Brace and Company, publishers.

term. And it may also suggest that the writer lacks a very important mental faculty—that of being able to separate his ideas into convenient but always coherent clusters. The person who writes on and on, without noticing when he has completed a logical subdivision of his exposition or argument, is as unfitted for his occupation as the one whose thoughts, as reflected in his writing, are excessively compartmented.

EXERCISE 11

What does the organization of each of the following passages suggest about the mind of the author?

1. I never in my life—and I knew Sarah Battle many of the best years of it—saw her take out her snuff-box when it was her turn to play; or snuff a candle in the middle of a game; or ring for a servant, till it was fairly over. She never introduced, or connived at, miscellaneous conversation during its process. As she emphatically observed, cards were cards: and if I ever saw unmingled distaste in her fine last-century countenance, it was at the airs of a young gentleman of a literary turn, who had been with difficulty persuaded to take a hand; and who, in his excess of candour, declared, that he thought there was no harm in unbending the mind now and then, after serious studies, in recreations of that kind! She could not bear to have her noble occupation, to which she wound up her faculties, considered in that light. It was her business, her duty, the thing she came into the world to do—and she did it. She unbent her mind afterwards—over a book.

2. Grouse, in my opinion, is the king of the game birds in Guernsey County, and the population seems to be on the increase. But grouse hunting hasn't been too popular. This is the result, I believe, of the lack of understanding the habits of the bird and the lack of good bird dogs. It's a great sport that has been ignored by the hunter. Sportsmen who are interested in grouse shooting, couldn't go wrong on a trip to Guernsey County.

    Rabbits, the top game animal in hill country, still is hunted and enjoyed by the greatest number of hunters. Many also set traps and hunt foxes and ducks.

The deer herd in Guernsey County is estimated to be in the neighborhood of 350 head. About 15 to 20 are killed annually on the highways. Hunting during the 1953 season should be fairly productive.

3. As a student he was eager to learn, and his recitations in class, though somewhat irrelevant to the matter under discussion at the moment, were so full of wit and odd miscellaneous informa- tion that teachers welcomed his presence. Rather taller than most boys his age, he had a thick mop of brown hair which had a tendency to become uncombed under the stress of ideas, and his brown eyes and wide humorous mouth had the power of putting people under his spell before he was with them for ten minutes. He had not yet got over the adolescent tendency toward awkwardness, and his hands, a little larger than the common run of hands, often sought refuge in his pockets. It was the fashion in his day to wear trousers above the ankles, but the fact that his trousers dangled not far below his calf may have been due more to the rapid, uncheckable upward expansion of his frame than to any conscious desire to be in style. What annoyed his teachers most was his invariable habit of gazing out of the window just when they were making the most important point in their day's lecture. Quite plainly his mind was a thousand miles away, yet when it came to a showdown he always turned out to have been listening—and retaining. He was too exasperating on occasion to be a model student, but no teacher ever regretted having had the chance to teach him.

4. The inductive method has been practised ever since the begin- ning of the world by every human being. It is constantly prac- tised by the most ignorant clown, by the most thoughtless school- boy, by the very child at the breast. That method leads the clown to the conclusion that if he sows barley he shall not reap wheat. By that method the schoolboy learns that a cloudy day is the best for catching trout. The very infant, we imagine, is led by induction to expect milk from his mother or nurse, and none from his father.

EXERCISE 12

Among the most spectacular best-sellers of the past twenty or thirty years have been books offering comfort and inspiration to unhappy, dissatisfied people. Among them have been Walter B. Pitkin's *Life Begins at Forty,* Marjorie Hillis' *Live Alone and Like It,* Dale Carnegie's *How to Win Friends and Influence People,* Joshua Loth Liebman's *Peace of Mind,* Norman Vincent Peale's *A Guide to Confident Living* and *The Power of Positive Thinking.* Examine one or two of these books, or a similar one that is riding high in the best-seller lists at the present moment, and analyze the tricks of sentence- and paragraph-structure, arrangement, and rhythm that help each author "put across his message." Do you think there is a correlation between the snappy prose and the quality of thinking that it embodies? Is the prose well adapted for the sort of reader the author presumably had in mind? How do you personally react to it?

EXERCISE 13

This is a review exercise, designed to help you draw together what you have learned about the length, arrangement, and rhythm of prose sentences and paragraphs. Analyze each passage for such things as the orderly movement of thought from sentence to sentence, the relative effectiveness of short and long sentences, the use of periodic and loose sentences, etc.

1. Society everywhere is in conspiracy against the manhood of every one of its members. Society is a joint-stock company, in which the members agree, for the better securing of his bread to each shareholder, to surrender the liberty and culture of the eater. The virtue in most request is conformity. Self-reliance is its aversion. It loves not realities and creators, but names and customs.

   Whoso would be a man, must be a nonconformist. He who would gather immortal palms must not be hindered by the name of goodness, but must explore if it be goodness. Nothing is at last sacred but the integrity of your own mind.

2. Apart from the peculiar tenets of individual thinkers, there is also in the world at large an increasing inclination to stretch unduly the powers of society over the individual, both by the force of opinion and even by that of legislation: and as the

tendency of all the changes taking place in the world is to strengthen society, and diminish the power of the individual, this encroachment is not one of the evils which tend spontaneously to disappear, but, on the contrary, to grow more and more formidable. The disposition of mankind, whether as rulers or as fellow citizens, to impose their own opinions and inclinations as a rule of conduct on others, is so energetically supported by some of the best and by some of the worst feelings incident to human nature, that it is hardly ever kept under restraint by anything but want of power; and as the power is not declining, but growing, unless a strong barrier of moral conviction can be raised against the mischief, we must expect, in the present circumstances of the world, to see it increase.

3. Persecution for the expression of opinions seems to me perfectly logical. If you have no doubt of your premises or your power and want a certain result with all your heart you naturally express your wishes in law and sweep away all opposition. To allow opposition by speech seems to indicate that you think speech impotent, as when a man says that he has squared the circle, or that you do not care wholeheartedly for the result, or that you doubt either your power or your premises.

But when men have realized that time has upset many fighting faiths, they may come to believe even more than they believe the very foundations of their own conduct that the ultimate good desired is better reached by free trade in ideas—that the best test of truth is the power of the thought to get itself accepted in the competition of the market, and that truth is the only ground upon which their wishes safely can be carried out. That, at any rate, is the theory of our Constitution. It is an experiment, as all life is an experiment. Every year if not every day we have to wager our salvation upon some prophecy based upon imperfect knowledge. While that experiment is part of our system I think that we should be eternally vigilant against attempts to check the expression of opinions that we loathe and believe to be fraught with death, unless they so imminently threaten immediate interference with the lawful and pressing purposes of the law that an immediate check is required to save the country.

4. Don't think you are going to conceal faults by concealing evidence that they ever existed. Don't be afraid to go in your

library and read every book as long as any document does not offend our own ideas of decency. That should be the only censorship.

How will we defeat communism unless we know what it is? What it teaches—why does it have such an appeal for men? Why are so many people swearing allegiance to it? It's almost a religion, albeit one of the nether regions.

Now we have got to fight it with something better. Not try to conceal the thinking of our own people. They are part of America and even if they think ideas that are contrary to ours they have a right to have them, a right to record them and a right to have them in places where they are accessible to others. It is unquestioned or it is not America.

5. I believe that that community is already in process of dissolution where each man begins to eye his neighbor as a possible enemy, where nonconformity with the accepted creed, political as well as religious, is a mark of disaffection; where denunciation, without specification or backing, takes the place of evidence; where orthodoxy chokes freedom of dissent; where faith in the eventual supremacy of reason has become so timid that we dare not enter our convictions in the open lists to win or lose. Such fears as these are a solvent which can eat out the cement that binds the stones together; they may in the end subject us to a despotism as evil as any that we dread; and they can be allayed only in so far as we refuse to proceed on suspicion, and trust one another until we have tangible ground for misgiving.

The mutual confidence on which all else depends can be maintained only by an open mind and a brave reliance upon free discussion. I do not say that these will suffice; who knows but we may be on a slope which leads down to aboriginal savagery. But of this I am sure: if we are to escape, we must not yield a foot upon demanding a fair field, and an honest race, to all ideas.*

The Rhythm of Verse

This is not a book on the "appreciation" of literature. We do not intend, therefore, to say much about the means by which

_____

* Quoted from an article by Judge Learned Hand, by courtesy of the *Saturday Review.*

the poet achieves the effects peculiar to poetry: you can read about that in a number of excellent books. But since we have just been saying a number of things that bear directly on the rhythm of verse, it will be worthwhile to go one step farther and show how you can apply the principles just outlined to your reading of verse.

To begin with, when we were talking about the rhythm of prose we remarked that prose has no recurrent beat—no regular system of accent, or meter. That is one vital difference between prose and verse—a much more real one than the commonly heard rule that "anything that is printed with straight right-hand margins is prose, and anything with irregular right margins is verse." Unlike prose, all true verse has an underlying regularity of accent.

Rhythm has a very special significance to human beings. Every moment of our lives, though we may seldom stop to consider it, we are involved in a whole complex of rhythmic cycles—the succession of day and night and of the seasons, the beat of the heart, the unending cycle of birth, maturity, decay, death, and renewal found throughout nature. We seem furthermore to have some innate receptivity to created rhythm. One of the most basic human impulses, even of the savage, is to express oneself in some rhythmic manner; and when a man thus expresses himself in the hearing of others, whether it be by beating a tom-tom or by reciting a sonnet, the influence of the rhythm spreads. The heightened emotion of one man becomes, by contagion, the heightened emotion of a whole group. An extreme instance of this is the manner in which, in revival meetings, rhythmic sermonizing, followed by singing and chanting, culminates in an often uncontrollable mass paroxysm of emotional fervor.

In a highly refined and subtle form, this is what happens when we read poetry, or hear it read. The regular recurrence of accent provides a rhythmic, and therefore at least potentially emotional, context. The reader is made more receptive to the emotional suggestions of the words themselves. Thus the total

emotional experience of poetry derives from two main sources
—the connotative effect of the words and the arrangement of
those words in a definitely rhythmic pattern.

But much damage has been done by teachers who have in-
sisted that pupils "scan" poetry—that is, mark off the accented
and the unaccented syllables into uniform groups which are
called "feet." In so doing, they have implied that verse is
nothing but a monotonous series of iambs or trochees or whatever: da-*dum,* da-*dum,* da-*dum,* da-*dum;* or *dum*-da, *dum*-da,
dum-da; or da-da-*dum,* da-da-*dum,* da-da-*dum.* While it is perfectly true that such a regular beat *underlies* verse, that is not
the most important thing.

We have seen that the various words and phrases which make
up a sentence receive all degrees of stress: some, like the articles
the and *a,* are passed over so lightly that often we almost fail to
hear them, while others, such as nouns and verbs, receive greater
emphasis. The amount of emphasis depends largely on the logical importance of each word in context. If you will now read
aloud the preceding sentences, you will hear how subtly your
accentuation is modified, from word to word, by the sense itself.

Keeping the all-important fact of sentence rhythm in mind,
let us now look at the first portion of Emerson's poem, "The
Snow-Storm":

> Announced by all the trumpets of the sky,
> Arrives the snow, and, driving o'er the fields,
> Seems nowhere to alight: the whited air
> Hides hills and woods, the river, and the heaven,
> And veils the farm-house at the garden's end.
> The sled and traveler stopped, the courier's feet
> Delayed, all friends shut out, the housemates sit
> Around the radiant fireplace, enclosed
> In a tumultuous privacy of storm.

If we read this passage aloud, according to the strict requirements of the meter alone, it would sound—as nearly as we can
reproduce sound on the printed page—something like this:

anNOUNCED by ALL the TRUMpets OF the SKY (*pause*)
arRIVES the SNOW and DRIVing O'ER the FIELDS (*pause*)
seems NOwhere TO aLIGHT the WHITed AIR (*pause*)
hides HILLS and WOODS the RIVer AND the HEAVen (*pause*)
and VEILS the FARMhouse AT the GARden's END (*pause*)
the SLED and TRAVeler STOPPED the COURier's FEET (*pause*)
deLAYED all FRIENDS shut OUT the HOUSEmates SIT (*pause*)
aROUND the RADiANT firePLACE enCLOSED (*pause*)
in A tuMULtuOUS priVAcy OF storm (*pause*)

Anyone who is not completely insensitive to the beauties of
sound would agree that that is a dastardly thing to do to any bit
of verse. By paying strict and absolutely unimaginative attention to the "notation" suggested by the metrical pattern, we
have destroyed the sense of the passage. All we have is an intolerably monotonous tick-tock, tick-tock, tick-tock.

We now assume for the moment that the passage is written
as prose:

Announced by all the trumpets of the sky, arrives the snow, and,
driving o'er the fields, seems nowhere to alight: the whited air hides
hills and woods, the river, and the heaven, and veils the farm-house
at the garden's end. The sled and traveler stopped, the courier's
feet delayed, all friends shut out, the housemates sit around the
radiant fireplace, enclosed in a tumultuous privacy of storm.

Since we are not forewarned—by the arrangement of the words
into lines of what we are accustomed to recognize as "verse"—
that the passage is written in iambic meter, five accents to a
line, we are under no compulsion to stress the beat. Instead,
we read it as we would read any prose, with predominant regard for the sense. Although no two persons will read the same
passage in exactly the same way—and fully recognizing the
inadequacy of using only two degrees of stress, light and heavy
—this is roughly the way it would sound, with a slanted line
indicating a short pause, and a double line, a full stop:

anNOUNCED by all the TRUMpets of the SKY / arRIVES the
SNOW / and / DRIVing o'er the FIELDS / seems NOwhere to
aLIGHT // the WHITed AIR HIDES HILLS and WOODS / the

RIVer / and the HEAVen / and VEILS the FARMhouse at the GARden's end // the SLED and TRAVeler STOPPED / the COURier's FEET deLAYED / all FRIENDS SHUT OUT / the HOUSEmates sit around the RADiant FIREplace / enCLOSED in a tuMULtuous PRIvacy of STORM //

Comparing this version with the one produced by uncompromising fidelity to the meter, you see that most of the metrical accents fall upon the syllables which are also accented by the sense. This is as it should be; the result otherwise would be monstrously artificial. But in the strictly metrical reading, many syllables are stressed which are left unstressed in the "sense" reading. The unimportant is given a false degree of emphasis. Finally, the first version provides for pauses only at the end of each line; but these pauses are not always called for by the sentence construction—indeed, they often break the normal flow of the sentence. In the "sense" version, however, the pauses are inserted where the sentence construction requires, regardless of their position in the line. Strict metrical reading, that is, disregards punctuation; reading for sense takes the punctuation into full account.

Obviously, the second version is better than the first; it is intelligible, and furthermore, because the metrical accents and the sense accents largely coincide, it preserves the essential rhythm. But it is impossible to represent typographically a much better reading—the ideal reading. We can only describe what it is like.

The *complete* rhythm of poetry, as distinguished from the rigidly mechanical recurrence of stressed and unstressed syllables, is a subtle blending of the two sorts of rhythm we have been discussing. The metrical pattern hovers always in the background; but above it, and along with it, moves the larger, more varied rhythm of the sentence as a whole. If you listen to the opening bars of the Brahms First Symphony, you will hear a musical analogue of this conjunction of two rhythms. The drums (the regular meter) beat a precise, unchanging accompaniment in the background as the strings (the sense-current)

weave a constantly varying fabric of sound. The two movements, taken separately, are unimpressive; but when they are
combined, the one "setting off" the other, they give a rich,
stately effect.*

This is the most important thing to remember about the
rhythm of verse. *Basic* regularity of stress is essential; but it is
tolerable only when combined with the varied stresses and
pauses dictated by the logic of the sentence. If we overemphasize the meter, we obscure the sense and the overtones of the
sense; if we overemphasize the normal intonations, we obscure the pleasurable regularity. Only when the two are fused
into a single harmonious pattern are the possibilities of rhythmic language fully realized.

EXERCISE 14

One of the passages printed below is an excerpt from a poem
famous for its lovely cadences, which combine a regular meter
(iambic pentameter) with the rhythms of natural speech. The
other passage is a rewritten, much inferior, version of the same
passage. Which is the original? How can you tell?

1.   . . . For I have learned
    To look on nature, not as in the hour
    Of thoughtless youth; but oftentimes hearing
    The music of humanity, sad, still,
    Nor grating nor harsh, though of ample power
    To subdue and chasten. And I have felt
    A presence that disturbs me with the joy
    Of elevated thoughts; a sublime sense
    Of something interfused far more deeply,
    Whose dwelling is the light of setting suns,
    And the ocean round and the living air,
    And the blue sky, and in man's mind:
    A spirit and a motion, that impels

---

* Another musical analogue is found in the second movement of the Tschai-
kowsky Sixth ("Pathétique") Symphony.

All thinking things, every object of every thought,
And rolls through all things.

2.   . . . For I have learned
To look on nature, not as in the hour
Of thoughtless youth; but hearing oftentimes
The still, sad music of humanity,
Nor harsh nor grating, though of ample power
To chasten and subdue. And I have felt
A presence that disturbs me with the joy
Of elevated thoughts; a sense sublime
Of something far more deeply interfused,
Whose dwelling is the light of setting suns,
And the round ocean and the living air,
And the blue sky, and in the mind of man;
A motion and a spirit, that impels
All thinking things, all objects of all thought,
And rolls through all things.

EXERCISE 15

Here are three more pairs of passages. Decide in each case
which of the two alternative passages is more pleasing to the
ear and which is more successful in matching the rhythm to
the mood.

1. (a) The sea is calm tonight.
The tide is full, the moon lies fair
Upon the straits;—on the French coast the light
Gleams and is gone; the cliffs of England stand,
Glimmering and vast, out in the tranquil bay.
Come to the window, sweet is the night-air!
Only, from the long line of spray
Where the sea meets the moon-blanched land,
Listen! you hear the grating roar
Of pebbles which the waves draw back, and fling,
At their return, up the high strand,
Begin, and cease, and then again begin,
With tremulous cadence slow, and bring
The eternal note of sadness in.

(b) Calm tonight, how calm the sea is!
　　Full's the tide, and fair the moon lies
　　On the straits; the lights of France first
　　Gleam, then go; the English cliffs stand
　　Glimm'ring, vast, o'er the tranquil bay.
　　Come, look out! how sweet the night air!
　　Only, from the line of spray,
　　Where the sea meets moonlit land,
　　Listen! hear the grating roar—
　　Pebbles, which the waves draw back,
　　Flinging then upon the strand—
　　Start, and stop, and start again,
　　Bringing, with slow and tremulous cadence,
　　Th' eternal note of sadness in.

2. (a) I hate to count the time I've spent in wooing,
　　In fruitless watching, in futile pursuing.
　　The light that people say always lies
　　In lovely but fickle woman's eyes,
　　Has proved to be my poor heart's undoing.
　　Though Dame Wisdom time after time has sought me,
　　I pushed aside the good advice she brought me;
　　To tell the truth, my only guide books
　　Were that woman's come-hither looks,
　　And, in short, folly's the total of what they taught me.

　(b) The time I've lost in wooing,
　　In watching and pursuing
　　　　The light that lies
　　　　In woman's eyes,
　　Has been my heart's undoing.
　　　Though Wisdom oft has sought me,
　　　I scorn'd the lore she brought me,
　　　　My only books
　　　　Were woman's looks,
　　　And folly's all they've taught me.

3. (a) I've travelled much in the realms of gold,
　　　And many goodly kingdoms and states seen;
　　　Round numerous western isles have I been
　　Which bards to Apollo in fealty hold.
　　Often of one wide expanse I'd been told

       That was ruled by deep-brow'd Homer as his demesne;
       Yet I never breathed its pure serene
   Till old Chapman spoke out loud and bold:
   Then I felt akin to some watcher of the skies
       When swimmeth a new planet into his ken;
   Or else like Cortez, when with eagle eyes
       At the Pacific star'd he—and every one of his men
   Look'd at one another with wild surmise—
       Silent, standing on a peak in Darien.

(b) Much have I travell'd in the realms of gold,
       And many goodly states and kingdoms seen;
       Round many western islands have I been
   Which bards in fealty to Apollo hold.
   Oft of one wide expanse had I been told
       That deep-brow'd Homer ruled as his demesne;
       Yet did I never breathe its pure serene
   Till I heard Chapman speak out loud and bold:
   Then felt I like some watcher of the skies
       When a new planet swims into his ken;
   Or like stout Cortez when with eagle eyes
       He star'd at the Pacific—and all his men
   Look'd at each other with a wild surmise—
       Silent, upon a peak in Darien.

CHAPTER FIVE

Tone

W E ARE NOW READY to apply the lessons of the preceding chapters to the subject of *tone*. Tone results from the interaction of almost everything we have been talking about up to this point; it is the total emotional and intellectual effect of a passage of writing. To it, connotation, diction, and rhythm all contribute. An important function of language, we have seen, is to mold a reader's attitude toward the subject discussed. Tone determines just what that attitude will be.

A writer's attitude toward what he discusses is not necessarily identical with the response he wants to produce in his reader. An advertising man, for instance, or a ghost writer for men in public life, may be completely indifferent to his subject, or he may have very different views from those he is expected to propagate. But since it is his job to make his reader feel a certain way toward his subject, he deliberately writes in a vein that he thinks is most likely to evoke that feeling. From the reader's standpoint it is highly desirable that such strategy be understood and taken into account before a decision is made and acted upon. That is one practical reason why you should know what tone is, and how it is created.

But a more important reason is that an understanding of tone and its contributory elements can enrich your enjoyment of imaginative literature. If you know how tone is achieved, you can discover what sort of attitude a poet or essayist or novelist has toward his subject. It may be that, once you have ascertained his position, you will be reluctant to share it as he desires you to do. That is all right; that is the sacred privilege of the genuinely critical reader. Or it may be that a similar consideration of tone will intensify your experience by clarifying the author's precise mood and thus revealing subtle meanings of whose existence you had been unaware. In any event, you have nothing to lose and everything to gain by always remembering that tone is meant to influence *you*.

The last two paragraphs should sound familiar to you, because, though put in somewhat different form, they say little more than was said in the very beginning of this book. And as we discuss various specific ways by which the tone of a piece of writing is determined, we shall be drawing constantly upon the ideas presented in earlier chapters. We shall take for granted that by this time you are adequately aware of the power of words in general. What we shall do now is show the influence on tone of two or three special sorts of language—metaphors, symbols, and allusions.

Metaphors

First, about metaphors. (We use the word here in its inclusive sense of all figures of speech.) You will have no trouble understanding how metaphors operate if you have mastered the two sections of this book which deal with analogy and connotation. The function of a metaphor is to suggest an analogy. If a writer wishes to make something clearer and more vivid, he draws into his discussion, if only by a single word or two, a concrete image which brings to mind one or more qualities possessed by the situation or object or person or abstract idea which needs illustration. For example, in describing the scene at a busy corner at various hours of the day and night, a feature writer may wish to impress his readers with several dominant characteristics of the crowd—its largeness, its appearance of oneness (people lose their individual identities and are swallowed up in the mass), its motion, and the fact that its size fluctuates at various hours. Now the writer *could* come right out and use

those words—"largeness," "oneness," "motion," "fluctuation."
But they are abstract words; they fail to make the reader "see."
And so the writer may fall back on a cliché which, even if it
lacks freshness, at least conveys the idea: he will speak of "the
tides of humanity." As every reader will realize if he thinks
about it, the tides of the sea have some of the same characteristics which the writer finds in the people who pass by the corner.
The writer makes his point by an implied analogy between the
sea and the crowd. The strength of the analogy lies in the readiness and vividness with which the reader recognizes the qualities that the two objects share—their bonds of similarity.

Writers use metaphorical language primarily as a means of
intellectual clarification. It makes abstract ideas concrete, complex ideas simple, unfamiliar ideas more comprehensible. But
it has an additional effect—one which may be, in the long run,
more important than the first. The thing to remember is that
metaphors evoke mental images; and mental images often have
powerful emotional qualities. Thus the selection of metaphors
has a great deal to do with the total emotional context—the
tone—of any passage of writing.

In our discussion of the cliché (pages 96-102) we saw one way
in which a writer's use of metaphor may give us a clue to his
thought processes. If he depends on hackneyed figures of speech
to convey his meaning, the probability is that he sees with the
eyes of others. By cultivating your awareness of trite language,
you are arming yourself against writers who seek to influence
you with second-hand ideas as well as with second-hand
language.

But a writer's metaphors may also tell you other things about
him and his own attitude, as well as the attitude he wishes you to
have. Ordinarily, metaphors should fulfill two requirements:
they should harmonize with the writer's intention and with the
subject and atmosphere he wants to portray, and within a brief
passage they should harmonize with each other. Metaphorical
language, then, should be appropriate and consistent—unless,

as we shall see, a writer has special reason for violating this general rule.

The following quotation from a newspaper report of a concert by the Pittsburgh Symphony Orchestra illustrates a writer's failure to observe either one of these principles:

Having opened the program with Moussorgsky's "A Night on Bald Mountain," a work which has been preserved for posterity by the brilliance of Rimsky-Korsakoff's orchestration, the orchestra launched into the main musical bill-of-fare for the evening, Brahms' second symphony. One could hardly have wished for more, for this Brahms masterpiece stands as a monument of musical architecture to the German master. From the opening, with its haunting principal theme, to the close, Mr. Reiner guided the big orchestra through the maze of sturdy contrapuntal fabric which is Johannes Brahms, with the skill of a harbor pilot steering a boat safely into port through familiar but treacherous waters.

Now the tone of the whole article (not reprinted here) is serious. The writer apparently wishes to present an accurate report of a concert, which is a delicate and complex imaginative experience. But does his choice of language and metaphor support this serious intent? Is it, indeed, at all consistent with the subject discussed? Scarcely. "Launch" has the connotation of impetuous, headlong, forceful, even somewhat disorderly action; one of its dictionary definitions is "to shove off." Can a symphony orchestra be said to "launch" into anything—unless (which is plainly not the case here) the writer wants to ridicule its performance? Is "bill-of-fare," with its connotation of restaurant food, appropriate in a report of an event in the concert hall? "Monument of musical architecture," although it cannot stand too much logical scrutiny and is, in any event, cliché, at least is more in keeping with the tone of the whole article. But above all, what about the metaphor by which the conductor is likened to a pilot and the Brahms symphony to an ocean liner, while the difficulties of the work are represented first as a maze (of fabric!) and then as the treacherous waters of a harbor? The continuity of tone is rudely disrupted as, against our expectation and our desire, we are forced to envision a grizzled pilot on the bridge of the *Queen Elizabeth* as she slowly makes her way among the tugboats and barges of New York harbor. What has happened to the Brahms symphony? The writer, it is quite plain, completely lacks a sense of fitness. As a result, his report, because it has no steady point of view, no coherent tone, fails to communicate his experience to his readers.

The skilled writer—one who fully understands what he wishes to accomplish and knows how to go about accomplishing it—always takes care that his metaphors make the same sort of impression on the reader as the passage would if stripped of its metaphors. The connotative function of the metaphor is to reinforce the tone established by the writer's choice of language in general. If the writer hopes to establish rapport with his reader on the basis of man-to-man talk, his metaphors will be drawn from common, everyday experience, just as his diction is designed to reflect the normal speech of the reader to whom he is addressing himself. But if he wishes to elevate his reader's feelings, his metaphors will themselves have that elevated quality. Unless each individual metaphor harmonizes with the tone of the whole, the reader will be distracted by the extraneous and irrelevant elements which are unexpectedly forced into his experience.

Metaphorical language which seems inappropriate to the general tone of the passage may suggest (as in the case of our music critic) that the writer simply does not have a clear idea of his purpose or of the way to achieve it. But there is another possibility: may not the writer be *deliberately* using incongruous metaphor for some purpose? For one thing, poets and prose writers often use an unexpected and superficially inappropriate metaphor for the sake of contrast. The tone (or "atmosphere") of *Hamlet* is largely derived from the abundance of metaphors referring to disease, corruption, and decay; there is much talk of the putrefaction of flesh, evil smells, and the unpleasant qualities of ulcers and blisters. Such metaphors effectively symbolize one theme of the play, which is the moral degeneration of the people in the court at Elsinore. But in the midst of these figures of speech suddenly occurs a passage (act IV, scene 5) in which the talk is of roses, pansies, columbines, daisies, and violets, whose sweet fragrance is in strange contrast to the noisome odors which have been so much talked of ("My offence is rank; it smells to heaven"). The effect of such seeming incongruity is not to destroy the dominant emotional tone; rather, the flower references intensify it by throwing the corruption-infection theme into stronger relief. The physical ugliness which symbolizes moral evil is made to seem even uglier by its juxtaposition with symbols of innocent beauty.

In one of his dispatches from the Spanish Civil War, Ernest Hemingway said of the German planes that were aiding the rebels: "If their orders are to strafe the road on their way home, you will get it. Otherwise, when they are finished with their jobs on their particular objective, they go off like bank clerks, flying home." And he continued: "Up toward Tortosa things looked quite deadly already from the way the planes were acting. But down here on the delta the artillery were still only warming up, like baseball pitchers lobbing them over in the bull pen."* Now the "bonds of similarity" between German planes and bank clerks (both are eager to get home after the day's work) and between the warming-up respectively of heavy guns and of baseball pitchers (leisureliness, no great attention to control) make Hemingway's metaphors effective so far as the clarification of ideas is concerned. But are not bank clerks and baseball pitchers incongruous in the grim context of war? They are: and that is why Hemingway used them. German planes, even in 1938, when this dispatch was written, epitomized ruthlessness—but there is scarcely a less harmful man alive than a bank clerk! By setting the two side by side, Hemingway sought to make the reader more acutely conscious of the sinister meaning of the German planes in contrast to the peaceful inoffensiveness of a homing bank clerk. And the mention of baseball pitchers in connection with artillery underscores the vast, tragic

* Quoted by permission of *The New Republic*.

difference between the motives of gunners and those of pitchers.
Hemingway, in a word, influenced his readers' attitude toward
war by his use of contrasting metaphors from peacetime.

Thus a careful consideration of the appropriateness of metaphor can throw light on a writer's attitude toward his subject
and the attitude that he expects us to have. In a similar manner
we can find clues in the consistency, or lack of consistency, of
the metaphors in a passage. The extended or repeated use of
concrete language evokes in the reader's mind a series of pictures. Just as the retina of the physical eye retains an after-
image, so does the eye of the imagination. When we read at
normal speed, the picture that occurs in our mind is not in-
stantly blotted out as soon as we have left the word that has
called it forth. Instead, it lingers for an instant; and if another
image is suggested before the first one has faded, the result will
be a sort of double exposure. Unless the two images are of the
same type, so that the second has a natural similarity to the first,
they will clash, and the total effect will be one of confusion. That
is what happened when our music critic spoke of a launching, a
bill-of-fare, a monument of musical architecture, and an arriv-
ing ocean liner—all in the space of a sentence or two.

In the daily newspaper of a famous university a few years ago
appeared these sentences:

Let's look at the two [Un-American Activities] committees already
established in both houses of Congress. They're run by Senator
McCarthy and Representative Velde—two peas in a pod. Both have
juggled hot potatoes in recent months. And the result is that too
many innocent persons have received burnt fingers while the Red-
hunting congressmen have walked off with the gravy of fat headlines.

Here we have a glorious riot of imagery! First the Senator and
the Representative are transformed into two peas in a pod.
Then the two peas snap out of their cozy pod and become jugglers (in a television act?), tossing hot potatoes around. The
"burnt fingers" of the next sentence would be consistent with

the "hot potatoes"—except that it is not the jugglers whose fingers are burnt, but the innocent persons (if "hot potatoes" refers to people as well as issues) whom they have tossed around. In other words, a reader taking the metaphor seriously would have to conclude that the hot potatoes themselves have received burnt fingers. Then, suddenly, the jugglers shoulder muskets and start hunting Reds; but what they walk off with is not game but gravy—gravy somehow obtained from "fat" headlines. How they got back into the kitchen is not explained. At least we do have some of the makings of a dinner—peas, potatoes, and gravy.

What happened was that in the student journalist's mind such terms as *peas in a pod, juggled, hot potatoes, burnt fingers, hunting, gravy,* and *fat* had lost whatever metaphorical force they once possessed for him; they were simply clichés that seemed to serve his purpose of writing vividly. Used singly, they would not have been so bad, though the writing would still be indefensibly trite. But jumbled together in this fashion, they form a passage that is not only hackneyed but hilarious.

Sometimes a writer uses a single metaphor to support and illuminate a whole long passage of his discussion. If he does it well, we are justified in thinking that he has an unusually agile mind, which can follow a single analogy into many ramifications, all of them germane to the argument. But extended metaphors are dangerous devices in the hands of the less skilled. A freshman writer of a thousand-word "autobiography," for instance, sometimes begins by likening his life, down to the age of seventeen or eighteen, to the building of a house, and he insists on using the metaphor in every paragraph. ("The ground was broken . . . the architects were my parents . . . slowly but surely the foundations were laid . . . when I began school, it may be said that the first floor was finished and ready for occupancy . . ." etc.) While the initial idea may have been sound, the attempt to show that the stages of childhood and youth are analogous at every point to the stages of building a house results only in absurdity. Even in more serious writing, for a wide audience, an extended metaphor may have the same result, if w

examine it closely enough. Some writers, who are more clever
than honest, begin with a perfectly acceptable implied analogy
in the form of a metaphor. They thus win the faith of their
readers, who are likely to accept without serious question every
ensuing application of that analogy, whether it is logical or not.

For practice in examining an extended metaphor, read the
following passage. Is the analogy sound at every point? Or does
the writer sometimes strain his metaphor to make it apply to
everything he is saying?

I find the great thing in this world is not so much where we stand,
as in what direction we are moving: to reach the port of heaven, we
must sail sometimes with the wind and sometimes against it—but we
must sail, and not drift, nor lie at anchor. There is one very sad
thing in old friendships, to every mind that is really moving onward.
It is this: that one cannot help using his early friends as the seaman
uses the log, to mark his progress. Every now and then we throw an
old schoolmate over the stern with a string of thought tied to him,
and look—I am afraid with a kind of luxurious and sanctimonious
compassion—to see the rate at which the string reels off, while he lies
there bobbing up and down, poor fellow! and we are dashing along
with the white foam and bright sparkle at our bows;—the ruffled
bosom of prosperity and progress, with a sprig of diamonds stuck
in it! But this is only the sentimental side of the matter; for grow
we must, if we outgrow all that we love.

Don't misunderstand that metaphor of heaving the log, I beg you.
It is merely a smart way of saying that we cannot avoid measuring
our rate of movement by those with whom we have long been in the
habit of comparing ourselves; and when they once become station-
ary, we can get our reckoning from them with painful accuracy. We
see just what we were when they were our peers, and can strike the
balance between that and whatever we may feel ourselves to be now.
No doubt we may sometimes be mistaken. If we change our last
simile to that very old and familiar one of a fleet leaving the harbor
and sailing in company for some distant region, we can get what we
want out of it. There is one of our companions;—her streamers were
torn into rags before she had got into the open sea, then by and by
her sails blew out of the ropes one after another, the waves swept
her deck, and as night came on we left her a seeming wreck, as we

flew under our pyramid of canvas. But lo! at dawn she is still in sight—it may be in advance of us. Some deep ocean-current has been moving her on, strong, but silent—yes, stronger than these noisy winds that puff our sails until they are swollen as the cheeks of jubilant cherubim. And when at last the black steam-tug with the skeleton arms, which comes out of the mist sooner or later and takes us all in tow, grapples her and goes off panting and groaning with her, it is to that harbor where all wrecks are refitted, and where, alas! we, towering in our pride, may never come.

EXERCISE 1

Here are a number of definitions of slang by eminent writers, past and present. How do the connotations of the metaphor used by each writer define his own attitude?

1. Slang is language that takes off its coat, spits on its hands, and gets to work.
2. Slang is a dressing-room in which language, having an evil deed to prepare, puts on a disguise.
3. Slang is the speech of him who robs the literary garbage-carts on their way to the dumps.
4. The language of the street is always strong. . . . Cut these words and they would bleed; they are vascular and alive; they walk and run.
.5. Slang is the wholesome fermentation or eructation of those processes eternally active in language, by which the froth and specks are thrown up, mostly to pass away, though occasionally to settle and permanently crystallize.

EXERCISE 2

In this miscellaneous group of metaphors from prose and poetry, examine each quotation for these points: (1) the vividness and freshness with which the metaphor illuminates the idea; (2) the appropriateness of the metaphor to the subject discussed; (3) the clues the metaphor offers to the attitude of the writer, or to the attitude he wishes the reader to have.

1. Her smile was silent as the smile on corpses three hours old.

2. [The question: Whom did Shakespeare address his sonnets to, and to what degree are they autobiographical?] There are many footprints around the cave of this mystery, none of them pointing in the outward direction. No one has ever attempted a solution of the problem without leaving a book behind him; and the shrine of Shakespeare is thickly hung with these votive offerings, all withered and dusty. No one has ever sought to gain access to this heaven of poetry by a privileged and secret stairway, without being blown ten thousand leagues awry, over the backside of the world, into the Paradise of Fools. The quest remains unachieved.

3.
> A tree whose hungry mouth is pressed
> Against the sweet earth's flowing breast;
>
> A tree that looks at God all day,
> And lifts her leafy arms to pray;
>
> A tree that may in summer wear
> A nest of robins in her hair;
>
> Upon whose bosom snow has lain;
> Who intimately lives with rain.*

4. [A visitor's impression of New York's East Side] The architecture seemed to sweat humanity at every window and door.

5.
> Day after day, day after day,
> We stuck, nor breath nor motion;
> As idle as a painted ship
> Upon a painted ocean.

6. I take great comfort in God. I think he is considerably amused with us sometimes, but that he likes us, on the whole, and would not let us get at the match-box so carelessly as he does, unless he knew that the frame of his Universe was fire-proof. How many times have I not seen the fire-engines of Church and State clanging and lumbering along to put out—a false alarm! And when the heavens are cloudy what a glare can be cast by a burning shanty!

* From *Trees and Other Poems*, by Joyce Kilmer. Copyright 1914 by Doubleday & Co., Inc.

7.   I saw eternity the other night
            Like a great ring of pure and endless light,
              All calm, as it was bright.

8. (a) He looketh on the earth, and it trembleth; he toucheth the
            hills, and they smoke.
   (b) The hills forget they're fix'd, and in their fright
            Cast off their weight, and ease themselves for flight;
            The woods, with terror wing'd, outfly the wind,
            And leave the heavy, panting hills behind.

9.   The meadow and the mountain with desire
              Gazed on each other, till a fierce unrest
              Surged 'neath the meadow's seemingly calm breast,
            And all the mountain's fissures ran with fire.

            A mighty river rolled between them there.
              What could the mountain do but gaze and burn?
              What could the meadow do but look and yearn,
            And gem its bosom to conceal despair?

            Their seething passion agitated space,
              Till lo! the lands a sudden earthquake shook,
              The river fled: the meadow leaped, and took
            The leaning mountain in a close embrace.

10.   That time of year thou mayst in me behold
            When yellow leaves, or none, or few, do hang
            Upon those boughs which shake against the cold,
            Bare ruined choirs, where late the sweet birds sang.
            In me thou see'st the twilight of such day
            As after sunset fadeth in the west,
            Which by and by black night doth take away,
            Death's second self, that seals up all in rest.
            In me thou see'st the glowing of such fire
            That on the ashes of his youth doth lie,
            As the deathbed whereon it must expire,
            Consumed with that which it was nourished by.
              This thou perceivest, which makes thy love more
                strong,
                To love that well which thou must leave ere long.

11. It is no matter what you teach children first, any more than what leg you shall put into your breeches first. You may stand disputing which is best to put in first, but in the mean time your breech is bare. While you are considering which of two things you should teach your child first, another boy has learnt them both.

12. Selling and buying are a pitched battle: the consumer erects his sales resistance (as he might a stockade in Indian country) and the manufacturer tries to knock it down.

EXERCISE 3

In the light of what has been said about consistency of metaphor, comment on the effect of each of the following passages:

1. At season's close, end Jim Castle was elected captain for 1954, and Munger put the quietus on various draft movements attempting to pull him back into the grid wars. The ensuing "search for a coach" would have given Messrs. Gilbert and Sullivan food for several operatic parodies. In a free-wheeling policy of "come one, come all," hordes of candidates were interviewed, discussed, speculated about, photographed, fingerprinted, and everything but hired. Leaks and counter-leaks gave press representatives copy for dull afternoons, but the little bouncing ball refused to light. Thus, by mid-January, the athletic scene had thoroughly shifted. In addition, Pennsylvania's fortunes were firmly cast with the fast-jelling Ivy League, and her "suicide schedules" for '54 and '55 recognized as anachronisms already.

2. [Concerning a certain philosophical controversy] As it was, Newman easily turned his flank. No other instance probably can be found of a game in which one player held all the trumps, and another took all the tricks. Had Huxley been Newman's opponent the breaking of lances would have been a joy to witness. But Huxley would never have made Kingsley's initial mistake; and, but for that mistake, Newman would never have taken up the glove.

3. The defendant, in presenting his alibi, chose the alley he was going to bowl on—and the jury wouldn't swallow it.

4.   Tomorrow, and tomorrow, and tomorrow
            Creeps in this petty pace from day to day
            To the last syllable of recorded time;
            And all our yesterdays have lighted fools
            The way to dusty death. Out, out, brief candle!
            Life's but a walking shadow, a poor player,
            That struts and frets his hour upon the stage
            And then is heard no more. It is a tale
            Told by an idiot, full of sound and fury,
            Signifying nothing.

5. Suppose it were perfectly certain that the life and fortune of
every one of us would, one day or other, depend upon his winning or losing a game of chess. Don't you think that we should
all consider it to be a primary duty to learn at least the names
and the moves of the pieces; to have a notion of a gambit, and
a keen eye for all the means of giving and getting out of check?
Do you not think that we should look with a disapprobation
amounting to scorn, upon the father who allowed his son, or the
state which allowed its members, to grow up without knowing a
pawn from a knight?

Yet it is a very plain and elementary truth, that the life, the
fortune, and the happiness of every one of us, and, more or less,
of those who are connected with us, do depend upon our knowing something of the rules of a game infinitely more difficult and
complicated than chess. It is a game which has been played
for untold ages, every man and woman of us being one of the
two players in a game of his or her own. The chessboard is the
world, the pieces are the phenomena of the universe, the rules
of the game are what we call the laws of Nature. The player on
the other side is hidden from us. We know that his play is always fair, just, and patient. But also we know, to our cost, that
he never overlooks a mistake, or makes the smallest allowance
for ignorance. To the man who plays well, the highest stakes are
paid, with that sort of overflowing generosity with which the
strong shows delight in strength. And one who plays ill is check-
mated—without haste, but without remorse.

. . . Well, what I mean by Education is learning the rules of
this mighty game. In other words, education is the instruction
of the intellect in the laws of Nature, under which name I include not merely things and their forces, but men and their

ways; and the fashioning of the affections and of the will into an earnest and loving desire to move in harmony with those laws.

EXERCISE 4

Decide how appropriate and effective the metaphors in the following quotations are:

1. A word is not a crystal, transparent and unchanged; it is the skin of a living thought, and may vary greatly in color and content according to the circumstances and the time in which it is used.

2. If you detect the ridicule, and your kindliness is chilled by it, you are slipping into the grasp of Satire.

   If, instead of falling foul of the ridiculous person with a satiric rod, to make him writhe and shriek aloud, you prefer to sting him under a semi-caress, by which he shall in his anguish be rendered dubious whether indeed anything has hurt him, you are an engine of Irony.

   If you laugh all round him, tumble him, roll him about, deal him a smack, and drop a tear on him, own his likeness to you and yours to your neighbor, spare him as little as you shun, pity him as much as you expose, it is a spirit of Humor that is moving you.

3. What I like in a good author is not what he says, but what he whispers.

4. Adjectives are sirens; they betray all whom their music beguiles. Enslave them and you are master of the poetic art. Their talents are four: they have sound, meaning, decorative value and emotional value.

5. No language after it has faded into *diction*, none that cannot suck up the feeding juices secreted for it in the rich mother-earth of common folk, can bring forth a sound and lusty book. True vigor and heartiness of phrase do not pass from page to page, but from man to man, where the brain is kindled and the lips suppled by downright living interests and by passion in its very throe. Language is the soil of thought, and our own especially is a rich leaf-mould, the slow deposit of ages, the shed foliage of feeling, fancy, and imagination, which has suffered an

earth-change, that the vocal forest, as Howell called it, may clothe itself anew with living green. There is death in the dictionary; and, where language is too strictly limited by convention, the ground for expression to grow in is limited also; and we get a *potted* literature, Chinese dwarfs instead of healthy trees.

EXERCISE 5

The following are excerpts from a newspaper account of a concert by the Cincinnati Symphony Orchestra. Judge the appropriateness of the metaphors and the accuracy of the language generally:

The story of every song was written in the movements of his [the conductor's] body. The violins bounced like trampolins through the first section, Overture to the Opera "Oberon" by Weber, and made latecomers forget they were standing and not resting in their seats.

Minus the red faces they must have worn in the afternoon when the instruments didn't arrive, the musicians played their "gems" on a stage shrouded with curtains.

The program in its softness didn't leave the grandeur of a symphony orchestra in the minds that left the theatre. There wasn't a number that would have stirred the heart of a Sousa fan.

The last piece, "The Moldau" by Smetana, was light and gay enough to make concertgoers request two encores. At first it reminisced until it reached a roaring that rocked the stage, then it died to a theme similar to the "Flight of the Bumble Bee," and finally into a gay twirling dance with every twirl returning to a greater climax.

The concert was offered by the musicians in the manner of a seven-course dinner. The first numbers sharpened the appetite and as the program went on it got heavy with the entree until finally the first encore was like apple pie.

The surprise came when the pie was served a la mode with the final encore, No. 15 in C Major, Opus 72 by Dvorak.

Symbols

Down to this point, we have been concerned primarily with metaphors whose significance in context depends upon the situ ation which they are called upon to clarify. A metaphor involving a rose, for example, may serve one or more of a number of purposes. It may emphasize the idea of color: "Her cheek like the rose is, but fresher, I ween." It may emphasize the idea of odor:

> What's in a name? That which we call a rose
> By any other name would smell as sweet.

Or it may emphasize the idea of softness:

> There is sweet music here that softer falls
> Than petals from blown roses on the grass.

The special quality of the rose which is recalled by the comparison depends upon what quality is being emphasized by the context.

But now consider these other passages in which the rose is mentioned:

> When this, our rose, is faded,
>   And these, our days, are done,
> In lands profoundly shaded
>   From tempest and from sun;
> Ah, once more come together,
>   Shall we forgive the past,
> And safe from worldly weather
>   Possess our souls at last?*

> Loveliest of lovely things are they,
> On earth, that soonest pass away.
> The rose that lives its little hour
> Is prized beyond the sculptured flower.

> The fairest things have fleetest end,
>   Their scent survives their close:
> But the rose's scent is bitterness
>   To him that loved the rose.

---

* Reprinted by permission of Dodd, Mead & Co., Inc.

This world that we're a-livin' in
   Is mighty hard to beat;
You get a thorn with every rose,
   But ain't the roses sweet!

———

Gather ye rosebuds while ye may,
   Old Time is still a-flying,
And this same flower that smiles today
   Tomorrow will be dying.

In these instances the rose is not used for the sake of specific comparison. Instead, it "stands for" or symbolizes something: namely, physical beauty (with a frequent suggestion of impermanence). Our response to the mention of the rose is determined not so much by the emotional context as by our well-established habit of thinking of the rose as a symbol of beauty.

Symbols, therefore, are metaphors whose associative meaning is more or less permanently fixed. They are important in communication, above all in imaginative prose and poetry, because writers often allow them to bear the full meaning of a passage rather than to act as accessories and commentaries, as is the case with other metaphors. Symbolism, skillfully used, is far more effective than bald literal statement. This is true for two reasons. The first is that symbols, like other kinds of metaphor, call forth an emotional reaction by way of sensuous imagery; the second is that, because most symbols have figured in literature for centuries, they are surrounded by an aura of literary association which evokes in the well-read man a host of reminiscences of passages in older literature, with all that they themselves connote. The use of a river as a symbol of the eternal flux of life, of the absence of anything really permanent and substantial in our human existence, goes all the way back to Plato and Heraclitus, and countless writers of prose and poetry have used it since. One who reads Matthew Arnold's "The Future" finds in Arnold's extended use of the symbol, echoes of a hundred other men who have set down the same poignantly melancholy reflections on earthly vanities. Again, the symbolic mean-

ing of *serpent* has at least a twofold origin, in the story of the
Garden of Eden and in the classical myth of Medusa, who had
snakes for hair. It combines two tragic ideas: moral transformation—the fall from innocence into a state of sin, brought about
by deceit (Satan, Adam, and Eve), and physical transformation
—of a living being into stone (Medusa). Which aspect of the
symbol is emphasized depends on the context where it occurs.

It is impossible to read imaginative literature with genuine
understanding unless we keep constantly on the alert for these
pregnant symbols, which "mean" much more than they seem
to say on the surface. In a simple word or two, they sum up
the most important ideas in life. Here are a few common ones:

gold
: The symbol of wealth, of material (as opposed to
spiritual) possessions; also of happiness, hope, youth.
(See Exercise 7, part 3.)

moon
: Peace, serenity, chastity, romantic love; also (paradoxi-
cally) loneliness, changefulness.

star
: Remoteness, purity, permanence. (What is the meaning implied in Shelley's line, "The desire of the moth
for the star"?)

> Bright star, would I were steadfast as thou art!
> Not in lone splendor hung aloft the night,
> And watching, with eternal lids apart,
> Like Nature's patient, sleepless eremite,
> The moving waters at their priestlike task
> Of pure ablution round earth's human shores,
> Or gazing on the new soft-fallen mask
> Of snow upon the mountains and the moors:
> No—yet still steadfast, still unchangeable,
> Pillow'd upon my fair love's ripening breast,
> To feel forever its soft fall and swell,
> Awake forever in a sweet unrest,
> Still, still to hear her tender-taken breath,
> And so live ever—or else swoon to death.

crossroads
: A choice between two or more courses of action—usually a critical decision.

Two roads diverged in a yellow wood,
And sorry I could not travel both
And be one traveler, long I stood
And looked down one as far as I could
To where it bent in the undergrowth;

Then took the other, as just as fair,
And having perhaps the better claim,
Because it was grassy and wanted wear;
Though as for that the passing there
Had worn them really about the same,

And both that morning equally lay
In leaves no step had trodden black.
Oh, I kept the first for another day!
Yet knowing how way leads on to way,
I doubted if I should ever come back.

I shall be telling this with a sigh
Somewhere ages and ages hence:
Two roads diverged in a wood, and I—
I took the one less traveled by,
And that has made all the difference.*

ice   Coldness, and therefore often death. Also hardness,
and therefore the word can imply a personal attitude.

Some say the world will end in fire,
Some say in ice.
From what I've tasted of desire
I hold with those who favor fire.
But if it had to perish twice,
I think I know enough of hate
To say that for destruction ice
Is also great
And would suffice.*

The use of symbols like these adds much to the emotional tone of any piece of writing. Sometimes they reinforce an impression which is produced by other means. At other times they are used for ironic contrast, as when a novelist who has just described a sordid occurrence in the London slums suddenly shifts the reader's vision to the stars shining tranquilly in the skies, and thus intensifies, by contrast, the evil quality of what he has just been talking about.

While the general import of a symbol usually is fixed, its precise connotation varies with the tone of the passage in which it occurs. Thus symbolism and tone—the part and the whole—interact one upon the other. Take for example three abiding symbols of death—the words *sleep, grave,* and *worm*. Each word implies a different sort of attitude toward the fact of death. *Sleep* is almost wholly favorable in its attitude; it connotes relief from physical and mental pain, welcome oblivion. *Grave* has less of the warmth, the comfort, that *sleep* suggests. It implies, above all, silence, lack of motion, coldness. *Worm* is the least pleasant of the symbols, with its grisly suggestion of the physical disintegration of the body after death.

But note how, in the following passages, the precise feeling we are expected to adopt toward death is determined, not alone by the selection of one symbol rather than another, but by the context, which subtly modifies the connotation of the symbol:

> From too much love of living,
>   From hope and fear set free,
> We thank with brief thanksgiving
>   Whatever gods may be
> That no life lives for ever;
> That dead men rise up never;
> That even the weariest river
>   Winds somewhere safe to sea.
>
> Then star nor sun shall waken,
>   Nor any change of light:
> Nor sound of waters shaken,
>   Nor any sound or sight:

> Nor wintry leaves nor vernal,
> Nor days nor things diurnal;
> Only the sleep eternal
> In an eternal night.

Here the poet—Swinburne—plainly regards death as a narcotic
sleep. It is welcomed, not because it promises anything positive, but because at least it will blot out all the disappointed
hopes, the frustrations and uncertainties, of life. The meaning
of *sleep*, then, is colored by the lines that lead up to it.

> Our revels now are ended. These our actors,
> As I foretold you, were all spirits, and
> Are melted into air, into thin air;
> And, like the baseless fabric of this vision,
> The cloud-capp'd towers, the gorgeous palaces,
> The solemn temples, the great globe itself,
> Yea, all which it inherit, shall dissolve
> And, like this insubstantial pageant faded,
> Leave not a rack behind. We are such stuff
> As dreams are made on, and our little life
> Is rounded with a sleep.

To Shakespeare, in these lines, the sleep of death promises
nothing more than it promised to Swinburne; but death is
viewed not as a release from life, but as a natural culmination
of an existence which is itself unsubstantial and illusory. The
meaning of *sleep* in the last line is compounded of the meanings of many words that preceded it, all to the same effect—
*spirits, melted, thin air, baseless, vision, cloud-capp'd, dissolve,
insubstantial, faded, rack* [cloud fragment], *dreams*. Death and
life are two parts of a perfectly harmonious whole.

> To die; to sleep;
> No more; and by a sleep to say we end
> The heart-ache and the thousand natural shocks
> That flesh is heir to. 'Tis a consummation
> Devoutly to be wish'd. To die; to sleep;—
> To sleep? Perchance to dream! Ay, there's the rub;
> For in that sleep of death what dreams may come,

> When we have shuffl'd off this mortal coil,
> Must give us pause. There's the respect
> That makes calamity of so long life.

Here Shakespeare uses the same basic idea that Swinburne sets forth. But he finds in the symbol of sleep elements that Swinburne did not consider. Mention of dreams as a part of sleep in effect nullifies the usual meaning of the symbol. Compare the total effect of this passage with the preceding one, which also speaks of dreams. What is the difference?

EXERCISE 6

Here is a further group of passages in which the idea of death is represented by one or another of the symbols we have just mentioned—sleep, grave, and worms. By weighing the emotional tone of the whole passage, including the connotation of the other metaphors, try to decide just what attitude each writer wishes us to adopt toward death:

1. Is not short pain well borne, that brings long ease,
   And lays the soul to sleep in quiet grave?
   Sleep after toil, port after stormy seas,
   Ease after war, death after life does greatly please.

2. I must go down to the seas again to the vagrant gypsy life,
   To the gull's way and the whale's way where the wind's like a whetted knife;
   And all I ask is a merry yarn from a laughing fellow-rover,
   And quiet sleep and a sweet dream when the long trick's over.*

3. Wherever literature consoles sorrow or assuages pain; wherever it brings gladness to eyes which fail with wakefulness and tears, and ache for the dark house and the long sleep—there is exhibited in its noblest form the immortal influence of Athens.

4. Sleep is a death; oh make me try,
   By sleeping, what it is to die,
   And as gently lay my head
   On my grave, as now my bed.

* From *Poems*, by John Masefield. By permission of The Macmillan Company, publishers.

5.   Let's dry our eyes; and thus far hear me, Cromwell,
             And when I am forgotten, as I shall be,
             And sleep in dull cold marble, where no mention
             Of me more must be heard of, say, I taught thee.

6. Your worm is your only emperor for diet. We fat all creatures else to fat us, and we fat ourselves for maggots. Your fat king and your lean beggar is but variable service, two dishes, but to one table; that's the end. . . . A man may fish with the worm that hath eat of a king, and eat of the fish that hath fed of that worm. . . . [and thus] a king may go a progress through the guts of a beggar.

7.   He'd have the best, and that was none too good;
             No barrier could hold, before his terms.
             He lies below, correct in cypress wood,
             And entertains the most exclusive worms.

8. The place and the object [Rome viewed from the Capitoline hill] gave ample scope for moralising on the vicissitudes of fortune, which spares neither man nor the proudest of his works, which buries empires and cities in a common grave; and it was agreed that in proportion to her former greatness the fall of Rome was the more awful and deplorable.

9. *Romeo* [to Mercutio, who is badly wounded]:
Courage, man; the hurt cannot be much.
Mercutio: No, 'tis not so deep as a well, nor so wide as a church-door, but 'tis enough, 'twill serve. Ask for me tomorrow, and you shall find me a grave man.

EXERCISE 7

1. What is the usual meaning of the following symbols?

Sunrise, noon, twilight, autumn, April, seed, tear, tinsel, drum, snow, eagle, laurel, crown, crucifix, tide, wine, poppy, white, purple, red, gray, green, lion, nightingale

2. Read Ivan Bunin's short story, "The Gentleman from San Francisco," and compile a list of the many symbols it contains.

3. Examine the various ways in which the symbols of gold and

twilight (along with gray, silver, etc.) add emotional depth
to the situation in Browning's poem "Andrea del Sarto." In
line 26, what does "serpentining beauty" denote, and what
does it symbolize?

EXERCISE 8

Explain the symbolism of the following quotations:

1. [Of Dickens' *Pickwick Papers*] The thing is aimed at the dia-
   phragm, and, by ricochet, touches the heart.

2. After all, what laws can be laid down about books? . . . To admit
   authorities, however heavily furred and gowned, into our libraries and let them tell us how to read, what to read, what value to
   place upon what we read, is to destroy the spirit of freedom
   which is the breath of those sanctuaries.* [What is the symbolic
   meaning of "furred and gowned"?]

3.
    > Snow falling and night falling fast oh fast
    > In a field I looked into going past,
    > And the ground almost covered smooth in snow,
    > But a few weeds and stubble showing last.
    >
    > The woods around it have it—it is theirs.
    > All animals are smothered in their lairs.
    > I am too absent-spirited to count;
    > The loneliness includes me unawares.
    >
    > And lonely as it is that loneliness
    > Will be more lonely ere it will be less—
    > A blanker whiteness of benighted snow
    > With no expression, nothing to express.
    >
    > They cannot scare me with their empty spaces
    > Between stars—on stars where no human race is.
    > I have it in me so much nearer home
    > To scare myself with my own desert places.†

* From *The Second Common Reader*, by Virginia Woolf. By permission of
Harcourt, Brace & Co., publishers.
  † From *Complete Poems of Robert Frost*, 1949. Copyright, 1916, 1923, 1949,
by Henry Holt and Company, Inc.; copyright, 1936, 1942, 1943, by Robert Frost.

Allusions

In Chapter One we said, "Often a single line or two may contain a wealth of suggestiveness. To one who knows the story of the fall of Troy, Marlowe's lines

> Was this the face that launched a thousand ships,
> And burnt the topless towers of Ilium?

contain all the emotional values implicit in the story of a beautiful woman for whose love a civilization was almost destroyed." This was an anticipatory example of another important source of tone: the allusion, which is a reference to specific places, persons, literary passages, or historical events that, like metaphorical symbols, have come to "stand for" a certain idea. Every writer of anything more complicated than a comic strip relies to a greater or less extent upon the device of allusion. The degree of understanding with which anyone reads is directly proportional to the readiness with which he recognizes allusions when he encounters them—and recognizes not only their bare, literal meaning, but also their connotation. This readiness depends, in turn, upon the fund of general knowledge he has at his command. The more familiar he is with history and literature, the better prepared he is to receive the full message which the writer intends for him. The only way to cultivate such a familiarity is to read and read and read—and then to remember. It is possible, of course, to identify some allusions by going to books of reference, like Brewer's *Reader's Handbook,* the same compiler's *Dictionary of Phrase and Fable,* and Benét's *Reader's Encyclopedia.* But only a few conscientious souls will go to the trouble of constantly interrupting their reading to "look things up," and too frequent recourse to reference books is a dismal business anyway. The only genuinely satisfactory way to handle allusions is to be prepared for them when they come—so that one may have the justifiable pride of recognizing the already familiar.

We can illustrate the importance of allusions by referring to an entertaining essay by Wallace Stegner, called "Turtle at Home," which appeared a few years ago in a national magazine. "Turtle at Home" is an intimate report of the life of a turtle named Achilles, which survived innumerable encounters with trucks in the street but was crushed (metaphorically if not literally) by the irresistible force of Love in the person of another turtle. Unless we know who the Achilles of Homeric story was and what he represents, we miss the appropriateness of the turtle's name.

In the essay occurs this paragraph:

But strawberries were his real fleshpots. They left him giddy, speeded up his reactions, put him almost in a frenzy of bliss. I shall cherish to my last hour the picture of Achilles munching large Marshall strawberries with the juice running down his rhythmic jaws and his whole face beatific. He was Greek, he was Dionysiac, he was young Keats bursting Joy's grape against his palate fine, he was a Rabelaisian monk with his robe tucked up, glutting himself with pagan pleasures. What reflections of a like charm could one get from the sight of a dog wolfing his carnivorous meals, or a cat washing her face after meat with a fussy, old-maid, New England nasty-neatness?*

Here is a whole series of allusions, and the humor of the passage is completely lost if the reader cannot interpret them. Remember that Mr. Stegner is describing the sinful appetite of a pet turtle. "His real fleshpots": the dictionary may define the word, but it may not recall the historical association—the fleshpots of Egypt, with their place in Biblical story (*Exodus* xvi:3). "He was Greek, he was Dionysiac": an allusion to the festivals of ancient Greece in which the physical senses, particularly those connected with eating and drinking, were indulged to a point of frenzy. "He was young Keats . . .": we must recall Keats's "Ode on Melancholy":

> Ay, in the very temple of Delight
> Veil'd Melancholy has her sovran shrine,
> Though seen of none save him whose strenuous tongue
> Can burst Joy's grape against his palate fine.

* Reprinted by permission of Mr. Stegner and *The Atlantic Monthly.*

"He was a Rabelaisian monk . . .": an allusion to Friar John, that celebrated figure in Rabelais who took a healthy delight in the pleasures of the flesh.

Thus we have, in a single paragraph, a series of four allusions, drawn from the Old Testament, the history of ancient Greece, early nineteenth-century English literature, and Renaissance French literature: all of them connoting indulgence in the joys of the table and the cup. Mr. Stegner might have said, in sentences devoid of metaphor and allusion, that Achilles went wild over strawberries; but how much more vivid is this allusive paragraph—*if* the reader fully reacts to the allusions! Each symbol (because many allusions are just that) summons up, in the well-read man's consciousness, a whole complex of associations. He remembers the story that lay behind the fleshpots of Egypt; he recalls from his miscellaneous reading the nature of the Dionysiac revels; he knows that young Keats was enamored of sensuous pleasure; he sees again Rabelais' robust descriptions of the far from ascetic monk. In effect, therefore, Achilles' strawberry debauch is the sum of all the palatal orgies in human history.

But all this of a *turtle!* What can the gargantuan appetites of a pleasure-loving monk have in common with the quantitatively minute strawberry consumption of a turtle? Nothing, except the gusto. And that is the point. Mr. Stegner has carefully chosen his allusions for a particular purpose. First, they translate Achilles' unrestrained sensuality into a series of human equivalents, and thus induce the reader to regard Achilles in human terms. Secondly, the patent exaggeration and incongruity of the allusions have the ultimate effect of kindly humor. The reader's attitude toward Achilles' gormandizing has been determined by the connotative quality of the allusions.

Probably you think that this explanation has been laborious; and it has. But the very fact that we have labored in trying to explain the function of a few simple allusions in a contemporary essay has its own point, which is that allusions, like metaphors and symbols, are not meant to be analyzed; when they are thus examined, much of their power evaporates. They are meant to be apprehended automatically. The truly accomplished reader, when he encounters such a paragraph as we have quoted, does not stop to wonder what each allusion means; his acquaintance with literature and history enables him spontaneously to react as the writer intends him to. He *knows*.

There are three major sources of allusions, together with lesser sources which are as numerous as the fields of knowledge themselves. Those three major sources are mythology, literature (including the Bible), and history.

In the twentieth century it is hard for us to realize how important a part mythology played in the imaginations of writers and readers down through the ages. The gods and goddesses of Olympus, the heroes of ancient legend, were as familiar to the people who created the literature of the western world as are popular movie stars to us. Their very names—Juno, Hercules, Prometheus, Vulcan, Jupiter—had the power to evoke rich emotions which sprang from recollection of the wondrous stories in which these figures had their being. Unless you can somehow re-create for yourself the emotional experience a mythological reference brought to readers in older generations, your reading of noncontemporary literature will lack much of the pleasure and understanding it would otherwise possess. One practical way to learn more about mythology is to go to a focus-point of a great many of the myths and legends we have received from ancient Greece and Rome—the poems of Ovid, of which there are many translations. Another way is to browse in such collections as Bulfinch's *Age of Fable*. And in any event, you should read widely in English poetry; if you do, the individual attributes of the mythological figures, and the stories in which they occur, will gradually become familiar to you.

The main reason why modern men and women know so little about mythology is that few of them ever have, or take, the opportunity to read classical (i.e., Latin and Greek) literature, in which these myths are embodied. But even apart from its connection with mythology, a little knowledge of classical literature can be of tremendous help in equipping you to understand allusions even in everyday reading. The *Iliad* and the *Odyssey* of Homer, for instance, are full of episodes and personages that are frequently referred to in ordinary journalism, to say nothing of the permanent monuments of our literature. If we read of a certain political figure who is "sulking in his tent" because he has not got what he wanted, the meaning is far clearer if we recall the episode of Achilles (the fighter, not the turtle) sulking in his tent because he had captured in battle a beautiful girl whom his general, Agamemnon, would not let him keep. Or if someone's prophecies of doom have earned him the name of a Cassandra, it means much to know just who Cassandra was—and to do that we must know something of Greek tragedy. (What is the difference in implied attitude between "Cassandra" and "Jeremiah"?)

Naturally, allusions to our own English and American literature are more frequently encountered nowadays than classical allusions. Not the least of the purposes of a college course in literature is to show how a knowledge of older writing is essential to a full comprehension of present-day writing. Mr. Stegner, in the essay about the turtle, speaks of Achilles, after "he" has been discovered to be a "she," as "that Rosalind in boy's clothing." He expects his reader to recognize the allusion to the disguised heroine of *As You Like It,* and to enjoy the implied incongruity. And he concludes his essay with the simple statement, *"Amor vincit omnia."* One misses much if he does not recollect the fact—humorous in itself—that this motto was also inscribed on a brooch worn by the Prioress in Chaucer's *Canterbury Tales.*

In such a way, literary allusions help influence the precise effect of any piece of writing. In the case of references to characters in literature, we must know just what part they play in the poem or drama or novel in which they appear, and how their creator wished his readers to regard them in the first place. We then transfer this attitude to the new situation. If a man is called "a veritable Micawber," we are expected to react toward

him as we react toward Dickens' magniloquent, genial, shiftless
Micawber himself: our attitude is expected to be a mixture of
annoyance and amused tolerance. If, in his description of a
woman, a writer refers to Becky Sharp or to Scarlett O'Hara, we
know we are to look upon her as a selfish, willful woman. Instances could be multiplied almost indefinitely. We often run
across references to Mr. So-and-so's "Man Friday." The allusion,
of course, is to the friend and servant of Robinson Crusoe, and
originally it connoted only helpfulness and devotion. Today,
however, the implication has changed, and "Man Friday" has
something of a derogatory tone; it suggests not only man-of-all-
work but also someone akin to a stooge. Similarly the term
"young Lochinvar" ("Young Lochinvar came out of the west"—
Scott's *Marmion*) has suffered a change of connotation. Whereas
it originally symbolized manliness, nowadays it carries a suggestion of priggishness and unpleasant precocity—as when it is
used of a new and untried political leader whose virtues have
been proclaimed with suspicious fervor.

Quotations embedded in the text are a type of allusion. The
pleasure and profit of our reading are increased when we recognize such stray phrases and recall their full meaning in their
original context. In his classic description of a prize fight,
William Hazlitt uses both simple allusion and direct quotation
to good purpose to emphasize the attitude which he maintains
throughout the essay—that this is no ordinary fight, but a battle
of supermen worthy of Homeric epic. And so he draws into his
narrative echoes both of Homer and of Milton, whose *Paradise
Lost* is partially modeled upon Homer's epics.

He [Tom Hickman, the "Gas-man"] strutted about more than
became a hero, sucked oranges with a supercilious air, and threw
away the skin with a toss of his head, and went up and looked at
Neate, which was an act of supererogation. The only sensible thing
he did was, as he strode away from the modern Ajax, to fling out his
arms, as if he wanted to try whether they would do their work that
day. By this time they had stripped, and presented a strong contrast
in appearance. If Neate was like Ajax, "with Atlantean shoulders,

fit to bear" [*Paradise Lost,* ii, 306] the pugilistic reputation of all Bristol, Hickman might be compared to Diomed, light, vigorous, elastic, and his back glistened in the sun, as he moved about, like a panther's hide.

And then Hazlitt gives a wonderful blow-by-blow account of the epic encounter, which continued until

The Gas-man went down, and there was another shout—a roar of triumph as the waves of fortune rolled tumultuously from side to side. This was a settler. Hickman got up, and "grinned horrible a ghastly smile," [*Paradise Lost,* ii, 846] . . .

But although "all one side of his face was perfect scarlet, and his right eye was closed in dingy blackness," the bout went on.

The wonder was the half-minute time. If there had been a minute or more allowed between each round, it would have been intelligible how they should by degrees recover strength and resolution; but to see two men smashed to the ground, smeared with gore, stunned, senseless, the breath beaten out of their bodies; and then, before you recover from the shock, to see them rise up with new strength and courage, stand ready to inflict or receive mortal offence, and rush upon each other "like two clouds over the Caspian" [*Paradise Lost,* ii, 714–16]—this is the most astonishing thing of all:—this is the high and heroic state of man!

"This is the high and heroic state of man": and the quotations from *Paradise Lost* admirably underscore that theme. A reader of Hazlitt who remembers his Milton will transfer to his witnessing of the great fight the same feelings of awe with which he watched the titanic encounter between Satan and Death at the gates of hell. Which is exactly what Hazlitt intended.

The third major source from which writers draw their allusions is history. When the WPA sponsored low-priced theatrical performances in the middle 1930's, critics of the New Deal referred caustically to "bread and the circus." They did so because they believed that most of their readers would recognize the allusion to the device by which the Roman emperors tried to keep their rebellious subjects' minds off their woes. The use of free food and free entertainment as a sop to popular discontent was a symptom of the decline of Roman power; it was followed in time by the complete collapse of Roman civilization—and the anti-New Dealers trusted that people would complete the analogy. That is one of the uses of historical allusions—to suggest a parallel (however incorrect it may be) between a current situation and a historical one, for the sake of proving a point.

But even when it is not a question of argument, historical allusions often have powerful connotations to those who understand them. A whole library of romantic stories—or, to be more prosaic, a whole year's college course in history—is summed up in Stephen Vincent Benét's lines, at the beginning of *John Brown's Body*, which refer to the motley crowd who founded America:

> Stepchild of every exile from content
> And all the disavouched, hard-bitten pack
> Shipped overseas to steal a continent
> With neither shirts nor honor to their back.
>
> Pimping grandee and rump-faced regicide,
> Apple-cheeked younkers from a windmill-square,
> Puritans stubborn as the nails of Pride,
> Rakes from Versailles and thieves from County Clare,
>
> The black-robed priests who broke their hearts in vain
> To make you God and France or God and Spain.*

We shall not stop to discuss the main allusions, which should be obvious to every high-school graduate; but we should call attention to one or two points overlooked by all except the most alert readers. Assuming that you know who the regicides were among America's founders, what about "rump-faced"? In addition to the visual image the epithet suggests, there is also a punning allusion to the Rump Parliament which figures promi-

* From *John Brown's Body*, published by Rinehart & Co., Inc. Copyright, 1927, 1928, by Stephen Vincent Benét.

nently in the history of the English civil war; and in "the nails
of Pride" there is an allusion to the leader of the *coup* which
resulted in the Rump Parliament.

EXERCISE 9

1. What are the meaning and effect of the mythological allusions in the following quotations?

   (a) So excellent a king; that was, to this,
       Hyperion to a satyr; so loving to my mother
       That he might not beteem the winds of heaven
       Visit her face too roughly . . .
                   Frailty, thy name is woman!—
       A little month, or e'er those shoes were old
       With which she followed my poor father's body,
       Like Niobe, all tears—why she, even she—
       O God! a beast, that wants discourse of reason,
       Would have mourned longer—married with mine uncle,
       My father's brother, but no more like my father
       Than I to Hercules . . .

   (b) The world is too much with us; late and soon,
       Getting and spending, we lay waste our powers:
       Little we see in Nature that is ours;
       We have given our hearts away, a sordid boon!
       The Sea that bares her bosom to the moon;
       The winds that will be howling at all hours,
       And are up-gathered now like sleeping flowers;
       For this, for everything, we are out of tune;
       It moves us not.—Great God! I'd rather be
       A Pagan suckled in a creed outworn;
       So might I, standing on this pleasant lea,
       Have glimpses that would make me less forlorn;
       Have sight of Proteus rising from the sea;
       Or hear Old Triton blow his wreathèd horn.

2. What is the symbolic or connotative meaning of the following names which are taken from mythology or ancient literature?

Narcissus, Arcadia, Aphrodite, Nestor, Pan, Tantalus, Maecenas,
Phoebus Apollo, the Lotus Eaters, Penelope, Mercury, Parnassus,
Lethe, Cerberus, Atalanta, Elysium, Hydra

EXERCISE 10

Suppose you encounter each of the following words or phrases
in a contemporary magazine article or book. What is the original source of the allusion? In what sort of modern context
would it be found? What sort of event or person or situation
might be described? What attitude (if any) is implied? (For
example: An allusion to the lion and the lamb lying down together [*Isaiah,* xi:6] might today be found in a discussion of the
reconciliation of two hostile factions of a political party.) Don't
hesitate to use reference books.

1. Mammon; a dove and an olive branch; the mantle of Elijah;
   Nimrod; sow the wind and reap the whirlwind; the handwriting
   on the wall; kill the fatted calf; the road to Damascus; a Judas.
2. Olympian detachment; Oedipus complex; rise phoenix-like from
   the ashes; Socratic dialogue; sailing between Scylla and Charyb-
   dis; sowing the dragon's teeth; Trojan horse; cleansing the
   Augean stables; Procrustes' bed; a stoic attitude.
3. A plague on both your houses; Lilliputian; a Portia; a Polly-
   anna attitude; Machiavellian policy; a Casper Milquetoast; a
   modern Mrs. Malaprop; a word used in the Pickwickian sense;
   a Babbitt; tilting at windmills.
4. An Armada; Bedlam; a mugwump; scorched earth policy; crossing the Rubicon; a modern Dreyfus; sitting with Mark Hopkins
   on a log; a Beau Brummell; make a journey to Canossa; the iron
   hand in the velvet glove; a second Elizabethan age.

EXERCISE 11

What is the meaning of the following stanza from Gray's "Elegy
Written in a Country Church-Yard"? (It would help to have
the whole poem at hand, to show the context in which these
lines occur.)

Some village-Hampden, that with dauntless breast
The little Tyrant of his fields withstood;
Some mute, inglorious Milton here may rest,
Some Cromwell guiltless of his country's blood.

—————

It is impossible, in a book of this scope, to acquaint you with all the ways in which writers communicate their attitudes to their readers and thus influence the readers' own attitudes. One cannot become a truly intelligent reader simply by remembering a few rules and principles; rather, one reaches reading maturity only through long and well-directed practice. In the rest of this chapter we shall suggest the general direction of that practice by selecting for discussion and illustration a few more common means by which tone is determined. But remember that these in no way exhaust the list; a whole book the size of this one would be inadequate for that task.

Deviations from "Normal" Style

First, what about that particular type of writing which almost every college student condemns as "flowery"? It presents so frequent a stumbling block to the immature, and is so intimately associated with the question of tone, that we should devote some space to it.

Precisely what *flowery* means, the average student cannot tell, any more than a certain immortal writer could specify why he did not like Dr. Fell. But patient cross-examination often will reveal that writing is regarded as "flowery" when it is over-decorated, contains many figures of speech and other rhetorical devices, and, perhaps most important of all, is characterized by language peculiar to older (i.e., pre-twentieth century) poetry. The question is, What is the reader to make of such writing?

Tastes and fashions in writing change from generation to generation. What once was thought to be "fine writing," today seems unbearably stiff and artificial, full of unnecessary flounces and furbelows. On the other hand, the plain, relatively undecorated style in fashion among most contemporary writers who address themselves to a fairly wide audience would undoubtedly have been called "low" and "vulgar" by people in some other ages. In every epoch there is a "norm" of literary diction just as there is of sentence-length. When you read certain Elizabethan poems, for example, or De Quincey's elaborate flights of prose, or some of Tennyson's verse, it is completely unfair to dismiss such masterpieces as "flowery," simply because they do not conform to our contemporary standards of diction. You have a very definite obligation to learn what criteria of style prevailed when these pieces were written—to understand exactly what sort of effects their writers were striving for. You must, in a word, put yourself in the place of the audience for which each work was originally composed. If, by thoughtful study of books about literature and of representative poetry and prose from various epochs, you begin to understand that different ages have different literary fashions, you will see that a wholesale condemnation of unfamiliar styles of writing as "flowery" is unjust.

But what about contemporary writing that has the same "flowery" manner? To discover what the writer means by thus deviating from the present-day norm of diction, consider all that we have already said about the function of words in setting the tone of writing, and recall also, from Chapter Four, the function of rhythm. Here is a sample of writing that is both contemporary and "flowery":

Isolt the abandoned one, fair princess of Brittany, stands forlorn on her native strand. Her wide eyes linger long on the empty horizon of the gray North Sea, where last she has seen her beloved Tristan, dropping over the rim of the world and out of sight.

The good King Howel, fond father of Isolt, stands silent on the headland, watching. His great heart swells with compassion, and as he turns away to his castle, he knows that he will never forget this poignant picture of her loneliness. It had been etched indelibly in his memory.

And yet, as the years unfurl, he remembers much more than her dejection. In his mind's eye he sees her standing there, with white birds circling in the sunlight overhead. He sees the majestic roll of the waves on the eternal sea. He sees the fleecy clouds drifting aloft in the blue, and the blossoming heather blowing in the wind. And so the magnificence of Nature surrounding the lonely Isolt tempered the melancholy of his memory with a glow of enduring beauty.

Plainly the author of those paragraphs wishes to stir his reader's emotions. In attempting to do so, he has pulled out all the stops: he has used connotative words galore, and he has manipulated the sentence rhythms to try to induce the contemplative feelings that are associated with poetry. Perhaps the trick succeeds with the untutored reader; but what about your own reactions? Probably you have marveled at the lavish array of clichés spread out before you: clichés which are intended to make you respond in a certain way, but to which you, as a critical reader, refuse to respond. Remembering what we said in Chapter Two about the implications of cliché language, you will not be surprised to discover that this effusion was written for a crass purpose:

Such is the comfort, the blessing, the benediction, that beauty bestows on memory. The provision of such beauty has ever been the goal of our earnest endeavors at G—— Funeral Homes. To invest a beauty of memory in our every deed, sparing no conceivable effort in providing services of immaculate refinement, always has been our ideal.

In that example, as in the advertisements quoted on pages 204-5 and 210-11, the writer plainly wanted to achieve a serious tone. His purpose was to hypnotize his uncritical reader into believing in the superiority of his employer's mortuary arrangements. And that is one frequent present-day use (or abuse) of the deliberately "poetic" tone, against which it is not at all hard to be fortified.

The use of language that is inappropriately elevated and "poetic" is one aspect of the general topic of incongruity; another is the use of language that is too colloquial or too prosaic for the subject and occasion. A funeral sermon, for instance, should not be "flowery"; it is most effective when its language is simple, unpretentious, and above all not trite. But on the other hand, it should not contain slang or other language which suggests distinctly different occasions. When an incongruous word or phrase suddenly intervenes to break the prevailing tone of the passage, we have anticlimax, as in Joaquin Miller's poem "Myrrh," on the anguish of his parting from his wife Minnie:

> And you and I have buried Love,
> A red seal on the coffin's lid;
> The clerk below, the court above,
> Pronounce it dead: the corpse is hid
> And I who never cross'd your will
> Consent . . . that you may have it still.
> Farewell! a sad word easy said
> And easy sung, I think, by some . . .
> . . . I clutch'd my hands, I turned my head
> In my endeavour and was dumb;
> And when I should have said, Farewell,
> I only murmured, "This is hell!"

The contemporary American writer H. L. Mencken is a past master of the use of both kinds of incongruities—the pretentious and the colloquial—for comic effect. His three volumes of autobiography (*Happy Days, Newspaper Days,* and *Heathen Days*) can teach the observant reader more about the function of word-connotations than can volumes of commentary:

Today the fear of cops seems to have departed teetotally from American boys, at least on the level of the bourgeoisie. I have seen innocents of eight or nine go up to one boldly, and speak to him as if he were anyone else. Some time ago the uplifters in Baltimore actually organized a school for Boy Scouts with cops as teachers, and it did a big trade until the cops themselves revolted. What happened was that those told off to instruct the Scouts in the rules of traffic, first aid, the operation of fire-alarm boxes, etiquette toward the aged and blind, the elements of criminal law and other such branches got so much kidding from their fellows that they were

covered with shame, and in the end the police commissioner let out
the academy *sine die,* and restored the faculty to more he duties.*

Irony

Mr. Mencken's staple device of dead-pan humor brings us naturally to another element of tone—one which causes more trouble to the immature reader than any other. That element is
irony, which is an affirmation, written in apparent seriousness,
of what one does *not* believe.† Irony differs from hypocrisy in
that the user of irony expects his reader to see beneath his
surface pretensions; he does not wish to be taken seriously. The
effect of irony lies in the striking disparity between what is said
and what is meant. The most famous example of sustained irony
in English literature is "A Modest Proposal" by Jonathan Swift,
which you should read. In it, Swift describes the economic and
social advantages that would accrue to the Irish if they would
use a new supply of food—namely, their own children. With all
the sobriety and objectivity of a professional economist, he
enumerates the benefits of such a practice—the increased income to prolific parents, the lessened demands on public charity, the introduction of a succulent table dish, and so on—and
he deftly meets all objections that could be raised to the scheme
Horrified by this cold-blooded advocacy of cannibalism, the
reader is forced finally to conclude that Swift could not possibl
mean what he says. Only then does the reader realize that Swif
is writing in the bitterest vein of irony; that "A Modest Pro
posal" is really a statement of the terrible poverty which existe
in eighteenth-century Ireland; and that at every point Swift i

* From *Happy Days,* by H. L. Mencken. By permission of Alfred A. Knop
Inc., publisher.

† In the following discussion we are concerned only with *verbal* irony. Th
term *irony* is also applied to (1) a situation or turn of events that is the opposi
of what is expected or fitting ("an ironic twist of fate") and (2) to a devi
in fiction and the drama, in which the reader or spectator knows more abo
the true situation than do the characters, whose unawareness of the real sta
of affairs gives their actions and utterances extra ("ironical") meaning. The
are called, respectively, *irony of situation* and *dramatic irony.*

denouncing the political and economic practices which resulted
in the plight of his countrymen.

Arthur Hugh Clough's "The Latest Decalogue" (you must,
of course, know what the title means) offers a very simple example of irony. Remember that the ironist is a man who writes
with his tongue in his cheek:

> Thou shalt have one God only; who
> Would be at the expense of two?
> No graven images may be
> Worshipped, except the currency:
> Swear not at all; for, for thy curse
> Thine enemy is none the worse:
> At church on Sunday to attend
> Will serve to keep the world thy friend:
> Honour thy parents; that is, all
> From whom advancement may befall;
> Thou shalt not kill; but need'st not strive
> Officiously to keep alive:
> Do not adultery commit;
> Advantage rarely comes of it:
> Thou shalt not steal; an empty feat,
> When it's so lucrative to cheat:
> Bear not false witness; let the lie
> Have time on its own wings to fly:
> Thou shalt not covet, but tradition
> Approves all forms of competition.

In this sardonic poem, Clough expresses some very profound
social criticism. If you can explain, on the basis of these lines,
how he feels about the morality of his age, you have made a
long step toward understanding how irony functions.

EXERCISE 12

How does the diction of each of the following passages deviate
from the "norm" of present-day diction? How does that difference affect the reader's attitude toward what is said?

1. All the world loves a lover and when that lover loves the loveliest
    the loveliest spot on earth produceth, the world is circumscribed
    to local environment, and a status of affairs exists exuding ex-
    uberant joyfulness to the point of exquisiteness. Tilghman's
    Island reveled in the throes of such conditions, Wednesday eve-
    ning of last week, when Miss Ida Howeth, daughter of Capt. and
    Mrs. Charles J. Howeth, became the bride of Rev. Thomas C.
    Jones, of Oklahoma, at the M. E. Church South, at Fairbanks.

    The joyousness was as universal as it was intense; for she who
    was about to cross the threshold of wedlock, had by her kindness
    of heart, amiability and utter unselfishness endeared herself to
    all, from the toddling child, to those whose whitened hairs told
    the story of time's ravages.

    Naught was omitted to make the occasion the event of the
    years and success crowned effort. As the mellifluous notes fell
    from the lips of the wedding bells and mingled with the zephyrs
    of night, the little church even seemed to grasp the spirit of the
    hour and stood glorious in its diminutive dignity. As the in-
    spiring strains of Mendelssohn's wedding march sprang from the
    artistic finger-touch of Miss Helen May, the very flowers became
    transmogrified and perfume leaped from the rose bloom decora-
    tions and fanned the cheeks of Tilghman's gathered beauty. The
    waves of the bay danced with delight as they mingled with those
    of the Choptank—clapped their hands and were glad. That Miss
    Ida was the idol of the island was made manifest. Verity, there,
    had drawn aside the curtain of doubt and pinned it with the
    star certitude.

2. Has it been duly marked by historians that the late William
    Jennings Bryan's last secular act on this globe of sin was to catch
    flies? A curious detail, and not without its sardonic overtones.
    He was the most sedulous fly-catcher in American history, and
    in many ways the most successful. His quarry, of course, was not
    Musca domestica but *Homo neandertalensis*. For forty years he
    tracked it with coo and bellow, up and down the rustic backways
    of the Republic. Wherever the flambeaux of Chautauqua
    smoked and guttered, and the bilge of Idealism ran in the veins,
    and Baptist pastors dammed the brooks with the sanctified, and
    men gathered who were weary and heavy laden, and their wives
    who were full of Peruna and as fecund as the shad (*Alosa sapi*

dissima)—there the indefatigable Jennings set up his traps and spread his bait. He knew every country town in the South and West, and he could crowd the most remote of them to suffocation by simply winding his horn. The city proletariat, transiently flustered by him in 1896, quickly penetrated his buncombe and would have no more of him; the cockney gallery jeered him at every Democratic convention for twenty-five years. But out where the grass grows high, and the horned cattle dream away the lazy afternoons, and men still fear the powers and principalities of the air—out there between the corn-rows he held his own puissance to the end. There was no need of beaters to drive in his game. The news that he was coming was enough. For miles the flivver dust would choke the roads. And when he rose at the end of the day to discharge his Message there would be such breathless attention, such a rapt and enchanted ecstasy, such a sweet rustle of amens as the world had not known since Johann fell to Herod's sardonic ax.*

EXERCISE 13

How much irony is there in each of the following selections? How does what the writer says differ from what he really means?

1. [From an article by an astronomer, addressed chiefly to scientists and entitled "The Principles of Poor Writing"] Write hurriedly, preferably when tired. Have no plan; write down items as they occur to you. The article will thus be spontaneous and poor. Hand in your manuscript the moment it is finished. Rereading a few days later might lead to revision—which seldom, if ever, makes the writing worse. If you submit your manuscript to colleagues (a bad practice), pay no attention to their criticisms or comments. Later resist firmly any editorial suggestions. Be strong and infallible; don't let anyone break down your personality. The critic may be trying to help you or he may have an ulterior motive, but the chance of his causing improvement in your writing is so great that you must be on guard.†

* From *Selected Prejudices,* by H. L. Mencken. By permission of Alfred A. Knopf, Inc., publisher.
† Quoted by permission of the author, Dr. Paul W. Merrill, and the publisher, *Scientific Monthly.*

2. [From an article called "How to Hate Americans," written by an American and published in an American periodical, but allegedly addressed to Europeans. You might enjoy writing a paragraph in the same vein to develop each of these pieces of advice.]
    1. Hate Americans because they are rich.
    2. Hate Americans because they drink too much.
    3. Hate Americans because they are always thinking and talking about business and work.
    4. Hate Americans for their movies and commercial radio and television.
    5. Hate Americans because they do not produce great art and literature.
    6. Hate Americans for "McCarthyism."
    7. Hate Americans because they want to run the world.

3. If you can't prove what you want to prove, demonstrate something else and pretend that they are the same thing. In the daze that follows the collision of statistics with the human mind, hardly anybody will notice the difference. The semiattached figure is a device guaranteed to stand you in good stead. It always has.

You can't prove that your nostrum cures colds, but you can publish (in large type) a sworn laboratory report that half an ounce of the stuff killed 31,108 germs in a test tube in eleven seconds. While you are about it, make sure that the laboratory is reputable or has an impressive name. Reproduce the report in full. Photograph a doctor-type model in white clothes and put his picture alongside.

But don't mention the several gimmicks in your story. It is not up to you—is it?—to point out that an antiseptic that works well in a test tube may not perform in the human throat, especially after it has been diluted according to instructions to keep it from burning throat tissue. Don't confuse the issue by telling what kind of germ you killed. Who knows what germ causes colds, particularly since it probably isn't a germ at all?

In fact, there is no known connection between assorted germs in a test tube and the whatever-it-is that produces colds, but people aren't going to reason that sharply, especially while sniffling.*

---

* From Darrell Huff's *How to Lie with Statistics;* by permission of the publishers, W. W. Norton & Co., Inc.

4. The clear brown eyes, kindly and alert, with 12-20 vision, give
   confident regard to the passing world through R. K. Lampert
   & Company lenses framed in gold;
   His Soul, however, is all his own;
   Arndt Brothers necktie and hat (with feather) supply a touch
   of youth.

   With his soul his own, he drives, drives, chats, and drives,
   The first and second bicuspids, lower right, replaced by bridge-
   work, while two incisors have porcelain crowns;

   (Render unto Federal, state, and city Caesar, but not unto time;
   Render nothing unto time until Amalgamated Death serves final
   notice, in proper form;
   The vault is ready;
   The will has been drawn by Clagget, Clagget, Clagget, and
   Brown;
   The policies are adequate, Confidential's best, reimbursing for
   disability, partial or complete, with double indemnity should
   the end be a pure and simple accident)

   Nothing unto time,
   Nothing unto change, nothing unto fate,
   Nothing unto you, and nothing unto me, or to any other known
   or unknown party or parties, living or deceased;
   But Mercury shoes, with special arch supports, take much of the
   wear and tear;
   On the course, a custombuilt driver corrects a tendency to slice;
   Love's ravages have been repaired (it was a textbook case) by
   Drs. Schultz, Lightner, Mannheim, and Goode,
   While all of it is enclosed in excellent tweed, with Mr. Baumer's
   personal attention to the shoulders and the waist;

   And all of it now roving, chatting amiably through space in a
   Plymouth 6,
   With his soul (his own) at peace, soothed by Walter Lippmann,
   and sustained by Haig & Haig.*

---

* From *Collected Poems*, by Kenneth Fearing. Copyright, 1940, by Random
House, Inc. Reprinted by permission of Random House, Inc.

Sentimentality

So much for one or two of the ways in which humor, conscious or unconscious, is related to the tone of writing. Now we turn to the subject of sentimentality, which, in its extreme manifestations, can also be funny.

Many situations in life are always fraught with emotion, no matter who participates in, or observes, them: innocent childhood viewed by an adult, young love, betrayal, married happiness, unfulfilled ambition, the conflict between ideals and circumstances, pathetic accidents, poverty, old age, death. They are the situations that form the basic material of literature; they include, indeed, most of the important things in life. Everybody wants to write about them, but since they have been written about over and over, from the very beginning of civilization, comparatively few people have anything new to say concerning them. Those who rework the old themes without adding fresh perspective often take refuge in sentimentality.

Sentimentality can be defined as shallow and exaggerated emotion. Taking an emotional symbol or situation—home, mother, death of a pauper, return of a wanderer—the sentimentalist, perhaps from the sincerest of motives, extorts more feeling from it than a reasonable person would find there, and dwells upon it longer and more insistently than he should.

Furthermore, the sentimentalist, lacking fresh ideas, depends heavily upon the cliché in all its forms—upon the tried-and-true devices by which too many preceding writers have stirred their readers' feelings. But those images and phrases are now emotionally dehydrated; they have been used so often that they have lost their power to affect. And so the effect of sentimentality, to the reader who has a sense of proportion, is the opposite of what is intended. Depending upon the precise quality of the passage, the reader is either exasperated or amused. But he is not touched.

We can illustrate the nature of sentimentality by quoting two accounts dealing with the same material but differing radically in point of view. Not long ago a social worker, after visiting a "case" in a large eastern city, wrote a report from which the following excerpts are made, all proper names having been changed. The tone, whatever else it may be, is not sentimental:

The unfinished frame summer-kitchen addition to the dilapidated farmhouse Mrs. Denby occupies on the outskirts of Birchdale is a mute reminder of the ambition Mr. Denby had entertained to remodel the property and make it more habitable: an ambition interrupted last autumn by his fatal three-month illness. He left his family in quite sorry straits. There are five children, the youngest only fourteen months old. They must live on their Mothers' Assistance Fund grant of $55 a month. Mrs. Denby, a no more than moderately intelligent woman, mingles a somewhat vulgar streak with strong Baptist religiosity. Her house is kept clean, but, with the exception of a shining new electric refrigerator in one corner of the kitchen, it is poorly furnished.

One of Mrs. Denby's elder sons was badly burnt in an accident some years ago and missed a year and a half of school. His sister, Elizabeth, is now living with Mr. Denby's relatives nearby, an arrangement which Mrs. Denby is willing to tolerate at least temporarily, although she has no truck with her numerous "in-laws."

Mr. Denby, the oldest of fifteen children, left school to go to work. He held various jobs, but none for long. He was constantly chasing the will o' the wisp of "more money," and as a result got nowhere. He was a notoriously poor provider, Mrs. Denby says, but despite this shortcoming her life with him was serene.

Their son George is said by his teachers to be retarded in his school work. He has not yet had an intelligence test, but his native ability seems possibly lower than average. He will have some difficulty in keeping up with his age-group.

Soon after the social worker's visit, the Denby house burned down, and one of the city newspapers ran the following story:

WIDOW SOBS AS FLAMES DESTROY ALL

A 38-year-old widow, mother of five children, poked aimlessly through the fire-blackened ruins of her little home at Center Road

and Delaney Street yesterday and wept bitter tears of utter hope-
lessness.

"What are we to do?" Mrs. Hannah S. Denby sobbed. "The fire
took everything except the clothes on our backs. It even burned my
picture of my husband . . . and he died only six months ago."

And for Mrs. Denby, the loss of that picture seemed even harder
to bear than the destruction of all but a few pieces of their furniture
in the blaze which broke out Sunday afternoon shortly after the
family had returned from church.

For her tow-headed, five-year-old daughter, Beth, the fire had
meant another heart-rending loss, for her only doll and her doll
coach were consumed by the flames.

And for 17-year-old Frank, now the man of the family, for 11-
year-old James and seven-year-old George, the fire meant the end
of the happiness they had just started to recapture in family life
since the death of their father.

Only 16-month-old Robert was unaware of the feeling of family
tragedy. He cooed gaily in his mother's arms.

For the time being the widow and her children have found a
home with her sister. "But she is very ill," Mrs. Denby said, "and
it is hardly fair for us to stay there. I wish I knew what we could
do, where we could turn. Perhaps the good Lord will find a
way. . . ."

Compare the two accounts, and you will have a good notion of
the elements of sentimentality: the selection of detail to maintain a certain impression, whether wholly or partly false; the
use of cliché symbols (e.g., the little girl and the burned doll
coach); and the trite language itself ("bitter tears of utter hope
lessness"). Do you think the writer of the newspaper account
was sincerely moved by the Denbys' plight?

What is sentimental to one person may not be sentimental to
another; it all depends upon how fine a sense of fitness the
reader has. A reader who is ready to respond to any appeal to
emotion, merely because it has something to do with babyhood
or the first stirrings of pure young love, will not discriminate
between the sentimental and the genuinely emotional. To him
it is the subject that counts, not the treatment or the motive

behind the treatment. But a more mature reader will instinctively reject an appeal which applies a pressure pump to his tear
ducts. What do you think of this poem?

> She knelt upon her brother's grave,
>   My little girl of six years old—
> He used to be so good and brave,
>   The sweetest lamb of all our fold;
> He used to shout, he used to sing,
> Of all our tribe the little king—
> And so unto the turf her ear she laid,
> To hark if still in that dark place he play'd.
>   No sound! no sound!
>   Death's silence was profound;
>   And horror crept
>   Into her aching heart, and Dora wept.
>   If this is at it ought to be,
>   My God, I leave it unto thee.*

Do not think for a moment that we mean to depreciate the
expression of emotion in literature. Our point is simply that
writing which expresses emotion in hackneyed and excessive
terms not only is far inferior to writing which expresses that
same emotion with dignity and restraint, but also can give us
valuable warning that our generous and warm-hearted natures
are about to be imposed upon.

Restraint

If there is one lesson which we have emphasized, over and over
again, it is this: The real meaning of writing that matters most
is not found on the surface, in the actual, literal significance of
the words. It hovers beneath the surface, in the delicate shadings of connotation and rhythm, in the precise effect of metaphor and symbol and allusion. Sometimes that surface is so
highly decorated, so full of a certain kind of meaning, that we
are content with its own delights, and neglect to pierce beneath

* From *Collected Poems*, by T. E. Brown. By permission of The Macmillan
Company, publishers.

it to the deeper undercurrents. But often (and this is what we mean by restraint) writers leave the surface comparatively bare; the meaning on that level is plain and simple. The untrained reader in all probability will consider this to be the *only* meaning. But underneath that simple exterior of restraint there lies a rich hidden treasure of suggestion and implication, which the mature reader will appreciate the more because it has not been publicly advertised. It is his reward for being a perceptive and sensitive reader.

The best place to try out your ability to read deeply—to get out of a passage everything that the author packed into it for you—is a poem that describes a situation or a state of mind: not a narrative poem, in which things happen, but a poem in which someone is seen before or after events, or without reference to events. If no events are described, then you are confronted with the problem of telling what the poem is "about." Almost any good lyric poem can test your reading faculty. Some of Browning's shorter dramatic monologues also are admirable for this purpose: "Soliloquy of the Spanish Cloister," "My Last Duchess," "Fra Lippo Lippi," and "The Laboratory." And so too are A. E. Housman's poems, one of which we select for illustration.

> On moonlit heath and lonesome bank
>   The sheep beside me graze;
> And yon the gallows used to clank
>   Fast by the four cross ways.
>
> A careless shepherd once would keep   5
>   The flocks by moonlight there,
> And high amongst the glimmering sheep
>   The dead man stood on air.
>
> They hang us now in Shrewsbury jail;
>   The whistles blow forlorn,   10
> And trains all night groan on the rail
>   To men that die at morn.

There sleeps in Shrewsbury jail to-night,
    Or wakes, as may betide,
A better lad, if things went right,   15
    Than most that sleep outside.

And naked to the hangman's noose
    The morning clocks will ring
A neck God made for other use
    Than strangling in a string.   20

And sharp the link of life will snap,
    And dead on air will stand
Heels that held up as straight a chap
    As treads upon the land.

So here I'll watch the night and wait   25
    To see the morning shine,
When he will hear the stroke of eight
    And not the stroke of nine;

And wish my friend as sound a sleep
    As lads' I did not know,   30
That shepherded the moonlit sheep
    A hundred years ago.*

To begin with, the reader must take full advantage of whatever
small hints the poet offers outside the poem itself. In this case,
Housman appended a note to the poem, saying simply, "Hanging in chains was called keeping sheep by moonlight." This
brief sentence really sums up the irony, or bitter contrast, which
underlies the whole poem—the association of sheep-watching by
moonlight (the most peaceful and inoffensive of occupations
and the most tranquil of settings) with the gruesome practice of
hanging convicted criminals† in chains (an especially severe
punishment). It is the interplay of these two sets of completely
diverse associations which gives the poem its dominant tone.

* From A. E. Housman, *A Shropshire Lad*, Henry Holt & Company.
† Or, perhaps, specifically sheep-stealers. But whichever was in Housman's
mind, the poem's impact is unaffected.

The basic contrast of the poem is brought out in the first two stanzas. Consider the implications of *moonlit heath, sheep,* and *graze* as against *gallows* and *clank* (what is the effect of the sound of the word?); and of *careless* (carefree), *shepherd, flocks, moonlight,* and *glimmering sheep* as against *the dead man stood on air.* The language is very simple, but the clashing associations of those two groups of words give us a key to the very intense emotions that lie beneath the surface. What is the effect of the grotesque image suggested by "The dead man stood on air"?

With mention of Shrewsbury jail, the whistles blowing, and the trains groaning all night, a new note enters—another contrast, this time between the stillness of the old rural setting at the crossroads and the new conditions under which condemned criminals are executed. Does the speaker approve or disapprove of the new system?

In the fourth stanza the precise situation is made clear: the speaker, the sheep-herder, is thinking of someone in particular who is awaiting execution in Shrewsbury jail. What is the attitude implied in the *us* of line 9, the *lad* of line 15, the *chap* of line 23, and the *lads'* of line 30? What do the lines "A better lad, *if things went right,* / Than most that sleep outside" do to clarify that attitude?

In the fifth stanza there is a pun (*ring* in two senses). Is a pun usually found in a poem about someone about to be hanged? Is it a humorous pun? Housman selected the word *string* in the last line of the stanza for a special reason: not merely because of the rime-scheme. What is the difference in implication between *rope* and *string,* and how does the effect of *string* harmonize with the tone of the whole?

The sixth stanza recalls to mind the earlier image of the criminal "standing on air." The earlier reference was to the gallows at the crossroads; here it is to the modernized gallows in the jailyard. But the effect of hanging is the same under both conditions. And that is a point Housman wishes to make.

Suddenly, at the beginning of the seventh stanza, we are taken back to the original setting—the moonlit heath and lone-

some bank, with the sheep peacefully grazing beside the speaker.
The idea of death is now conceived of as the difference between
hearing the stroke of eight o'clock and not hearing the stroke of
nine. Of all the ways in which Housman might have epitomized
the fact of death, why do you think he chose that one?

Finally, the speaker alludes to the men who were hanged long
years ago and thus "kept sheep by moonlight." And we realize
with a shock—if we have not done so before—that he too is
"keeping sheep by moonlight." In other words, the ultimate
effect of the poem is centered in the double meaning of the
phrase. If the phrase can be applied with equal accuracy to both
the speaker and the condemned man, as the speaker implies,
what, in the last analysis, is the speaker thinking?

One other note. The rhythm of this poem is as incongruous
to the subject as is the highly colloquial diction: instead of
having a measured, grave tempo, it fairly skips along. The short
line is aided by the simple rime-scheme (*a-b-a-b*). The stanza
sounds almost like something children memorize in kinder-
garten.

Therefore to the superficial reader, the poem seems, perplex-
ingly enough, to be a more or less flippant treatment of a serious
subject. There is some sort of humor in the image of the dead
man standing on air, in the pun on *ring,* in the familiar *lad* and
chap, in the offhand way in which death is imaged in the seventh
stanza. But the careful reader will realize that the humor is of a
peculiar and significant kind: it is humor without the faintest
suggestion of a smile; on the contrary, it is grim, bitter humor.
And the lightness suggested by the colloquial diction and the
lilting rhythm is just as deceptive.

The effect of Housman's poem lies in the complete incongruity between what is said, for anyone to read, and what is left
unsaid, for the attentive reader to discover. The flippancy, the
offhand manner, point not to any callousness on the part of the
speaker. On the contrary, they are simply camouflage for very
deep and bitter feelings. The truth about the speaker's emotions resides almost completely in the implications, rather than

the external meaning, of what he says. The half-humorous tone makes the actual subject of the poem—the impending execution —all the more terrible.

Even the most conscientious and intelligent reader finds it difficult to put into words the impression a poem or an essay or a scene in a play or novel makes upon him. That is why such vague and essentially meaningless words as "flowery" are so often called into use. We shall end by offering a short list of serviceable adjectives by which tone may be described. There is no rule of thumb by which you can learn how to use them with accuracy and discrimination; but you can begin by learning their dictionary definitions, and from then on you should be careful to observe how other writers use them. Above all, try your hand at fitting them to a wide variety of selections from writing, old and new. After you have read a short poem, for example, try to find the adjective which you think best describes the tone of the poem as it strikes you. Exercise 18 offers a small assortment of passages for practice. Here are some of the terms you should know and train yourself to use:

whimsical, grave, fanciful, bantering, rhapsodic, ironical, devotional, intemperate, fervent, tender, cynical, indignant, meditative, bitter, wry, sentimental, satirical, light-hearted, solemn, patronizing, didactic, flippant, reminiscent, sardonic, elegiac, eulogistic, resigned, colloquial, affected.

This list is far from exhaustive, but it will aid you in your efforts to put into words your sense of the emotional tone and intention of what you read. From now on, make it a point of pride never to say, "I know what my impression is, but I can't find the right words to express it!"

―――――――――――

EXERCISE 14

How sentimental do you think each of the following selections is?

1.   "THEN THE DRAGON CAME . . ."

Nobody tells a story like Daddy. The everyday world fades away as his words lead you into a new and shining land.

And what if the Dragon is a bit scary? You need only climb into Daddy's arms to be safe and secure again before it's time to sleep.

To make those we love safe and secure is the very core of homemaking. It is a privilege known only in a country such as ours, where men and women are free to work for it.

And taking care of our own is also the way we best take care of our country. For the strength of America is simply the strength of one secure home touching that of another.

If you've tried to save and failed, chances are it was because you didn't have a *plan*. Well, here's a savings system that really works—the Payroll Savings Plan for investing in U.S. Savings Bonds.

2.   They stood side by side on the granite step in the soaring brightness. In front of them were the seaweedy rocks of the cove and the spruces and the pointed firs and the dark bay and islands and the line of the ocean heaving with light. The waves breathed in the cove. "Husband," she said. "Wife," he said. The words made them bashful. They clung together against their bashfulness. "Today we begin," he said, "to make . . ." "This wilderness our home," she said. The risen sun over the ocean shone in their faces.

3.   Western wind, when wilt thou blow,
                        The small rain down can rain?
                  Christ, if my love were in my arms,
                        And I in my bed again!

4.   As thro' the land at eve we went,
                        And pluck'd the ripen'd ears,
                  We fell out, my wife and I,
                  O we fell out I know not why,
                        And kiss'd again with tears.
                  And blessings on the falling out
                        That all the more endears,
                  When we fall out with those we love
                        And kiss again with tears!

For when we came where lies the child
  We lost in other years,
There above the little grave,
O there above the little grave
  We kiss'd again with tears.

5.   Why so pale and wan, fond lover?
        Prithee, why so pale?
     Will, when looking well can't move her,
        Looking ill prevail?
        Prithee, why so pale?

     Why so dull and mute, young sinner?
        Prithee, why so mute?
     Will, when speaking well can't win her,
        Saying nothing do 't?
        Prithee, why so mute?

     Quit, quit, for shame! This will not move;
        This cannot take her.
     If of herself she will not love,
        Nothing can make her.
        The devil take her!

6.   Sweet is the hour that brings us home,
        Where all will spring to meet us;
     Where hands are striving, as we come,
        To be the first to greet us.
     When the world hath spent its frowns and wrath,
        And care been sorely pressing:
     'Tis sweet to turn from our roving path,
        And find a fireside blessing.
     Oh, joyfully dear is the homeward track,
     If we are but sure of a welcome back.

     What do we reck on a dreary way,
        Though lonely and benighted,
     If we know there are lips to chide our stay,
        And eyes that will beam love-lighted?
     What is the worth of your diamond ray,
        To the glance that flashes pleasure;

When the words that welcome back betray,
We form a heart's chief treasure?
Oh, joyfully dear is our homeward track
If we are but sure of a welcome back.

EXERCISE 15

Following are two short passages from famous novels. The effect of each is centered in the final sentence. How do the two passages differ in tone? What is the author's purpose in the last sentence?

1. It is not my intention to breathe a word against the character of Mrs. Proudie, but still I cannot think that with all her virtues she adds much to her husband's happiness. The truth is that in matters domestic she rules supreme over her titular lord, and rules with a rod of iron. Nor is this all. Things domestic Dr. Proudie might have abandoned to her, if not voluntarily, yet willingly. But Mrs. Proudie is not satisfied with such home dominion, and stretches her power over all his movements, and will not even abstain from things spiritual. In fact, the bishop is henpecked.

2. Unscared by the thunder of the artillery, which hurled death from the English line, the dark rolling column pressed on and up the hill. It seemed almost to crest the eminence, when it began to wave and falter. Then it stopped, still facing the shot. Then at last the English troops rushed from the post from which no enemy had been able to dislodge them, and the Guard turned and fled.

   No more firing was heard at Brussels—the pursuit rolled miles away. Darkness came down on the field and city; and Amelia was praying for George, who was lying on his face, dead, with a bullet through his heart.

EXERCISE 16

The following poem, "To His Coy Mistress," illustrates the way in which tone can dramatically shift within the course of relatively few lines. (1) How would you describe the attitude of the poet to his "coy mistress" as the poem begins? (Be sure you

understand what *coy* and *mistress* meant when this was written,
in the latter part of the seventeenth century.) By what devices
of diction and allusion does he communicate this feeling? (2)
Exactly where does the shift occur? What is the tone henceforth?
(3) Does the change in tone actually mean that the poet's attitude toward his beloved suddenly changes, or can we say, on
the other hand, that his *underlying* feeling is consistent
throughout, despite the contrast of tone? (4) Study carefully the
figures of speech to see how each contributes to the intended
effect at the point where it occurs.

Had we but world enough, and time,
This coyness, lady, were no crime.
We would sit down, and think which way
To walk, and pass our long love's day.
Thou by the Indian Ganges' side
Shouldst rubies find: I by the tide
Of Humber would complain. I would   [*complain:* sing of love]
Love you ten years before the flood,
And you should, if you please, refuse
Till the conversion of the Jews.   10
My vegetable love should grow   [*vegetable:* plant-like]
Vaster than empires and more slow;
An hundred years should go to praise
Thine eyes, and on thy forehead gaze;
Two hundred to adore each breast,   15
But thirty thousand to the rest;
An age at least to every part,
And the last age should show your heart.
For, lady, you deserve this state;   [*state:* honor]
Nor would I love at lower rate.   20
But at my back I always hear
Time's wingèd chariot hurrying near;
And yonder all before us lie
Deserts of vast eternity.
Thy beauty shall no more be found,   25
Nor, in thy marble vault, shall sound
My echoing song; then worms shall try
That long preserved virginity,
And your quaint honor turn to dust,   [*quaint:* proud]

And into ashes all my lust: 30
The grave's a fine and private place,
But none, I think, do there embrace.
Now therefore, while the youthful hue
Sits on thy skin like morning dew,
And while thy willing soul transpires 35
At every pore with instant fires, [*instant:* eager]
Now let us sport us while we may,
And now, like amorous birds of prey,
Rather at once our time devour
Than languish in his slow-chapped power. [*slow-chapped:* 40
Let us roll all our strength and all slowly devouring]
Our sweetness up into one ball,
And tear our pleasures with rough strife
Through the iron gates of life:
Thus, though we cannot make our sun 45
Stand still, yet we will make him run.

EXERCISE 17

These three poems have the same general theme. By a close examination of their diction, figures of speech, rhythm, and other characteristics, decide how they differ in meaning, mood, and effect.

1.　　　　If yet I have not all thy love,
　　　　Dear, I shall never have it all;
　　　　I cannot breathe one other sigh to move,
　　　　Nor can intreat one other tear to fall,
　　　　And all my treasure which should purchase thee,
　　　　Sighs, tears, and oaths, and letters, I have spent.
　　　　Yet no more can be due to me
　　　　Than at the bargain made was meant;
　　　　If then thy gift of love were partial,
　　　　That some to me, some should to others fall,
　　　　　　Dear, I shall never have thee all.

　　　　Or if then thou gavest me all,
　　　　All was but all which thou hadst then;
　　　　But if in thy heart, since, there be or shall
　　　　New love created be by other men,

Which have their stocks entire, and can in tears,
In sighs, in oaths, and letters outbid me,
This new love may beget new fears,
For this love was not vowed by thee;
And yet it was, thy gift being general;
The ground, thy heart, is mine, whatever shall
    Grow there, dear; I should have it all.

Yet I would not have all yet;
He that hath all can have no more,
And since my love doth every day admit
New growth, thou shouldst have new rewards in store;
Thou canst not every day give my thy heart;
If thou canst give it, then thou never gavest it:
Love's riddles are that, though thy heart depart,
It stays at home, and thou with losing savest it:
But we will have a way more liberal
Than changing hearts, to join them; so we shall
    Be one, and one another's all.

2.   Yes! in the sea of life enisled,
With echoing straits between us thrown,
Dotting the shoreless watery wild,
We mortal millions live *alone*.
The islands feel the enclasping flow,
And then their endless bounds they know.

But when the moon their hollows lights,
And they are swept by balms of spring,
And in their glens, on starry nights,
The nightingales divinely sing;
And lovely notes, from shore to shore,
Across the sounds and channels pour—

Oh! then a longing like despair
Is to their farthest caverns sent;
For surely once, they feel, we were
Parts of a single continent!
Now round us spreads the watery plain—
Oh, might our marges meet again!

Who ordered that their longing's fire
Should be, as soon as kindled, cooled?
Who renders vain their deep desire?—
A God, a God their severance ruled!
And bade betwixt their shores to be
The unplumbed, salt, estranging sea.

3.   I

I wonder do you feel to-day
    As I have felt since, hand in hand,
We sat down on the grass, to stray
    In spirit better through the land,
This morn of Rome and May?

                                    II

For me, I touched a thought, I know,
    Has tantalized me many times,
(Like turns of thread the spiders throw
    Mocking across our path) for rhymes
To catch at and let go.

                                    III

Help me to hold it! First it left
    The yellowing fennel, run to seed
There, branching from the brickwork's cleft,
    Some old tomb's ruin: yonder weed
Took up the floating weft,

                                    IV

Where one small orange cup amassed
    Five beetles—blind and green they grope
Among the honey-meal: and last,
    Everywhere on the grassy slope
I traced it. Hold it fast!

                                    V

The champaign with its endless fleece
    Of feathery grasses everywhere!

Silence and passion, joy and peace,
    An everlasting wash of air—
Rome's ghost since her decease.

VI

Such life here, through such lengths of hours,
    Such miracles performed in play,
Such primal naked forms of flowers,
    Such letting nature have her way
While heaven looks from its towers!

VII

How say you? Let us, O my dove,
    Let us be unashamed of soul,
As earth lies bare to heaven above!
    How is it under our control
To love or not to love?

VIII

I would that you were all to me,
    You that are just so much, no more.
Nor yours nor mine, nor slave nor free!
    Where does the fault lie? What the core
O' the wound, since wound must be?

IX

I would I could adopt your will,
    See with your eyes, and set my heart
Beating by yours, and drink my fill
    At your soul's springs—your part my part
In life, for good and ill.

X

No. I yearn upward, touch you close,
    Then stand away. I kiss your cheek,
Catch your soul's warmth—I pluck the rose
    And love it more than tongue can speak—
Then the good minute goes.

XI

Already how am I so far
    Out of that minute? Must I go
Still like the thistle-ball, no bar,
    Onward, whenever light winds blow,
Fixed by no friendly star?

XII

Just when I seemed about to learn!
    Where is the thread now? Off again!
The old trick! Only I discern—
    Infinite passion, and the pain
Of finite hearts that yearn.

EXERCISE 18

Here is a group of passages of very diversified tone. How would you characterize the tone of each, and what specific means (diction, metaphor, allusion, rhythm, etc.) does the writer use to create that tone?

1. [The novel *End as a Man* deals with] life in a southern military academy. A drinking party and crooked poker game finally result in the expulsion of several cadets, including the wily and un-moral ringleader. The retired general in charge of the academy is the stereotype of military martinet, whose conception of the narrow and rigid discipline necessary to produce "a man" is set in bold relief against the energy of growing boys. The result is a fair picture of the frustration inherent in an overdose of discipline and in the license and disobedience that is largely engendered by it.

   No one would care to send his son to such an institution.

2.   O darling room, my heart's delight,
   Dear room, the apple of my sight,
   With thy two couches soft and white,
   There is no room so exquisite,
   No little room so warm and bright,
   Wherein to read, wherein to write.

For I the Nonnenwerth have seen,
And Oberwinter's vineyards green,
Musical Lurlei; and between
The hills to Bingen have I been,
Bingen in Darmstadt, where the Rhene
Curves toward Mentz, a woody scene.

Yet never did there meet my sight,
In any town, to left or right,
A little room so exquisite,
With two such couches, soft and white,
Not any room so warm and bright,
Wherein to read, wherein to write.

3. Why has our author selected such a theme? Why, amid all the
suggestive incidents of life in a wilderness; of a retreat from
civilization to which, in every individual case, a thousand circumstances must have concurred to reconcile human nature with
estrangement from home and country; or amid the historical
connections of our history with Jesuit adventure, savage inva-
sion, regicide outlawry, and French aggression, should the taste
of Mr. Hawthorne have preferred as the proper material for
romance, the nauseous amour of a Puritan pastor, with a frail
creature of his charge, whose mind is represented as far more
debauched than her body? Is it, in short, because a running
under-tide of filth has become as requisite to a romance, as death
in the fifth act to a tragedy? Is the French era actually begun
in our literature? And is the flesh, as well as the world and the
devil, to be henceforth dished up in fashionable novels, and
discussed at parties, by spinsters and their beaux, with as un-
concealed a relish as they give to the vanilla in their ice cream?
. . . We are painfully tempted to believe that [*The Scarlet Letter*]
is a book made for the market, and that the market has made
it merchantable, as they do game, by letting everybody understand that the commodity is in high condition, and smells
strongly of incipient putrefaction.

4.   Come sleep! O sleep, the certain knot of peace,
        The baiting place of wit, the balm of woe,
        The poor man's wealth, the prisoner's release,
        Th' indifferent judge between the high and low;

With shield of proof shield me from out the prease
  Of those fierce darts despair at me doth throw;
  O make in me those civil wars to cease;
  I will good tribute pay, if thou do so.
Take thou of me smooth pillows, sweetest bed,
  A chamber deaf to noise and blind to light,
  A rosy garland and a weary head;
And if these things, as being thine by right,
  Move not thy heavy grace, thou shalt in me,
  Livelier than elsewhere, Stella's image see.

5.   Wilt thou forgive that sin where I begun,
    Which is my sin, though it were done before?
   Wilt thou forgive those sins, through which I run,
    And do run still: though still I do deplore?
     When thou hast done, thou hast not done,
      For I have more.

   Wilt thou forgive that sin by which I have won
    Others to sin? and made my sin their door?
   Wilt thou forgive that sin which I did shun
    A year, or two: but wallowed in, a score?
     When thou hast done, thou hast not done,
      For I have more.

   I have a sin of fear, that when I have spun
    My last thread, I shall perish on the shore;
   Swear by thyself, that at my death thy sun
    Shall shine as he shines now, and heretofore;
     And, having done that, Thou hast done,
      I fear no more.

6. It cannot at this time be too often repeated—line upon line,
precept upon precept—until it comes into the currency of a proverb: *to innovate is not to reform.* The French revolutionists
complained of everything; they refused to reform anything; and
they left nothing, no, nothing at all *unchanged.* The consequences are *before us*—not in remote history; not in future prog-
nostication;—they are about us; they are upon us. They shake
the public security; they menace private enjoyment. They dwarf
the growth of the young; they break the quiet of the old. If

we travel, they stop our way. They infest us in town; they pursue
us to the country. Our business is interrupted; our repose is
troubled; our pleasures are saddened, our very studies are poisoned and perverted, and knowledge is rendered worse than
ignorance, by the enormous evils of this dreadful innovation.
The revolution harpies of France, sprung from Night and Hell,
or from that chaotic Anarchy which generates equivocally "all
monstrous, all prodigious things," cuckoo-like, adulterously lay
their eggs, and brood over, and hatch them in the nest of every
neighboring state. These obscene harpies, who deck themselves
in I know not what divine attributes, but who in reality are foul
and ravenous birds of prey (both mothers and daughters), flutter
over our heads, and souse down upon our tables, and leave
nothing unrent, unrifled, unravaged, or unpolluted with the
slime of their filthy offal.

7.   How do I love thee? Let me count the ways.
            I love thee to the depth and breadth and height
            My soul can reach, when feeling out of sight
            For the ends of Being and ideal Grace.
            I love thee to the level of every day's
            Most quiet need, by sun and candle-light.
            I love thee freely, as men strive for Right;
            I love thee purely, as they turn from Praise.
            I love thee with the passion put to use
            In my old griefs, and with my childhood's faith.
            I love thee with a love I seemed to lose
            With my lost saints—I love thee with the breath,
            Smiles, tears, of all my life!—and, if God choose,
            I shall but love thee better after death.

8. In order to supply the constant and increasing demand for
   "subjects" [for dissection by medical students], there had grown
   up an ancillary branch of research, carried out behind the
   scenes by the professional riflers of graves, known by the expressive names of Body Snatchers or Resurrectionists. . . . Many
   and gruesome are the tales told of their adventures, some not
   without a certain grisly humor; but one necessary result of such
   pursuits was a coarsening of the moral grain, an indifference to
   decent feelings, and a callous recklessness regarding human life
   which, as we shall see, was to bear fearful fruit.

Index

297